D1602233

THE PSYCHOLOGY
OF LEISURE

THE PSYCHOLOGY OF LEISURE

OF LEISURE

SECOND EDITION

By

JOHN NEULINGER
The City College of
The City University of New York

CHARLES C THOMAS · PUBLISHER
Springfield · *Illinois* · *U.S.A.*

Published and Distributed Throughout the World by

CHARLES C THOMAS • PUBLISHER

2600 South First Street

Springfield, Illinois 62717, U.S.A.

ISBN 0-398-04492-9

Library of Congress Catalog Card Number: 81-1744

With THOMAS BOOKS careful attention is given to all details of manufacturing and
design. It is the Publisher's desire to present books that are satisfactory as to their physical
qualities and artistic possibilities and appropriate for their particular use. THOMAS
BOOKS will be true to those laws of quality that assure a good name and good will.

Library of Congress Cataloging in Publication Data

Neulinger, John.
　The psychology of leisure.

　Bibliography: p.
　Includes index.
　1. Leisure — Psychological aspects. I. Title.
GV14.4.N48　1981　　　　790'.01'32　　　　　81-1744
ISBN 0-398-04492-9　　　　　　　　　　　　　AACR2

Printed in the United States of America

AF-R-1

To my son, Ronald

"To be for one day entirely at leisure is to be for one day an immortal"

Chinese Proverb

So each day I pass judgment and sentence myself to remain among the living. Condemned to live, I must then ceaselessly create reasons for living. The judgment is not so severe, nor the task so difficult, as we imagine. We have only to be open to the world and it will pour its riches at our feet. Before this winter I had not known that the bark of a tree, caught in yellow sunlight, could be enough to restore a life.

(William Barrett, 1978, p. 345)

PREFACE TO THE SECOND EDITION

It was with a sense of excitement and satisfaction, as well as trepidation, that I approached the task of revising the original edition of this book. Excitement, because the need for a revision had become clear. The field of the psychology of leisure has burst upon us in full force; the past few years have made it clear that a psychological perspective has become an accepted, necessary, and absolutely unavoidable approach in many areas of the leisure domain. Satisfaction, because I feel stronger than ever the conviction that I am working in an area that is bound to increase in importance with time; it is also the satisfaction that accompanies the explorer venturing into unchartered territory. Trepidation, because so much has happened in these last few years. It has become a cliche´ to speak of the exponential rate of change in modern society. That very change, however, makes developments in the leisure domain so necessary and brings about a constant flow of them. Much work not only has been done in the traditional areas of leisure, but the profession also has moved into new ones. The socioeconomic-political environment continues to give leisure an ever increasing salience and opens up new targets and challenges. At this point, the only way to capture most of what is happening in the leisure domain would be to edit a handbook of leisure, as I have suggested on several occasions. Such a task is not the purpose of this revision, however.

Modifications in this volume arose from the following considerations. *One*, the basic chapter outline of the original edition continues to serve a useful purpose. There will always be the need for chapters on "The Conceptualization of Leisure," "The Measurement of Leisure," and so on; however, each of the chapters required revision and expansion in the light of new developments and research. *Two*, new chapters needed to be added to cover areas that have recently become more openly involved with psychological aspects of leisure. I am referring primarily to gerontology and the measurement as well as improvement of the quality of life. *Three*, and I consider this the most important reason for revising this book: my thinking about leisure (I like to think!) has progressed. The inevitable fact in writing a nonfiction work, particularly in a rapidly developing area such as leisure, is that the minute one sends off the final manuscript to the publisher one would like to have it back for revisions. After all, science is the continuing approximation of truth, and we still have a lot of approximating to do. In this respect I see one minor change and two major new emphases in this revision. I have somewhat revised my original leisure paradigm — not in its essence, but more in its form. The two emphases are: first, I have sharpened and made more explicit the crucial distinction between free time and leisure, the very basis for a psychological conception of leisure; and second, I have recognized and given appropriate exposition to the significant and intimate relationship of leisure to the quality of life.

Let me express gratitude here to all those who did review the first edition or who gave me valuable feedback and suggestions in other ways. As to new developments and research reported, appropriate references and acknowledgements are made as the instance arises. Much was gained from the many informal and formal comments received at conferences, seminars, and workshops I attended, and it is impossible, at this point, to sort out the sources of these ideas. To this list of anonymous contributors must be added the many students with whom I had most insightful discussions and sometimes heated arguments. The critical reading of some of the new sections of the book by Gabrielle Stutman and her several suggestions were extremely helpful.

This revised edition, then, represents an organic development of the psychology of leisure: the essence of the organism remains the same; yet the organism changes. It grows, it develops new branches and adds new dimensions, all in line with its basic structure and the demands of the environment in which it finds itself. The organism in question is still a young one; we are still at the very beginning of its blossoming. I feel convinced that it has taken firm enough roots in our discipline to ensure its continued growth.

New York, NY
November, 1980

J.N.

PREFACE
TO THE FIRST EDITION

This Book is the outcome of my involvement in leisure research for the past seven years. I was originally attracted to the area of leisure as a result of my interest in personality measurement and assessment. Leisure seemed the ideal place to investigate personality dynamics. Leisure may be compared to a Rorschach card onto which we project our fantasies, wishes, and dreams. In what area of life can one better determine behavior that is, or ought to be, primarily determined by the person's desires and motives?

Many people have contributed to the research reported, the ideas expressed, and the suggestions made. Among those who participated actively in research were the following honors students at the Psychology Department of The City College: Carl Berg, William Czander, Judith Elman, Miranda Breit Murray, David M. Schnarch, and Margit M. Winckler. Thomas Waller contributed as a graduate research assistant to the early stages of research. Among other students who have contributed in minor roles were Roberta Getz, Sandra Lieberman, Bernard Slome, Barbara Wald, and Judy Wolf. Charles Raps was co-researcher in the *Mensa* study and helped in many of the other computer analyses.

Research support is acknowledged for some of the early work from The Russell Sage Foundatin (Research Grants RF235 and RF291), and for computer time from The City College Computer Center.

The critical reading of sections of the book by Douglas Kimmel and Nan Walter and their valuable comments were extremely helpful in formulating the final version of the work. Acknowledgement must also be given to the many writers in this field whose works are cited in these pages and whose ideas have often so permeated my own thinking that I no longer know which thought is mine and which is theirs. I wish to acknowledge particularly the influence of the work of Thomas F. Green whose distinction between *a work* and *a job* is very much a part of my conceptualization of leisure.

New York, NY
1974

J.N.

INTRODUCTION

Leisure has been our concern throughout the ages. The nature of this interest, however, has undergone quite a change. While in antiquity, leisure was close to an ultimate goal, a life of tranquility and contemplation, in modern days it seems to be turning into our ultimate problem: how to cope with a life that has set us free from the daily struggle for survival, but has not taught us to be ourselves and take advantage of never-before existing opportunities.

The metamorphosis of leisure from goal to problem was paralleled by a change in the meaning of leisure. Leisure once referred to a way of life, a state of being. Today, leisure is generally defined in opposition to work, as time left over, as a residue.[1] This shift in meaning is also responsible for our habit of calling the problem of free time the problem of leisure, a conceptualization that has been shown to be quite inappropriate (Green, 1968; Nahrstedt, 1972).

Leisure, viewed from a state of mind perspective (the orientation taken here), represents a positive experience. The problem of leisure becomes its absence, a state we have labelled *leisure lack*. Such a state is related to the individual's dissatisfaction with oneself; it is accompanied by the awareness that one's life is empty, one's work meaningless. *To leisure* means to be engaged in an activity performed for its own sake, freely and without pressure or coercion; it means doing something from which one derives meaning and satisfaction, and which involves one to the very core of one's being. To leisure means to be oneself, to express one's talents, one's capacities, and one's potentials.

How many people are fortunate enough to have a job that allows them to leisure. One of the often quoted problems of in-

---

[1]This statement is becoming less and less valid, and we hope to be contributing to this trend. It is, however, still quite appropriate for the general population.

dustrial society is that it has alienated us from our work, or as I prefer to call it, our jobs. Yet, we are still taught that there, on the job, we are to find meaning and fulfillment in life. For most, this is a frustrating and unrealistic demand. When we openly admit that in modern life (i.e., the postindustrial society) the job may no longer have the capacity to offer the basis for self-fulfillment and self-definition and when we recognize that it not only may be, but hopefully will be, in our "free time" that most of us shall fulfill themselves, only then shall we begin to solve what now tends to be known as "the problem of leisure."

This book is about the psychology of leisure. It deals with leisure from a certain viewpoint and suggests certain approaches to the investigation of leisure that derive from this orientation. It also examines the role that leisure plays in the individual's life as well as in society at large. While we are concerned primarily with leisure as a psychological phenomenon, this does not imply that we shall restrict ourselves to psychological subject matters. Psychological phenomena (if you will, subjective aspects) are imbedded in, affect, and are affected by nonpsychological phenomena (objective aspects), Lewin's (1951) *outer hull* or *ecology*. The very conditions that bring about the state of leisure, as we shall see, tend to be extremely dependent on environmental factors. In addition, a discussion of leisure cannot be oblivious that for a long time leisure has been viewed as a primarily sociological term, an issue that will need considerable attention.

The person new to this field tends to be amazed at the amount of literature on leisure. Professional works primarily originate not only from disciplines such as sociology, recreation, and physical education but also from philosophy, economics, political science, theology, and others. There are professional journals devoted to leisure research (e.g., the *Journal of Leisure Research, Leisure Sciences, Society and Leisure*) and many others covering applied or leisure related areas in the United States and throughout the world. It should be emphasized that the vast growth in this field is not restricted to the United States. Note should also be taken of the emergence of a new discipline, namely *leisure studies*, in a number of colleges and universities.

This book is organized around the framework of a broad program of leisure research (Neulinger, 1971). To the original eight areas two new ones have been added in this revision, gerontology and the quality of life. There is, of course, overlap among the areas and no claim is made to being exhaustive of all potential topics. While research approaches are being discussed throughout, some chapters are more oriented toward applied aspects than others.

Following are brief indications of chapter contents in order to give the reader an overview of what to expect.

THE CONCEPTUALIZATION OF LEISURE (Chapter 1). The *sine qua non* of any research is an adequate conceptualization of the terms used. This axiom is particularly relevant to the field of leisure research in which a confusion of terms is abundant, but it is equally applicable to leisure planning, policy, and applied fields. It is absolutely essential that we are clear and that we make it clear what it is we denote when we use the label *leisure*. This chapter presents only a brief historical sketch of the concept of leisure, since a considerable number of writers have offered quite extensive histories already. A number of leisure definitions are presented and several theories are referred to. A psychological paradigm of leisure is set forth. Empirical approaches to the conceptualization of leisure are discussed and data from our own research are reported.

THE MEASUREMENT OF LEISURE (Chapter 2). The most fundamental problem in any research effort is that of adequate measurement. Unless we can measure reliably and validly what we wish to research, we might as well quit before we start. In this chapter various approaches to the problem of measuring leisure are discussed. Emphasis is placed on the measurement of psychological aspects of leisure, although other approaches are examined as well. The measurement of leisure attitudes is described in the light of the development of an instrument that measures five basic leisure dimensions. Other attempts in that area are regarded as well. The possibilities of developing leisure types, that is, groupings of people in terms of similar leisure patterns, are explored. The emphasis here is on the characterization of the person as regards the leisure domain rather than on the abstraction of leisure attitudes or dimensions per se. Reference also is made to an instrument designed to measure the leisure experience rather than leisure attitudes.

THE COLLECTION OF LEISURE FACTS (Chapter 3). What do we actually know about leisure? What are some leisure facts, and what kind of information is being collected? A number of leisure surveys are discussed, and findings of our own are presented. The need for longitudinal national surveys of leisure within the context of the quality of life is emphasized. This chapter does not intend to be a summary of leisure findings; its purpose is to serve as a springboard for discussions about the kind of research that is going on and the nature of data that are being collected and invites suggestions for improvements and innovations.

LEISURE IN THE SOCIAL-PSYCHOLOGICAL CONTEXT (Chapter 4). While the distribution of leisure facts and attitudes and the identification of leisure types is of intrinsic interest, it is clear that this information takes on much more meaning when it is related to social and psychological background variables of the respondents involved. Such relationships serve both to formulate and confirm or disconfirm hypotheses about the nature and function of leisure.

Rather than summarizing findings relating to covariates of leisure, the relevance of some of the variables studied is discussed, and suggestions are made for the inclusion in future studies of certain other variables that may be important for an understanding of the dynamics of leisure. Again, some of our own findings are presented.

THE MEASUREMENT OF THE QUALITY OF LIFE: SOCIAL INDICATORS (Chaper 5). If we accept the premise that leisure is *the* criterion (or at least one of the criteria) of the quality of life, then all efforts of measuring this quality become relevant to our domain. This chapter outlines the history of *social indicators* and the *social indicators movement* and examines some of the issues and problems involved. It is designed to alert the reader to the common interests and concerns shared by this field with leisure studies.

THE FORMATION OF LEISURE ATTITUDES (Chapter 6). To ascertain prevailing leisure attitudes is one thing; to investigate how these attitudes may have developed is another. A knowledge of the covariates of leisure attitudes certainly is necessary and helpful to such an enterprise; however, an adequate theory of the formation of leisure attitudes must take into account developmental factors, general factors relating to attitude change and maintenance, and also the cultural and subcultural context of the persons involved. Similarly, the capacity to experience leisure will be affected by developmental, situational, and cultural factors. This chapter offers speculations in regard to these aspects of leisure.

EXPERIMENTAL LEISURE RESEARCH (Chapter 7). It is good to be able to report that experimental leisure research is on the increase. Considerable work has been done recently, although many researchers are still not aware that their work is relevant to the leisure domain. To the studies that relate to leisure in a tangential manner (e.g. studies on boredom and sensory deprivation), we can now add a number of others that deal directly with leisure and were designed to test leisure hypotheses.

LEISURE AND GERONTOLOGY (Chapter 8). It seemed feasible in 1974, to write a book on leisure and not have a chapter devoted to issues of the elderly; it no longer does in 1980, especially if we are concerned with the broader implications of leisure for the quality of life. Not only do changing population statistics make the issue more relevant, but political developments such as the changes in the mandatory retirement age make it practically mandatory that one consider these matters in terms of their implications for leisure. Consideration is given to the beautiful prospect that the elderly could become the forerunners of a leisure elite of the future that eventually will include all of the people.

LEISURE LACK AND FREE TIME AS SOCIAL PSYCHOLOGICAL PROBLEMS (Chapter 9). This chapter addresses itself to two types of problems related to leisure. One refers to the way free time may affect people in quite negative ways; the other has to do with the absence of leisure, or as we have called it leisure lack. How do these quite different problems manifest themselves? Do they affect everyone the same way, or can we observe variations as a function of individual differences or societal settings? What research approaches are best suited to study these issues? These and similar questions are discussed in this chapter.

LEISURE AND THE QUALITY OF LIFE (Chapter 10). If we accept the premise that leisure is a criterion of the quality of life, then the promotion of leisure becomes an individual as well as a societal goal. Experiencing leisure is an individual phenomenon, but it is highly dependent on one's position in society. Leisure education, thus, addresses itself both to the individual and to society at large; leisure counseling is primarily concerned with individuals. We must recognize, however, that the creation of a leisure society, while dependent on changing values, is still foremost a sociopolitical matter. The leisure professional will inevitably have to deal with the political domain.

The above is a brief indication of what this book is about. Our treatment is not encyclopedic; it is not our intention to be so. Rather, we like to feel that we have helped the novice in this area to put a multitude of facts, and some fiction, into perspective, and that the person already active in this area may find it stimulating to look at familiar issues in a new light.

The most important point that this author is trying to get across is that leisure is not to be seen in opposition to work. It is not necessary that we downgrade work in order to raise the value of leisure. Leisure is not *not-work*; leisure is not time left over after work! Leisure is a state of mind; it is a way of being at peace with oneself and what one is doing. Not all the things that need to be done in life can lead to leisure, nor is it feasible or even desirable to attain a steady state of leisure. But, let us strive for a society in which our major efforts are at least directed toward the goal of leisure, a society in which a person at work is a person at leisure and in which the job is left to be done during the time one must, of necessity, take off from one's work.

TABLES

CONTENTS

THE PSYCHOLOGY
OF LEISURE

CHAPTER 1

THE CONCEPTUALIZATION
OF LEISURE

WHAT IS LEISURE? Perhaps it is best to realize that there is no answer to this question, or better, that there is no one correct answer, just as there is no one answer to the question, what is happiness or what is success, or even, what is a table? Definitions are what we make them; they are labels about which a number of people agree. Not everybody will agree to use the same label for a given phenomenon, nor will everybody use a given label for only one thing. This is the denotative problem of the definition of leisure. Equally troublesome, however, is the connotative problem, namely the many meanings the term, leisure, carries for different people. Thus, to one person it may mean something good, to another something bad, to one, something active, to another, something passive, still to another something noble and worthwhile, while to another something to be frowned upon, nay, immoral. In this chapter we shall be dealing with the problem of the conceptualization of leisure. However, rather than trying to come up with *the one* definition of leisure, we shall delineate differences in the various ways leisure has been defined in order to alert the reader that different authors may be referring to different phenomena when using that same label. Not only may that be the case between authors, but the reader also may find the same author using leisure to denote different phenomena at various instances.[1]

---

[1] A worthwhile exercise in sensitizing oneself to that problem is to peruse a number of works on leisure (e.g. recent articles in the leisure education or counseling literature) and identify such inconsistent uses of the term *leisure*.

1

WHAT IS LEISURE: LEISURE DEFINED

The Classical Perspective on Leisure

The classical conception of leisure as a state characterized by meaningful and nonutilitarian activity seems to have originated with the Greeks.[2] For them, leisure was a concern to which labor, as well as the daily toil of life, were subordinate. Work was *a-scolia*: the state of being unleisurely. Leisure is defined by Aristotle as the state of being free from the necessity of being occupied and is characterized by the performance of activity "for its own sake or as its own end" (de Grazia, 1962, p. 13). Music and contemplation were viewed as being the only two activities worthy of leisure: music, because it cultivates the mind, and contemplation, because it leads to truth and true happiness. "The man in contemplation is a free man. He needs nothing. Therefore nothing determines or distorts his thought. He does whatever he loves to do, and what he does is done for its own sake" (p. 18).

---

[2]Most of the material in this section is based on Sebastian de Grazia, *Of Time, Work and Leisure* (New York, Twentieth Century Fund, 1962), and Joseph Pieper, *Leisure: The Basis of Culture* (New York, The New American Library, 1963). For interesting detail, see "Leisure, according to the Oxford English Dictionary," and "Leisure, according to the Encyclopedia of the Social Sciences," in Eric Larrabee and Rolf Meyersohn (Eds.), *Mass Leisure* (Glencoe, IL, The Free Press, 1958).

The history of leisure and recreation is described at some length in Norman P. Miller and Duane M. Robinson, *The Leisure Age* (Belmont, CA, Wadsworth, 1963). For a short treatment, see Thomas Woody, "Leisure in the Light of History," *The Annals of The American Academy of Political and Social Science, 313: 4-10 (1957)*. An attempt to relate modern needs to historical perspectives of leisure is made by Graham C. Taylor, "Work and Leisure in the Age of Automation," *Humanitas, Journal of the Institute of Man, 3:*57-65 (1967).

A most enlightening treatise on the way the term *free time* has taken on the meaning of *leisure* during the eighteenth and nineteenth century is given by W. Nahrstedt, in *Die Entstehung der Freizeit* (Gottingen: Vandenhoeck & Ruprecht, 1972).

For attempts to bring order into the various viewpoints on leisure by sorting them into categories and characterizing the nature of their differences, see the following: J.F. Murphy, *Concepts of Leisure* (Englewood Cliffs, NJ, Prentice-Hall, 1974); M. Kaplan, *Leisure: Theory and Policy* (New York, Wiley, 1975); and R. Kraus, *Recreation and Leisure in Modern Society* (Santa Monica, CA, GoodyearPublishing Co., 1978). For an overview of these categorizations, see J. Neulinger, *To Leisure: An Introduction* (Boston, MA, Allyn & Bacon, 1981).

The Greek ideal of leisure was expressed in Rome only through the writings of Seneca. The majority of Latin authors conceptualized leisure (*otium*) in terms of rest and recreation, thereby defining it as a type of nonactivity rather than by its intrinsic qualities. This activity-leisure distinction has its counterpart in the modern work-leisure dichotomy.

The Middle Ages still reflect the Aristotelian emphasis on activity performed for its own sake. St. Thomas Aquinas, in his commentary on Aristotle's *Metaphysics* defines the liberal arts as those concerned with pure knowledge whereas those arts "concerned with utilitarian ends that are attained through activity . . . are called servile" (Pieper, 1963, p. 34). The early Christians absorbed from their Greco-Roman heritage the ideal of contemplation, but with a different focus. Contemplation became specifically the search for religious truth and thereby a pathway to happiness; work was secondary in importance to the goal of salvation. "Work in a sense was something one did in his free time. Any activities other than those bearing on salvation were strictly speaking not essential" (de Grazia, 1962, p. 24). Work fulfilled needs for self-purification, repentance or charity, and was considered best when it distracted least from the primary goal of salvation.

Progressively, however, the ideal of contemplation was replaced by the search for understanding of nature's laws through alchemy, astrology, magic, and medicine.

"From the twelfth to the fourteenth century man came to grips with the stars, stones, sand, plants, and animals, and, in experiments, sought their transformation" (de Grazia, 1962, p. 27). Concomitantly, a new philosophy of work emerged in which pride in craftsmanship replaced the contemplative life. This change was partially facilitated by the dignification of labor in the monasteries.

The proposition that it is the duty of *all* men to work, and the corresponding possiblity of a shorter workweek, appeared his-

3

torically for the first time in Thomas More's *Utopia*, written in 1516. In *Utopia*, all must work, but none work more than six hours a day. The foundation of a work society based on the necessity of work and consequent restriction of leisure to free time was completed by Adam Smith, in the eighteenth century. In the *Wealth of Nations*, Smith defined the productive act solely in terms of the transformation of raw materials into "something useful to man" (de Grazia, 1962, p. 29). Consequently, the ability to produce and even to know could be realized only by work, which soon became the right and duty of every man. The new "work ethic" formed the matrix of all meaningful activity and the ideal of leisure "had long before taken its exit" (p. 30).

Nineteenth century accounts of leisure deal increasingly with topics such as the length of the workweek or hours per day spent at work. The concepts of leisure and free time became thoroughly confounded. This development had been made possible by the assumption that the only necessary condition for freedom (which is required for the experience of leisure) is a period of free time. Nahrstedt (1972) describes how the philosophers of the Enlightenment saw free-time periods as the workers' chance to partake in the classical experience of leisure. A noble thought, but one that could not work, since it is based on a fatal fallacy.

Twentieth Century Leisure Conceptions

Ushering in the sociology of leisure is Veblen's *The Theory of the Leisure Class* (1899). For Veblen, leisure connotes

> . . . non-productive consumption of time. Time is consumed non-productively (1) from a sense of the unworthiness of productive work, and (2) as an evidence of pecuniary ability to afford a life of idleness (p. 46).

Thus, leisure has become the very antithesis of work.

The studies that best characterize early twentieth century leisure research are those of Lynd and Lynd (1929; 1937); Lundberg, Komarowski, and McInerny (1934); Sorokin and Berger (1939); and Warner and Lunt (1941). These studies set the tone for the large amount of empirical research that prevails to this day and that is concerned primarily with the determination of leisure-time habits or activities. The conceptualization of leisure underlying these studies is a residual one: leisure is a residual — what is left of the twenty-four hours of the day when time devoted to work, sleep, and other necessities of life are subtracted. The following are examples of such definitions:

> By leisure, we mean all time beyond the existence and subsistence time (Clawson, 1964, p. 1).
>
> Leisure time is that portion of the day not used for meeting the exigencies of existence. No one has leisure who has no time he can dispose of as he will (Weiss, 1964, p. 21).
>
> Leisure is time beyond that which is required for *existence*, . . . and *subsistence*, . . . (Brightbill, 1960, p. 4).

Thus, leisure has become a frame or container that we fill up with things, i.e. so-called free-time activities. These activities become leisure, not because of their intrinsic characteristics, but because they are carried out during a period of time designated as leisure or free time. This type of conceptualization represents, however, only one of two major schools of thought concerning the definition of leisure (Smigel, 1963). This group equates leisure with free time, and according to Smigel, this is the meaning assigned to the term *leisure* by most modern sociologists.

The second school is best represented by de Grazia (1962). De Grazia renounces the residual definition of leisure. He admits that work is the antonym of free time, but not of leisure. By equating free time with leisure we make the claim that anybody who can have free time can also have leisure. Not so! "Leisure refers to a state of being, a condition of man, which few desire and fewer achieve" (p. 5). Can we be more specific as to the nature of this state? De Grazia is somewhat pessimistic in that respect. "Something as personal as leisure cannot be pinned down" (p. 6). He points out that

> The word leisure has always referred to something personal, a state of mind or a quality of feeling. It seemed that in changing from the term leisure to the term free time we had gone from a qualitative to a quantitative concept. We now had something that could be measured with ease (p. 59).

5

However, the gain was illusory since the subjective element remains in the term *free*.

A similar view of leisure as a state of mind or a way of being is taken by Pieper (1963). Leisure does not automatically accrue to the person who has free time.

> Leisure, it must be clearly understood, is a mental and spiritual attitude—it is not simply the result of external factors, it is not the inevitable result of spare time, a holiday, a week-end or a vacation (p. 40).

We shall refer to this type of leisure conceptualization as the *subjective definition of leisure*, in contrast to the residual type of definition, which we shall call the *objective definition of leisure*.

A somewhat different conception of leisure emphasizes what leisure does for the person rather than what it is. The importance of leisure activities for the formation and expression of man's character, for example, is emphasized by Riesman, Glazer, and Denney (1950) in *The Lonely Crowd*: "Play may prove to be the sphere in which there is still some room left for the would-be autonomous man to reclaim his individual character from the pervasive demands of his social character" (p. 314).

The role that leisure plays in the formation of personality had similarly been stressed by Bogardus (1934):

> Leisure time has been pronounced "the architect of character." If "work makes the worker," then leisure makes the rest of personality. As leisure hours become more numerous than work hours, then leisure (other things being equal) exceeds work in molding personality (p. 275).

The functional view of leisure is also evident in Wilensky's (1960) conceptualization, which has leisure fulfill certain personal needs.

What, then, is leisure? We have seen that we may define it *quasi* objectively by delimiting its duration and qualifying what it is not. In the eyes of some, however, this residual definition of leisure leaves out the very essence of leisure. We have subjective definitions of leisure that describe it as a state of mind but that are so evasive in their tone that it would be extremely difficult to derive an operational definition from these conceptualizations.

Still others speak of the functions leisure fulfills without clarifying what that leisure of which they speak is. Perhaps the complexity of the problem of leisure does not permit a "single principle" explanation or, what Allport (1968) calls, "a simple and sovereign theory" approach. Maybe all we can hope for is a delineation of the conditions for leisure along with an elaboration of its many functions. We shall close this brief survey of leisure conceptions by giving two examples that approach leisure in such a multiconditional manner.

Sutherland (1957) lists six "conditions for the enjoyment of leisure during time not sold for pecuniary reward": integrity of purpose, liberty to review goals, objectivity, equality in fellowship, common command of skills, and growth. Thus, he tries to combine objective and subjective aspects of leisure and be specific enough to permit the identification of leisure versus non-leisure behavior.

The most ambitious attempt of a multivariable approach to leisure is that of Kaplan (1960, 1975). Following is an example of his earlier conceptualization that already emphasizes the interrelationship of leisure with various social factors, such as the family, work, social class, religion, and sociability, and introduces the societal and cultural context as important determinants of leisure behavior. Here are the essential elements of leisure, according to Kaplan (1960):

(a) an antithesis to "work" as an economic function,
(b) a pleasant expectation and recollection,
(c) a minimum of involuntary social-role obligations,
(d) a psychological perception of freedom,
(e) a close relation to values of the culture,
(f) the inclusion of an entire range from inconsequence and insignificance to weightiness and importance,
(g) often, but not necessarily, an activity characterized by the element of play. (p. 22)

Leisure, Kaplan states, "is none of these by itself but all together in one emphasis or another."

Traces of the above elements are clearly perceptible in a later, more formal definition of leisure (Kaplan, 1975, p. 26):

7

> Leisure, we might say, consists of relatively self-determined activity-experience that falls into one's economically free-time roles, that is seen as leisure by participants, that is psychologically pleasant in anticipation and recollection, that potentially covers the whole range of commitment and intensity, that contains characteristic norms and constraints, and that provides opportunities for recreation, personal growth, and service to others.

We shall return to Kaplan's work in the following section on leisure theories.

LEISURE THEORIES

While leisure definitions try to come to grips with the concept of leisure, leisure hypotheses attempt to represent more or less comprehensive explanations of leisure behavior. A formal deductive theory has been described by Hendrick and Jones (1972) as follows. It has a set of basic concepts, at least some of which must be given an *operational* definition. (By the operational definition of a concept we mean the ability to measure it objectively, to point to it or identify it unambiguously in the physical environment, or to state the conditions that will bring it about.) The concepts of the theory are then related to each other in the form of propositions. These propositions are assumed to be true without proof; they are the premises or assumptions of the theory. From these propositions, which in fact represent the theory, logical deductions or inferences are drawn: the hypotheses. These hypotheses are then put to the test, through the experimental or some other appropriate method.

There are two aspects to a theory. One is the logical or formal one: a theory can be a highly sophisticated network of propositions and hypotheses, internally valid and generating many ideas. The usefulness of a theory, i.e. its power to help understand and predict relationships, will depend, however, largely on the second aspect: the degree to which the concepts of the theory are anchored in the real world. The importance of operational definitions cannot be overemphasized.

In surveying leisure theories, it becomes clear that no such formal theories as yet exist. It may be soothing to hear that, according to Hendrick and Jones (1972, p. 11), no such formal

8

theories exist anywhere in social psychology at this stage of the game. Rather, most researchers start with a hypothesis based on some intuitive feeling, perhaps derived from previous research. Such hypothesis testing is to be encouraged and may eventually lead to more formal theory building.

None of the theories listed next qualify as formal deductive theories. Some of them are of historical interest; others, and particularly the more recent ones, may furnish the basis for hypotheses testing and/or further conceptualizations.

Play Theories

To the degree that play is related to leisure, play theories are relevant in this context.[3] Miller and Robinson (1963), in their chapter on Theories of Play, outline the following:

THE SURPLUS ENERGY THEORY — formulated by Friedrich Schiller (1875): play is an outlet for unneeded energy.

PREPARATION FOR LIFE THEORY — represented by Karl Groos (1901): play prepares the child for adult life; the child instinctively practices adult roles and situations.

RECREATION AND RELAXATION THEORY — described by G.T.W. Patrick (1916): play serves to relax the person and restore him for work.

RECAPITULATION THEORY — G. Stanley Hall (1904) saw play as a recapitulation of the cultural epochs in the development of the human race.

In addition, Miller and Robinson mention Joseph Lee (1929) and Luther Gulick (1920) as major pioneers of American play theory. Modern theories of play are classified by Miller and

---

[3]For a review of theories and other aspects of play, the reader may wish to consult Berlyne, D.E., "Laughter, Humor, and Play," in Gardner Lindzey and Elliot Aronson (Eds.) *The Handbook of Social Psychology, 2nd edition*, Vol. III (Reading, MA, Addison-Wesley, 1969) pp. 795–852. A numer of articles on play can be found in Eric Larrabee and Rolf meyersohn (Eds.) *Mass Leisure* (Glencoe, IL, The Free Press, 1958). An interdisciplinary research index on play, giving 1,500 social science references ot the topic of play, has been produced by David A. Sleet (1971) and is available through University Microfilms, Manuscript Abstracts Division, 300 N. Zeeb Road, Ann Arbor, MI 48103. For a review of play in the light of major general theories of behavior as well as an emphasis on applied aspects of play, see J. Levy, *Play Behavior* (New York, Wiley, 1978) and also Sutton-Smith 1980).

Robinson into *physiological theories* (John Dewey, 1925; Eugene W. Nixon and Frederick W. Cozens, 1941; Hans Selye, 1956), *psychological theories* (S.R. Slavson, 1948; Erik H. Erikson, 1950; Sapora and Mitchell, 1961), *sociological-anthropological theories* (Johan Huizinga, 1955; Martin H. Neumeyer and Esther S. Neumeyer, 1958; Harold D. Meyer and Charles K. Brightbill, 1956), *aesthetic theories* (Konrad Lange, 1901; Baker Brownell, 1939; Harold H. Anderson, 1959; Lawrence K. Frank, 1948; Abraham H. Maslow, 1959).

Play theories have been reviewed by Ellis (1971) with a rather critical outcome. "As a field we have not yet had the courage to face the reality that most of those theories are unacceptable as guides to action in research and in practice." In examining the classical theories of play, his verdict on the surplus energy, the instinct, the preparation, the recapitulation, and the relaxation theories is the same: all are inadequate. The trend for more recent theories of play seems to be to apply general theories of psychology or motivation to the specific area of play, rather than to develop play specific theories. Thus, the only two modern theories of play, according to Ellis (1971), are play as competence motivation and play as arousal-seeking, both derived from general theories of motivation (White, 1959 and Berlyne, 1967). These theories received a more positive verdict by Ellis, as they may be more useful in generating testable hypotheses in the area of play behavior. In sum, Ellis (1973, p. 119) indicates that any one explanation for play may be unacceptable or inadequate, but that "the most satisfying explanation seems to involve an integration of three: play as arousal-seeking, play as learning, and the developmentalist view of the child."

A similar view is expressed by Barnett (1978), in a critical review of extant theoretical models of play behavior. "None of the theories satisfactorily explain the causal antecedents to play or encompass all of the different types of play that have been observed, . . ." Barnett describes three clusters of play theories, the *biological view*, the *environmental view*, and the *cognitive view*, but sees these as lying on a continuum. A synthesis and integration of elements from each of the models is suggested so that play is

10

viewed as "a state of mind but that the typology of a playful encounter is strongly influenced by environmental factors."
Barnett closes her article with the recognition that the crucial
question still remains unanswered: "Why does man play?" This
conclusion seems to reflect the current state of the art: "We have
as yet only a nebulous grasp of play's manifold nature and its
control of our lives" (Brian Sutton-Smith, 1980).

Leisure Theories and Hypotheses

Similar to play theories, leisure theories differ in terms of their
conceptual approaches and in terms of their degree of com-
prehensiveness. Miller and Robinson (1963), in their chapter on
Theories of Leisure and Recreation, refer to a considerable
number of people who at one time or another elaborated some
idea about leisure and its functions. A number of themes stand
out: leisure has potential for self-fulfillment, personal growth
and creative expression; leisure permits personal autonomy; leisure fulfills functions that were once fulfilled by work; leisure
may be dangerous to the person since it leaves him to his own
devices; leisure may be dangerous to society since it may turn its
members into dull, pleasure-seeking automatons; leisure can be
a challenge both to the individual and society. None of these
ideas, however, have been worked out to the point that would
permit the testing of specific hypotheses about leisure behavior.

A number of leisure theories attempt to explain leisure behavior in relation to work behavior. Wilensky (1960) describes
two of these as follows:

> The *compensatory leisure* hypothesis: . . . the Detroit auto-worker, for
> eight hours gripped bodily to the main line, doing repetitive, low-
> skilled, machine-paced work which is wholly ungratifying, comes
> rushing out of the plant gate, helling down the super-highway at 80
> miles an hour in a second-hand Cadillac Eldorado, stops off for a beer
> and starts a bar-room brawl, goes home and beats his wife, and in his
> spare time throws a rock at a Negro moving into the neighbourhood.
> In short, his routine of leisure is an explosive compensation for the
> deadening rhythms of factory life.
>
> The *"spillover" leisure hypothesis*: Another auto-worker goes quietly
> home, collapses on the couch, eats and drinks alone, belongs to noth-
> ing, reads nothing, knows nothing, votes for no one, hangs around the

home and the street, watches the 'late-late' show, lets the TV pro-
grammes shade into one another, too tired to lift himself off the couch
for the act of selection, too bored to switch the dials. In short, he develops a spillover leisure routine in which alienation from work becomes alienation from life; the mental stultification produced by his
labour permeates his leisure (p. 544).*

A critical look at this type of leisure hypothesis was taken by
Burch (1969), who in the light of his research data examined the
explanatory power of two hypotheses, the *compensatory* and the
familarity hypotheses, and then added his own theory, which he
called the *personal community hypothesis*.

According to Burch (1969), "the compensatory hypothesis
suggests that whenever the individual is given the opportunity to
avoid his regular routine he will seek a directly opposite activity"
(p. 127). Burch directs attention to the similarity of this
hypothesis to the surplus energy theory of play and to its elaboration by Wilensky. The familiarity hypothesis "assumes that
persons have worked out a comfortable routine for social survival and that the rewards of security outweigh any possible rewards bought by the high costs of uncertainty" (p. 132). Burch
relates his hypothesis to "force of habit" and to the concept of
canalization. Although the two hypotheses predict rather opposite types of behavior, both contribute to an explanation of
Burch's data. Burch feels, however, that additional predictive
power can be added through his personal community hypothesis
that assumes "that gross social issues and psychological drives are
significantly filtered and redirected by the social circles of
workmates, family and friends" (p. 138). He adds, ". . . transactions with the socialization by one's workmates, parents, spouse
and friends will shape the nature of one's leisure style." The
value of the hypothesis was demonstrated in the light of available
research data.

We turn next to a number of writers whose definition of leisure implies a theory of leisure. For example, Dumazedier
(1967) states:

---

*Reprinted from *International Social Science Journal, XII:* 4 (1960), by permission of
Unesco. © Unesco 1960.

Leisure is activity — apart from the obligations of work, family, and society — to which the individual turns at will, for either relaxation, diversion, or broadening his knowledge and his spontaneous social participation, the free exercise of his creative capacity (pp. 16–17).

Implied are three major functions of leisure: relaxation, entertainment, and personal development. Since these three functions, according to Dumazedier, are interdependent and coexistent in everyone's life, a further elaboration is needed to specify under just what conditions a particular function will become the dominant one.

In *The Sociology of Leisure* (1974), Dumazedier presents a more extended conceptualization, placing his definition of leisure squarely into a sociological framework. "I prefer to reserve the word leisure for the time whose content is oriented towards self-fulfilment as an ultimate end" (Dumazedier, 1974, p. 71), excluding the activity categories of renumerated work, family obligations, and sociospiritual and sociopolitical obligations.[4]

Parker (1971) approaches the problem of defining leisure by considering two dimensions of the person's "life space," i.e. "the total of activities or ways of spending time that people have" (p. 25). The two dimensions are *time*, which is dichotomized into *work time* and *nonwork* time, and *activity*, which ranges from *constraint* (obligatory activity) to *freedom*. Since leisure is primarily a function of the constraint-freedom scale, this paradigm makes "leisure in work" possible.

Parker bases his model of leisure on the two commonly used dimensions of time and activity, thus staying within a sociological framework. Yet, he states that "As with other aspects of life and social structure, leisure is an experience of the individual, . . ." (Parker, 1976, p. 12). A difficulty, however, is perceived in applying any standard definition for measurement purposes to this experiential (*psychological*) aspect of leisure (p. 13).

Another sociological model of leisure, based on the two dimensions of relative freedom of choice and relationship to work

---

[4]For another thorough perspective on the sociology of leisure, the reader is referred to N.H. Cheek, Jr., and W.R. Burch, Jr., *The Social Organization of Leisure in Human Society.* (New York, Harper and Row, 1976).

(Kelly, 1972), has recently been revised by replacing work-relation with intrinsic-social meaning (Kelly, 1978). Kelly states that "the work-relation dimension did not aid in establishing a typology of leisure." Research indicated that instead "a second dimension emerged as salient to the meaning of leisure to participants. It is the focus of satisfaction on either the activity itself or on social relationships." Kelly's revised model thus has two dimensions, *freedom* (high and low) and *meaning* (intrinsic and social), leading to four types of leisure.

In comparing his model to that of others, Kelly (1978) concludes that

> The revised paradigm would appear to be more closely related than the original to the continuum of freedom and constraint proposed by Stanley Parker (1971), the perceived motivation and freedom model of social psychologist John Neulinger (1974a) and the stress on meaning and state-of-mind of recreation theorist James Murphy (1975). However, it differs from each of the others in its formulation and in the empirical evidence supporting the development.

At the conclusion of this section, I want to return once more to the work of Kaplan who not only has furnished us a definition of leisure but also has an elaborate theoretical model that attempts to integrate this concept into not only the personal and family context but also the group, societal, cultural, and even historical framework (Kaplan, 1975). Kaplan's model is complex, as it must be to be able to handle that multitude of variables that enter into the system. At the same time it is dynamic, allowing for the constant interaction of the many components. Our primary intention here is to alert the reader to its existence and recommend the study of the original source.[5] Perhaps it is reassuring to note that there is stability in all that flux. Just as Kaplan remains true to his 1960 leisure definition in his 1975 version, so does he remain faithful to the kind of leisure theory he suggests: ". . . ultimately a theory of leisure can be little less than a theory of man and a theory of the emerging culture" (Kaplan, 1960, p. 289).

---

[5]Summaries of both Dumazadier's (1974) and Kaplan's (1975) theoretical positions may be found in J. Neulinger, *To Leisure, an Introduction* (Boston, Allyn & Bacon, 1981).

14

A Leisure Paradigm

The following paradigm is an attempt to identify relevant variables of the leisure experience. It is not intended to be an all-inclusive theory of leisure, as is, for example, the model suggested by Kaplan (1975). It is solely concerned with factors that make a characterization of and distinction between leisure and nonleisure possible. In the narrower sense, then, it remains at all times at the psychological level and restricts itself to psychological variables. In the broader sense, however, this restraint is immediately transgressed. The operationalization of the variables and the very use of the paradigm for a test of its validity and usefulness or for an applied purpose requires the anchoring of the variables in observable phenomena and the objective environment.[6]

The model described is concerned with the analysis of *a state of mind* and the identification of the conditions that will bring about that state. The outcome is a classification of this state into different experiences, some labelled as a type of *leisure*, others as a type of *nonleisure*.

The primary defining criterion of leisure is freedom or, to be more specific, *perceived freedom*. By this we mean a state in which the person feels that what he/she is doing is done by choice and because one wants to do it. No philosophical definition of freedom is required. Everyone knows the difference between doing something because one has to and doing something because one wants to. Whether such a perception is true freedom or only the illusion of it is irrelevant, as Lefcourt (1973) has illustrated. Even illusions have real consequences and the crucial consequence of the illusion of freedom is leisure.

---

[6]Perhaps, an example from another area of psychological research might clarify this point. The well-known frustration-aggression hypothesis of Dollard, et al. (1939) dealt with psychological concepts and phenomena, frustration, and aggression. Nevertheles, the operationalization of the concept of frustration might have been achieved, in some instances, in terms of the use of a screen that prevented children from reaching desired toys. The psychological model, then, to be tested, to be useful, or to be applied is anchored in the "real" environment that consists of screens, toys, children, and other such objective phenomena.

15

Leisure, then, has one and only one essential criterion, and that is the condition of perceived freedom. Any activity carried out freely, without constraint or compulsion, may be associated with the experience of leisure. *To leisure* implies being engaged in an activity as a free agent and of one's own choice.

While this definition catches the essential characteristic of leisure, it does not allow for variations in the intensity nor the quality (timbre) of the leisure experience. Two additional factors must be considered. First, *perceived freedom* is not an all-or-nothing condition; there is always the question of degree and this will affect both the intensity and quality of the experience. For the sake of simplicity, *perceived freedom* is dichotomized in the paradigm but is to be definitely understood as a continuous variable.

Second, there is at least one other dimension that is useful in distinguishing among different types of leisure and nonleisure, and that is the *motivation* for the activity (*intrinsic* or *extrinsic*).[7] For purposes of explication, this dimension is also treated as if it were dichotomous and as if it were one variable. Not only, however, is continuity implied, but that cells with both *intrinsic* and *extrinsic* motivation are provided for suggests that it may be advisable to treat each of these as separate variables.[8] This issue will be further discussed in the chapter on experimental leisure research.

The source of the satisfaction gained distinguishes the two types of motivation for the activity. If the satisfaction stems from

[7]The revision of the leisure paradigm, as presented in this second edition, was first published in Neulinger, "The need for and the implications of a psychological conception of leisure." (*The Ontario Psychologist, 8*, 2: 13–20, 1976a.) The original paradigm had included a third independent variable, namely *goal of activity*. It had been stated from the start that "we do not consider this variable a critical differentiator of leisure and nonleisure, but see it as useful in strengthening the paradigm's predictive power" (Neulinger, 1974a, p. 20). The only other change is the use of different labels for cells five and six, intended to eliminate inconsistencies in the original model.

[8]We might treat *intrinsic* and *extrinsic motivation* as two separate variables with three levels each (low, medium, high) and maintain a dichotomy of *perceived freedom*. We might then consider only certain of the eighteen ensuing cells for analysis (a statistical nightmare!) or employ a full factorial design, and then become lost in the interpretation of eighteen cells. This method, however, would still not catch the hierarchical nature of the model.

engaging in the activity itself, then we are dealing with *intrinsic motivation;* if it results from some payoff from the activity, we have a case of *extrinsic motivation.* In other words, is the activity itself the reward or does the activity only lead to the reward? A picture comes to mind of a country fair at which children were searching through a haystack in which small gifts had been randomly distributed. Once the gift was found, the child could keep it but had to leave. Many a child did just that. They searched, found their reward, and left happily smiling. There were others, although few, who searched, found a gift, quickly hid it again in the straw, and continued searching. For them, searching, the very activity in which they had been engaging, seemed to have been the reward, the motivating force behind their actions.

Intrinsic motivation relates closely to the ideal of leisure in the classical sense: an activity done for its own sake. It also touches on the dimension of perceived freedom, since extrinsically motivated behavior *may* not be perceived as completely free behavior. Anything done *in order to* may lose degrees of perceived freedom. These issues are currently being investigated by social psychologists and will be taken up again later (Chapter 7). Purists may object to the confounding of our two independent variables (*perceived freedom* and *motivation*). They are, however, logically distinct even though, statistically, they may not always be orthogonal.

Table I presents the paradigm of leisure. The prime distinction between leisure and nonleisure is made along the dimension of *perceived freedom.* We then allow for three categories of motivation: *intrinsic, intrinsic and extrinsic,* and *extrinsic.* Behavior is nearly always multidetermined, and certain activities will be both intrinsically and extrinsically motivated. This may be unfortunate for the designer of paradigms but reflects the complexity of life. Our model, thus, lists six qualitatively different states of mind, three leisure and three nonleisure states, ranging from *pure job* to *pure leisure.*

Before we turn to a brief description of each of the six cells of the model, we want to stress the following. The labels used are

TABLE I

A PARADIGM OF LEISURE

Freedom					
Perceived Freedom			*Perceived Constraint*		
Motivation			Motivation		
Intrinsic	*Intrinsic and Extrinsic*	*Extrinsic*	*Intrinsic*	*Intrinsic and Extrinsic*	*Extrinsic*
(1) Pure Leisure	(2) Leisure- Work	(3) Leisure- Job	(4) Pure Work	(5) Work- Job	(6) Pure Job
Leisure			Nonleisure		

◄——————————————State of Mind——————————————►

Source: Adapted from J. Neulinger, The need for and the implications of a psychological conception of leisure, *Ontario Psychologist*, 1976, 8, no. 2, p. 15.

meant to be descriptive and not prescriptive. The paradigm is an attempt to classify states of mind only. These states may be of quite short duration, even fleeting, or they may be prolonged; a person may, of course, vascillate from one stage to another. It is tempting to classify people, activities, or life situations into these categories, and as an approximation, this may be useful. But this is neither the function nor within the power of the model.

PURE LEISURE (Cell 1). (A state of mind brought about by)[9] an activity freely engaged in and done for its own sake — truly leisure in the classical sense, an ideal to be striven for, but hardly ever attained. Not only does it require freedom in the sense of

---

[9]This phrase applies to the description of all cells.

absence of both external and internal constraints, but it also implies being able to enjoy the satisfaction derived from intrinsic reward without having to pay attention to potential extrinsic ones. Implicit is the notion that the person's basic needs (Maslow, 1954) have been satisfied to such a degree that they no longer represent an issue.[10]

LEISURE-WORK (Cell 2). An activity freely engaged in and providing both intrinsic and extrinsic rewards. The sense of leisure is present: one perceives one's behavior as self-determined. The activity, however, is satisfying not only in itself but also in terms of its consequences or payoffs. One's employment situation may, at times, fulfill these conditions for certain people. A Rockefeller holding a job as a bank president or moving into the slum areas of Harlem to do social work might experience this type of leisure. A person doing chores around the house that are enjoyable *and* do not need to be done would qualify also. The emphasis is on the fact that one knows that one does not have to do the activity, or any other instead, if one really does not want to.

LEISURE-JOB (Cell 3). An activity freely engaged in, but providing satisfaction only in terms of its consequences or payoffs. Recreation, in the literal sense, is an example: exercising in order to restore one's strength or to maintain one's health, not on doctor's order but simply because one likes to do it and chooses to do so. Playing cards for the sake of winning money (without, however, being in financial need!) is another example.

The above represent three types of leisure states; let us now turn to three types of nonleisure states.

PURE WORK (Cell 4). An activity engaged in under constraint, but providing entirely intrinsic rewards. A state that comes very close to leisure in terms of felt satisfaction, yet lacks the essential ingredient: *perceived freedom*. The student turned on by a homework assignment who does more than is necessary, as well as a professor steeped in research, yet aware of the need for a

---

[10]Note in this context a study by Rokeach (1973) that showed the median ranking of "a comfortable life" (among eighteen terminal values) to range from about seven for the lowest income group to about thirteen for the highest, in a national sample of 1,325 subjects.

19

paycheck, may experience this state.

It may be well to remind the reader here that cells one and six, as well as three and four, are abstractions that are unlikely to arise in their pure form in real life. They are needed, however, to delineate the range of possibilities.

WORK-JOB (Cell 5). An activity engaged in under constraint and providing both intrinsic and extrinsic rewards. The degree of satisfaction derived will vary as a function of the proportion of the intrinsic to the extrinsic reward.[11] Once again, there is an awareness of constraint, thus turning this situation into a nonleisure experience, no matter how satisfying it might be otherwise. The average employment situation may produce this state, given that one is aware of one's lot as a worker, that is, one's inability to quit if so desired.

PURE JOB (Cell 6). An activity engaged in under constraint and with no reward in and of itself, but only through a payoff resulting from it. The very opposite of pure leisure. The everyday situation that might bring about this state is the job (paid employment) in its most negative connotation: a job one must do to earn a living and that provides no satisfaction other than the paycheck.

Some further remarks about the paradigm need to be made, even though some may seem repetitious. The purpose of the model is to identify critical variables of the leisure experience so that we can better understand as well as predict and influence behavior in this domain. The paradigm is an abstraction. In any given person, the dimensions discussed will manifest themselves in varying and at times quite different degrees for the same activity. To say it once more: behavior is multidetermined; there are always many reasons why we do things, some of which we are probably not even aware of. It would be naive to imagine that the social scientist can find single and neatly orthogonal causes of behavior, given the intricate interrelationships of our values and motivations. In addition, we should not underestimate that

---

[11]This, obviously, is not to deny the potential satisfaction of an extrinsic reward. This whole issue will be discussed at a later point.

people, particularly when they are not sure about what they want, may base their choice of action on the slightest and often quite irrelevant circumstance. We might even suspect that at times such behavior is quite intentional; it is a rejection of the obligation to choose, a kind of escape from freedom.

The model deals at this point with a very limited number of variables. Others could be added. For example, we might once again add the *goal* of the activity, or perceived pleasure, time pressure, importance, or any other of a number of potential variables. These need not necessarily be orthogonal to the ones already used in order to contribute further to the amount of variance accounted for by the present model.

The model does not specify any particular statistical method to test its validity or usefulness in making predictions. The intent is to delineate the leisure experience in the closest possible way and then worry about appropriate statistical designs. The model, however, is clearly of a hierarchical nature, positing *perceived freedom* as the overriding and determining dimension of leisure, suggesting other dimensions as potential modifiers of either the leisure or the nonleisure state.

One more point before we turn to implications of the model. That psychological factors, people's perceptions and experiences, are critical phenomena of the leisure domain and must be taken into account in theorizing, as well as in planning and policy decisions, and in the provision of leisure services is by now a well-recognized fact. A broad model of leisure, such as Kaplan's (1975), is flexible enough to permit the incorporation of sociological, psychological, economic, and other hypotheses, and even mini-theories from different disciplines, within its overall framework. More restrictive theories, however, that attempt to remain within for example a sociological framework, yet want to cover psychological phenomena, may run into problems. Dumazedier (1974), clearly recognizing the issue, has quite explicitly selected to stay within a sociological framework. Others, however, have attempted to infer to psychological phenomena from models that are built with basically sociological

21

constructs. This can only lead to confusion rather than the needed explication of leisure phenomena at both levels of discourse.

What do we see as the implications of the model? First, it allows leisure once again to become a positive value. It achieves this by making a work/job distinction rather than a work/leisure one. Leisure is no longer defined in contrast to work; it is no longer the opposite of a positive value. Work may lead to a leisure as well as a nonleisure experience, a reality factor of which we are well aware. As a consequence we no longer need feel that we must fight the work ethic in order to establish a new and much needed positive leisure ethic. There is no longer a struggle between leisure and work, but rather a coexistence.

Second, the model helps to clarify the role the individual or society plays in creating the conditions for leisure. It is evident that, to a large degree, a person's perception of freedom is a function of one's position in society. It is the result of factors over which the individual has relatively little control. If we take monetary constraints, as one example of this type, we see that the number of people who are financially independent is extremely low, and very few people are likely to manage to pull themselves out of this condition. A major change, in this respect, would require a social or political act, for example, the establishment of a guaranteed annual income. No individual is likely to plan such a step as a means to increase one's perceived freedom.

A third and related implication is the model's role in leisure education and counseling. A psychological conception necessitates a shift in emphasis away from a concern with filling up empty time or simply providing an array of so-called leisure activities, to promoting the conditions that will help to generate a leisure experience. We shall have more to say about this in later chapters.

Finally, there are heuristic aspects, research implications of the model. The identification of variables involved in the leisure experience allows for their investigation. Freedom and motivation (as implied in this model) have been much researched topics of social psychology, and an extension of such research into the

22

leisure domain may well be encouraged by this or any similar type model. We are thinking particularly of areas such as the perception of causality and attribution theory, the role of intrinsic versus extrinsic rewards in determining behavior, and individual differences in the perception of freedom. We shall return to these issues in the chapter on experimental leisure research.

EMPIRICAL DEFINITIONS OF LEISURE

It must be obvious, by now, that there is considerable disagreement among so-called experts (sociologists, political scientists, philosophers, etc.) about the exact meaning of leisure. Yet, the word is used in everyday speech quite frequently, and people seem to be able to communicate about the subject with each other quite satisfactorily. Thus, there must be a common core of meaning in the word that is generally accepted.

What Is Leisure: The Denotation of Leisure

A preliminary survey on leisure (Neulinger, 1967a) attempted to probe into the meaning of leisure by asking two questions: "What is leisure?" and "Would you make a distinction between leisure and recreation?" and if so, "What is the distinction?" A word is in order about this preliminary survey. Its purpose was to obtain information about problems involved in constructing a questionnaire relating to issues of leisure. The primary intention was not to use the data to draw inferences about the distribution of opinions or responses, but to check out ways of phrasing questions and to get a feeling for the subject matter.[12] Accordingly, only a small sample was used, without any systematic method of sampling other than the attempt to make the sample

---

[12]It may be worthwhile to state explicitly that in certain types of studies, random sampling is not a critical condition. Given a fairly even distribution of 80 percent red and 20 percent white marbles in a population of marbles, and given a reasonable sample, it is very likely that one obtains at least one white marble in the sample. If I am only interested in what types of marbles there are, rather than their distribution or frequency in the population, this one marble will give me the information. Only when I want to draw inferences about the distribution of marbles in the population does random sampling become critical. Of course, if the sampling is so biased and unrepresentative that one would not even get a single white marble, one would be in trouble. But, this is not likely to be the case even if sampling is far from random.

as heterogeneous as possible. A total of sixty-nine subjects, twenty-four males and forty-five females, ranging in age from eighteen to sixty-eight years, with a mean age of 38.2 years, completed the questionnaire. Respondents included representatives of the professions, the entertainment field, white-collar and blue-collar workers, students, and housewives.

Responses to the question: "What is leisure?" could be categorized into three distinct types of answers according to the emphasis of the total response, as follows:

a. emphasis on leisure as discretionary *time* (77%)

b. emphasis on leisure as discretionary *activity* (18%)

c. emphasis on leisure as *a state of mind* (5%)

While the distribution of responses should not be taken to be representative of a larger population (since we did not use random sampling), they do take on some significance in the light of similar results by J. Dumazedier in a better controlled study of 819 French workers and employees.[13]

Following are examples of responses to the question "What is leisure?", for each of the three categories:

a. *Emphasis on leisure as discretionary time*

After working hours. Vacation and weekend.

Leisure is the time left to an individual after the demands of earning a living and responding to the demands of society have been met.

Time to spend in relaxation from work.

Time free from work in which one may do the things one likes to do.

Discretionary time — you have a choice of what to do, one alternative of which is nothing.

b. *Emphasis on leisure as discretionary activity*

Any activity (or nonactivity) one does (or does not do) at one's own direction — when, where and for how long one wants to.

Doing what you want to do, when you want to do it, in a relaxed carefree way.

---

[13]An investigation carried out on a sample of 819 French workers and employees in 1953 by J. Dumazedier showed that, where as the majority of them still thought of *leisure* as merely *time*, more than a quarter already considered it as an activity. Not one of them, we may note, thought of leisure as a *state* (Friedman, 1961, p. 109).

Doing whatever pleases a person, while he is not fulfilling his duties.

c. *Emphasis on leisure as a state of mind*
  A physical and mental state void of work and worries of financial character.

The most important element of leisure is a *state of mind*, i.e. the mind must be free of guilt feelings and ready to pursue any number of activities with the sole purpose of enjoyment for its own sake . . . and not feeling that you really should be doing something else.

Relaxing, restful, comfortable, peaceful.

On the question "Would you make a distinction between leisure and recreation?", respondents were fairly evenly divided. Fifty-three percent said "Yes," they would make a distinction, and 47 percent replied "No." When asked to describe the distinction between leisure and recreation, the most frequent reply was that leisure implies passivity or nonactivity, whereas recreation implies activity. Examples of this type of response are the following:

To me recreation seems to be more athletic — sports such as swimming and tennis in my opinion would be recreation.

Leisure is the spare time that you have when you don't have to do anything but sit around and relax. Recreation to me is when you're participating physically. It also could be mentally . . .

Recreation is active, leisure can be passive.

Some respondents defined leisure as the frame into which recreation can be fitted. Examples are the following:

Leisure is the free, spare time that an individual would fill with their chosen recreation activities. Leisure is the time; recreation is what would be done with this time.

Recreation or hobbies are what a person uses his leisure for.

Leisure is the time available. *Recreation* is an application of time.

There was also some indication that leisure implies a more serious purpose than recreation:

Leisure is time which may be devoted to recreation; recreation connotes an absence of serious purpose, whereas leisure can encompass activities of serious purposes.

Some additional light was thrown on the meaning of leisure by responses to a question on why leisure is considered a necessary

25

part of life. (There was near unamimous agreement, 97 percent, that leisure *is* a necessary part of life). The most frequently given reason was that leisure is necessary to re-create oneself, to gain new strength, or to maintain good health. The following are examples:

> It gives our minds and bodies a rest.
> It refreshes both body and mind.
> Leisure recharges and refreshes. It gives a person added motivation to return to work.
> It lets the mind and the body rest from work, so that one might return to work refreshed.

A somewhat less frequently given reason was that man needs variety and that leisure offers this variety.

> Because all work and no play makes Jack a dull boy.
> Because life is no fun without it. It tends to get drab or depressing.
> Because one must have a change of pace both mentally and physically.

Some respondents emphasized the opportunity that leisure offers for self-actualization, for a broadening of the self, or for self-reflection and contemplation.

> It is the only part of life in which the purpose of the other parts may be examined.
> It is the time for self-awareness and for the slow emergence of an understanding of the world.
> This is when an individual can indulge those interests which are not related to work or routine, and thus become a more educated and satisfied person.

Reflecting on the responses obtained we may conclude that the objective definition of leisure, i.e. leisure as a residual, is a generally accepted way of thinking about leisure. This fact will become important in later discussions of the relationship of work and leisure. Note, however, that we did find leisure definitions that reflected the more classical view of leisure, indicating that this ideal has not totally vanished from the scene.

What Is Leisure: The Connotation of Leisure

We shall next describe a study that addressed itself to the question: "What does leisure mean to you?" or "What does leisure imply?" It is an inquiry into the connotative meaning of lei-

26

sure. The method used was that of Osgood, Suci, and Tannenbaum (1957), who developed the *semantic differential* technique for this very purpose. This method requires persons to rate concepts on several bipolar scales. For example, the concepts might be *mother*, or *church*, or *police*, and the bipolar scales might be *good-bad, strong-weak, fast-slow,* or *beautiful-ugly*. Each scale is viewed as consisting of seven points. For example, the *good-bad* scale would be represented as follows:

good　　1 . . . . .2 . . . . .3 . . . . .4 . . . . .5 . . . . .6 . . . . .7　　*bad*
　　　　　　　　　　　　neutral
　　extremely quite slightly　　or　　slightly quite extremely
　　　　　　　　unrelated

Respondents then check off that point on the scale at which they would place the concept in question. In spite of the apparent difficulty of this task, most people seem to be able to perform it quite reliably. Osgood, Suci, and Tannenbaum, using factor analytic procedures, have shown that most concepts are heavily weighted by three major factors: *evaluation, potency,* and *activity*, as measured by scales such as *fair-unfair, weak-strong,* and *active-passive*. The real advantage of this method is that one can obtain quantitative comparisons between the meanings of different concepts, as well as between the way in which different groups view the same concept.

Hanhart (1964) had used a semantic differential approach to examine the connotations of the words *Arbeit, Musse, Spiel,* and *Freizeit* (work, leisure, play and free time). His work inspired the project described next that was carried out by David Schnarch and is described fully in his honor's thesis (Schnarch, 1969).

LEISURE REDEFINED (David M. Schnarch, 1969). Two aspects of the study will be described. One is the way in which the term *leisure* relates to other concepts in the leisure-work domain; the other is a comparison of leisure, work, and self-profiles for two groups of subjects. A brief description of the method used in this study follows:

Subjects. The sample consisted of 237 respondents, 132 students and 105 full-time working subjects. The student sample consisted of

27

fifty-eight male and seventy-four female students at The City College of New York, mean age 19.5 years. Median family income about $10,000; religious distribution — 62 percent Jewish, 23 percent Catholic, 12 percent no religious preference, 3 percent Protestant, and 1 percent other. Of the working sample, fifty-eight were male and forty-seven female. Mean age was 27.2 years; mean educational level 14.1 years. Median family income about $12,000; religious distribution — 57 percent Jewish, 18 percent Catholic, 11 percent no religious preference, 9 percent Protestant, and 5 percent other. Occupations ranged from teachers throught business managers to secretaries.

Questionnaire. A semantic differential questionnaire with instructions similar to those of Osgood, et al. (1957) was used, listing the following ten concepts in this order: *leisure, labor, recreation, work, rest, activity, free time, play, idleness, and me*. Twelve bipolar scales were selected: six from Osgood's evaluative factor, four from the potency factor, two from the activity factor.

Procedure. The questionnaires were administered on a nonpaid, voluntary basis to students during one of their regular class hours; workers completed the questionnaires either at home or at their job. The anonymity of the respondents was protected in either case.

Let us now look at some of the results obtained. First, this is how the data were used to investigate perceived similarity of the concepts. The semantic differential furnishes a profile for each concept, i.e. the position of the concept on each of the twelve bipolar scales. If two concepts had identical positions on all twelve scales, they were considered to have the same meaning, at least in terms of the characteristics investigated. To the degree that their positions are different on the various scales, the concepts become less and less similar. The measure used to express this degree of similarity is the D score (Osgood et al., 1957).[14] A score of zero expresses maximum similarity or identity; the higher the D value, the less the similarity of the two concepts.

$$D_{il} = \sqrt{\sum_j d_{il}^2}$$

---

[14]Such a measure is provided by the *generalized distance formula* of solid geometry: where D_{il} is the linear distance between the points in the semantic space representing concepts i and l and d_{il} is the algebraic difference between the coordinates of i and l on the same dimension or factor, j. Summation is over the k dimensions (Osgood, et al., 1957. p. 91).

Table II presents D scores for the ten concepts investigated. Three pairs of concepts show the greatest similarity: *work – labor* (0.8), *recreation – play* (0.8), and *leisure – free time* (0.8). The concept that stands out as being most dissimilar to all others is *idleness*, with *idleness – recreation* (9.4), *idleness – activity* (9.3), and *idleness – play* (9.1) showing the greatest dissimilarity. The most interesting aspect of the table is the position of the concept *me*. Note its relative closeness to the concepts *work* (2.0) and *labor* (2.5) compared to the concept of *leisure* (3.4). *Me* is associated with *activity* (1.9), not with *rest* (5.4), and *activity*, in turn, is associated with *work* (2.2) more than with *leisure* (3.4). These findings demonstrate how identification takes place primarily through work, a point that will be discussed in greater length in later chapters.

TABLE II
SIMILARITY SCORES (D) FOR TEN CONCEPTS
IN THE LEISURE-WORK DOMAIN (N = 237)

	Work	Labor	Me	Activity	Play	Recreation	Free Time	Leisure	Rest	Idleness
Work		0.8	2.0	2.2	3.0	3.6	3.8	4.3	6.0	8.0
	Labor		2.5	2.7	3.5	4.1	4.3	4.8	6.5	7.8
		Me		1.9	2.1	2.7	3.1	3.4	5.4	8.6
			Activity		1.4	2.0	3.0	3.4	5.7	9.3
				Play		0.8	2.0	2.3	4.8	9.1
					Recreation		1.8	1.9	4.4	9.4
						Free Time		0.8	2.8	8.0
							Leisure		2.8	8.4
								Rest		7.3
										Idleness

Source: Schnarch, 1969.

The second findings to be reported are differences in profiles between students and workers for three of the concepts: *work*, *leisure*, and *me* (Table III). (Note that this table also permits comparisons between concepts within students or workers.) Looking at factor score differences, we can say that workers have a much more positive evaluation of the concept *work* than do students, and they also see *work* as more active. Workers also see themselves as much more powerful than students, and this is reflected in a more powerful perception of the concept of *leisure*, but not

29

of the concept of *work*. Expressing these findings in a different way, we can say that students perceived themselves as quite impotent, compared to workers. And they viewed the work required of them in a rather negative light. These findings may well reflect students' general dissatisfaction with current curriculum requirements and their feeling of alienation from the mainstream of American life.

The method employed in this study, the *semantic differential*, provides us, then, with a way of quantifying the meaning of leisure and other concepts. It should be noted, however, that this first study had several limitations: a small sample size, nonrandom sampling, and adjective scales that were not necessarily relevant to leisure concepts. The technique was adopted for a later questionnaire (*A Study of Leisure*, Appendix A), described in the next chapter. Profiles for the concepts *leisure* and *work* were obtained from two samples and have been presented elsewhere (Neulinger and Raps, 1972). Probably the most significant finding from that study is that, while *leisure* is generally perceived as more positive than *work*, in an absolute sense *work* is still placed on the positive end of most scales. Could a society exist where this would not be the case? Probably not, as long as that society depends on *work* to maintain itself as a functioning organism.

At the conclusion of this chapter the reader may feel a certain amount of dissatisfaction that is shared by the author. We set out by stating that an adequate conceptualization of leisure is a *sine qua non* for any research on leisure. Have we come up with an adequate conceptualization? The answer, unfortunately must be unequivocally, no. We have listed a number of leisure definitions; we have suggested a paradigm of our own; we have pointed to differences in various leisure concepts and have tried to delineate some of the meanings implied by the word *leisure*. But, it must be clear by now that the term *leisure* is very much like the term *intelligence:* everybody uses it but hardly anyone can agree on what it means. It may be used in different ways and it has different implications depending on how it is being used.

What is the solution, then? Perhaps, it is best to state once more what the problem is. That the term *leisure* is used colloquially with different denotative meanings is something about which we can do very little, nor might we even want to do anything about it if we could. As I see it, there are two separate issues involved. One is the relatively negative connotation that the term *leisure* still carries in our society. This, of course, relates to leisure still being perceived by most in opposition to work. As we move evermore into a postindustrial society, such a view is becoming inappropriate and in many ways destructive to the individual, as will be pointed out in later chapters. We ought, therefore, to work consciously on improving the popular connotation of the concept leisure. Can this be done? Perhaps we might take a lesson from the connotative meaning of the term *black*, which certainly has undergone quite a change in recent history. Perhaps we need a "leisure is beautiful" movement.

The second issue is the use of the term *leisure* by professionals in the professional literature and in all professional communications. Here we should demand a clarity of denotative meaning — *not* a prescription on *how the term ought to be used*, but simply an explicit statement on *how it is being used*. The professional ought to make it quite unambiguous what is being denoted by the term *leisure*, specifically whether it points to a period of time, and activity, or a state of mind. I have elaborated on these issues elsewhere a great deal and want to repeat here only that such a demand seems a self-evident necessity in any discipline that wishes to have itself viewed as a science, social or otherwise.

There is another implication that derives from this multiplicity of leisure meanings. Unless endowed with unlimited research funds, perhaps one ought to narrow one's goals to restrict oneself to the study of specific aspects of leisure. For example, time is obviously an intricately related aspect of leisure. Thus, we may study time budgets or allocations, ways in which people spend or want to spend their time. In doing so, we must keep in mind that we are studying one aspect of leisure. The delineation of relevant aspects of leisure may well be one of the primary goals of future research. If we cannot study leisure as a global concept or if no such unitary thing exists, let us not invent it (and commit the

TABLE III
WORK, LEISURE AND SELF CONCEPTS, AS PERCEIVED BY 131 STUDENTS AND 104 WORKERS

Scales:[a]	Work			Leisure			Me		
	Student	Worker	t	Student	Worker	t	Student	Worker	t
good/bad	2.6	1.9	6.43***	1.9	1.7	2.74**	2.1	1.9	2.27*
beautiful/ugly	3.7	3.1	4.56***	2.2	2.0	1.30	2.9	2.8	.72
honest/dishonest	2.5	1.9	6.60***	2.6	2.5	.85	2.1	2.0	1.09
fair/unfair	2.8	2.6	1.84	2.5	2.6	1.08	2.1	1.7	4.68***
pleasant/unpleasant	3.4	2.7	5.87***	1.7	1.3	6.24***	2.2	1.9	3.98***
relaxed/tense	4.7	4.3	2.61**	2.1	2.0	.74	4.4	4.6	1.02
evaluative factor	3.3	2.7	6.38***	2.1	2.0	2.33*	2.6	2.5	2.46*
large/small	3.2	3.1	1.04	3.7	3.6	.17	4.0	3.6	3.04**
heavy/light	2.9	3.5	5.11***	5.0	4.8	1.08	4.4	4.0	2.77**
strong/weak	3.0	2.9	1.00	3.5	3.1	3.07**	3.4	2.7	6.78***
wide/narrow	3.8	3.4	3.46***	3.5	3.1	2.52*	3.8	3.4	3.82***
potency factor	3.2	3.2	.03	3.9	3.7	2.61**	3.9	3.4	5.43***
fast/slow	3.4	3.1	2.70**	4.0	4.0	.10	3.0	2.7	2.46*
active/passive	2.3	2.0	2.82**	3.5	3.2	2.29*	2.5	2.2	2.09*
activity factor	2.8	2.5	3.52***	3.8	3.6	1.51	2.7	2.5	2.70**

[a]Scales range from 1 to 7, with the first half of the pairs at the lower end of the continuum.

*p < .05
**p < .01
***p < .001

Source: Schnarch, 1969.

32

fallacy of reification), but let us search for meaningful dimensions in the leisure domain that are susceptible to investigation and even experimentation.

CHAPTER 2

THE MEASUREMENT
OF LEISURE

THERE ARE TWO QUESTIONS INVOLVED in the problem of
measurement: what are we measuring, and how are we going to
measure it. The first question implies classification. To measure
something we have to focus in on it; we must distinguish it from
its surrounding; we must isolate it, put it into a class by itself.
Once we have identified what we want to measure we can turn to
the question of how to measure it. The simplest form of measurement is counting. We establish the frequency with which a
particular object or event occurs. Very often, this is all we want to
do and all we need to do; sometimes, this is all we can do. At other
times, however, we may not be satisfied with a mere frequency
count. Our interest may be related to a characteristic or quality of
an object or event rather than to its mere existence or nonexis-
tence. We may want to know how much of a certain quality the
object or event possesses, for example, how large it is, how hot it
is, and so on. Here again, there are different degrees of precision
we may wish to achieve. We may be satisfied with being able to
say that A has more of some quality than B; for example, A is
larger than B, without being concerned with how much larger.
We may want to quantify differences between A and B and C in
such a way that we are able to say that the *difference* between A
and B is twice as large as the *difference* between B and C. In
neither case are we concerned with the absolute amount of the
quantity possessed by the object. If we are, if we want to be able to
say that A possesses twice as much of a certain quality as B, for
example that A is twice as large as B, we must also be able to measure the complete absence of the quality. Different types of
problems will be faced depending on which type of measure-

35

ment one wants to achieve.[1]

The science of the measurement of leisure is still at a stage where it is very much concerned with the problem of classification. In the previous chapter we discussed the conceptualization of leisure. Conceptualization implies classification, just as classification leads to conceptualization. We have concluded that the adequate conceptualization of leisure is a difficult, perhaps impossible, task and have argued that we should make it our task to study separate aspects of leisure. In this chapter, we concern ourselves with some of these aspects and explore ways in which they have been quantified. Our emphasis is on leisure attitudes and dimensions relevant to the leisure experience, but we shall begin by outlining ways in which other aspects of leisure have been measured.

TRADITIONAL APPROACHES

The classification of leisure research into activities, expenditures of time and money, and meanings follows Meyersohn's (1969) description of the sociology of leisure in the United States.

The Measurement of Leisure Activities[2]

The most common approach to the study of leisure is the study of leisure activities. Activities are concrete acts; they can be observed, and they have duration; they represent objective behavior. Relative to subjective phenomena they are more readily subject to all types of measurements. Meyersohn (1969) lists three ways in which activities have been studied: (a) the amount of time used in them (b) the amount of money spent on them, and (c) the amount of interest in them.

There is no question that to somebody interested in leisure, information about these three aspects of leisure activities can be

---

[1]The reader with a statistical background will recognize this discussion as the problem of scaling, and as referring to *nominal, ordinal, interval,* and *ratio* scales. Most textbooks of introductory statistics give treatments of this topic (e.g. Guilford, 1965; Harshbarger, 1971; Ferguson, 1966).

[2]The term *leisure activity* is used here in the traditional sense, implying a *free-time activity* intended to and presumably leading to a leisure experience.

very useful and desirable. For example, a city park is presumably a place where one might want to spend one's free time. Thus, to the superintendent of parks, the time people spend in parks is of interest. However, should we assume that the activity, "spending time in the park," is a leisure activity? How about the nurse who spends her time pushing the baby carriage through the park, the man who walks his dog, the child who is taken there by his mother, or the mother who is taken there by her child?

The first and most serious problem with this approach is the question of which activities to include as leisure activities. As we pointed out before, no activity is inherently not a leisure activity. Some activities are more likely to and do more frequently fulfill the criteria of leisure. Accordingly, some activities will be of greater interest than others to the researcher of leisure. But a mere list of activities will always be ambiguous as to its meaning. Unless further qualified, such a list will never enable us to make unequivocal inferences about a leisure experience, but only about so-called *leisure activities*.

A second problem, not quite as serious as the first, is the problem of categorization. There is an infinity of different activities. What are the criteria to form classes of activities? What are the boundaries of each activity? What constitutes a unit of activity? These and other questions are common to all attempts at categorization and one settles them usually in terms of one compromise or another. The important point to keep in mind is that somewhere along the line one has made arbitrary decisions and that one's findings will be limited by the system of classification one has chosen.

The Measurement of Expenditures of Time and Money

In this type of research, often referred to as *time-budget* or *money-budget* studies, the way a person spends resources, time, or money is investigated. The idea is to get an accurate, detailed, and complete record of the person's total time or money allocations. These studies often include investigations into work as well as free-time behavior, since work information is bound to be part of the data obtained, and since time spent at work is relevant to

37

the residual definition of leisure. As a by-product of these studies, one obviously also obtains information about leisure activities, but this information is usually limited to the amount of time spent on them.

Problems mentioned in the previous section, those of identification and classification of leisure activities, are still with us. The first problem, the identification of leisure, is presumably resolved by using the residual definition: leisure is all time spent beyond the fulfillment of subsistence and existence needs. However, even if we accept the validity of this definition, we are still faced with the problem of determining just what are and what are not existence and subsistence needs. For example, is a certain amount of affiliation *necessary* for existence? Could we survive as complete social isolates? Or when do we eat to satisfy existence needs and when to satisfy pleasure needs?

The second problem, the classification of leisure activities, takes on a new twist when we start measuring the time spent in each activity. The difficulty is that of overlapping and concurrent activities. A man may read a book, listen to the radio, eat his dinner, and converse with his wife, all at the same time. Is he doing all of these things, or perhaps none of them, since he may be daydreaming? It becomes necessary to distinguish between primary, secondary, or even tertiary activities. Such distinctions are not easy to make and may, at times, be irrelevant. Some people have their television set turned on from the minute they get home. Are they watching TV? What is the operational definition of watching TV or of listening to the radio?

Modern time-budget studies are also attempting to give more meaning to the data obtained by ascertaining the context within which an activity took place. What activity came before? What followed? Who was present? For example, the monumental work by Alexander Szalai (1972), *The Use of Time*, a cross-cultural, twelve-nation, time-budget project, investigated activities in terms of four temporal variables, *duration, frequency, timing* and *sequential order*; a spatial variable, *location; and a social variable, with whom.* It is obvious that both the collection and analyses of such data present formidable problems.

The Measurement of the Meaning of Leisure

This is the least studied of the three aspects of leisure. "This third approach has few empirical examples" (Meyersohn, 1969). One of the reasons for this may be that the very question asked presupposes a different definition of leisure than the traditional residual one generally used. Studies of this type are more akin to what we have called the *subjective* definition of leisure, as represented by Pieper (1963) and de Grazia (1962). The concern is the subjective experience of leisure. What does an activity mean to the person? How does he feel about it? Why does he do it? What satisfaction does he get out of it? These are subjective phenomena, and all the problems involved in measuring such phenomena become relevant.

It should be stressed that the meaning of leisure here is not the meaning of the concept of leisure per se, but rather the meaning that the activity we call leisure has to the person. We are concerned here with the function or implication of the activity for the person.

Meyersohn, recognizing the importance of a distinction between leisure and free time in respect to this type of study, lists four distinct meanings of leisure: (1) leisure as rest, respite, restoration; (2) leisure as entertainment; (3) leisure as self-realization; and (4) leisure as spiritual renewal (1972, p. 211). It is clear that to obtain information of this kind, we shall have to be concerned with inner states of the person, we shall need to deal with psychological variables, and we shall be faced with all the problems involved in such investigations.

It is not a far step to include motivational research within the context of the meaning of leisure. Asking what satisfactions a leisure activity may offer is another way of inquiring what needs are being fulfilled by that activity. This type of approach is in line with a humanistic orientation to recreation and leisure, and we do find an increasing number of such studies in the 1970s.

REPRESENTATIVE STUDIES

On the following pages are a number of studies that exemplify how researchers have attempted to solve the problems listed in the previous section. In this chapter, we limit ourselves to a discussion of methodology; the next chapter shall deal with the content of some of these studies, although sometimes the distinction is hard to maintain. We attempt to give information that may be helpful to persons involved in developing their own method of coping with these problems. For example, since there is no one best way to categorize activities, we report several, in the hope that readers may find one that is suitable for their particular needs. Although this makes for much detail, it may prove to be useful.

Time-Budget Studies

Studies dealing with the use of time have been reviewed by Robinson and Converse (1972). According to these authors

> The vast majority of these studies in retrospect seem haphazardly executed and/or confined to relatively narrow classes of activities (like housework, or industrial time-and-motion studies) or specialized samples (farmers, students, executives, rural housewives).
>
> At best, perhaps a half-dozen studies scattered over the past thirty-five years were sufficiently rigorous and multipurposive in nature to be of much interest, and even here methodological defects and incomparabilities abound (p. 21).

Studies which the authors judge as most valuable are those of Lundberg, et al. (1934), Sorokin and Berger (1939), J. A. Ward — Mutual Broadcasting (1962), Opinion Research Corporation (1962), and Converse and Robinson (1966).We are presenting here their most informative summary table of these studies (Table IV); the interested reader is encouraged to consult the original article for more detail.

The Lundberg, et al. (1934) work, *Leisure: A Suburban Study*, is probably the best known and earliest study of leisure activities in the United States. According to the authors, the uses of leisure time had never before been subjected to detailed study from the standpoint of the individual or the special group. The method chosen to obtain information about the respondents' activities was the individual's own account of his activities. Three major problems, inherent in that method, were recognized: (a) the voluntary cooperation of respondents is needed for something that

TABLE IV

MAJOR TIME USE STUDIES COMPARED ON VARIOUS CHARACTERISTICS

Study	Sample	Time Budgets	Interviewing Period	Coding Categories	Special Features	Major Shortcomings
Lundberg et al. (1934)	2,460 residents of Westchester County, New York (of these almost 1,600 were students)	3–7/person; total = 4,460	November–May 1931–32 and 1932–33	15 (but no code for shopping)	1. "Good time patterns" i.e., enjoyable parts of day	1. No day of week differences (possible over-sample of weekends) 2. Low response rate 3. Affluent community with no illiterates and few working-class respondents 4. No summer months 5. Respondents reconstruct days from memory 6. Possible restriction to activities over 30 minutes
Sorokin and Berger (1939)	176 adults in Boston	At least 28/person; total = 3,476	May–November 1935	55 (reduced to 8 general categories)	1. Predictability of budgets 2. Motivations for activities 3. Social contacts for activities	1. Oversampling of unemployed, young women 2. Summer months only 3. Low response rates 4. Differences due to sex, employment, marital status, etc. not available
J. A. Ward–Mutual Broadcasting (de Grazia, 1962)	Nationwide sample of all individuals over 5 years of age in 7,000 households	2/person; total = 17,000 for ages 20–59	March–April 1954	13 (no separate code for TV)	1. Nationwide probability sample 2. Day of week variations accounted for	1. Only 17 hours period covered 2. No summer months 3. Breakdowns by age, education, etc. not available

41

TABLE IV — Cont.

Study	Sample	Time Budgets	Interviewing Period	Coding Categories	Special Features	Major Shortcomings
Opinion Research Corporation (de Grazia, 1962)	Nationwide sample of 5,021 persons aged 15 and over	1/person total = 5,021	June–July 1957	20 (only certain leisure activities)	1. Participation only	1. Actual time spent not ascertained
Converse and Robinson (1966)	Urban probability sample of 1,244 adults in employed households + 788 adults in Jackson, Michigan	1/person total = 1,802 budgets 2/person total = 440 budgets	November–December 1965; March–April 1966	96 (reduced to 27 activities)	1. Part of 10 nation study 2. Activities most easily given up 3. Most enjoyable part of the day 4. Yearly participation figures	1. No data for rural areas or unemployed households 2. No summer months

Source: Table 2 of THE HUMAN MEANING OF SOCIAL CHANGE, by Angus Campbell and Philip E. Converse, editors, © 1972 by Russell Sage Foundation, New York.

is of little interest to them and that seems to be an invasion of their privacy; (b) the record must rely on the person's memory, even though it might be taken every few hours; (c) an accurate description of an activity in brief words is difficult to make and difficult to interpret. In developing a classification system of activities it is of utmost importance to keep in mind the purpose to which the data will be put.

The method used, then, was to keep detailed diaries of the activities of respondents for periods ranging from one to seven days, in all a total of 4,460 days. Subjects of the study were 2,460 individuals in Westchester County, New York.

Activities were first divided into two main categories: *leisure* and *nonleisure*. Under nonleisure were included those activities:

> which are usually considered in a high degree obligatory or necessary to the maintenance of life and which are on the whole instrumental to other ends rather than ends in themselves. Also, they are the activities which general current attitudes do not regard with that peculiar emotional tone with which they regard leisure.

The main subcategories of nonleisure were *sleep, paid work, care of self, transportation,* and *household and children.*

Leisure activities were classified under seventeen categories, seven of which took up 90 percent or more of the leisure of all classes (except students), namely: *eating, visiting, reading, public entertainment, sports, radio* and *motoring.* Three categories, namely playing cards, dancing, and sociability were included in the final tables under *visiting.* Active arts, church, club, correspondence and telephoning, idle, study, unaccounted for, were thrown into the category *miscellaneous.*

Daily averages were based on the total leisure and the total nonleisure for five workdays plus one Saturday and one Sunday, divided by seven, except in the case of high school students, for whom the figure for an additional Sunday per week was used instead of Saturday.

The authors obtained a schedule of time expenditures rather than money expenditures "on the theory that the distribution of time expenditure is an even more important index to the pattern of life, and possibly to the social well-being of the group, than is

43

the distribution of money expenditure." The interesting point was made that the total income per person in that case is constant, namely twenty-four hours per day, so that everyone starts with a common base line.

An important feature of a survey study is the degree to which the total sample is subdivided and data are reported for specific subgroups. The Lundberg, et al. study reported on the following subsets of their data: *labor* (males who used this term in designating their occupations; females in this category consisted mostly of factory women and about a dozen housemaids), *white-collar* (chiefly office employees of a public utility company, exluding executive positions), *professional and executive, unemployed, housewives, high school students,* and *college students.* Each subgroup was further divided into males and females, except college students who were all male.

The second study listed by Robinson and Converse (1972) in their summary table (Table IV) is another classic, the work of Sorokin and Berger (1939). This is also a diary study, based on about 3,500 days of 176 people in Boston, mostly unemployed females under thirty. Data were collected over a period of over four weeks. The authors did not break down their data by occupation; the nature of the sample would have made such an analysis not too meaningful.

Both the third and fourth study of the summary table (Table IV) are reported in more detail in de Grazia's (1962) *Of Time, Work and Leisure.* The J. A. Ward study, a national sample, also employed a diary method, covering every quarter-hour period from 6 AM to 11 PM, a total of seventeen hours per day. The authors used two major breakdowns of activities, subdivided further as follows:

> *Away from home* — at work; traveling; shopping; at restaurant, tavern, barber, etc.; at friend's or relative's house*; leisure (games, sports, church, etc.)*
>
> *At home* — leisure (other than reading)*; reading*; miscellaneous work at home; household chores or housekeeping; eating or preparing food; dressing, bathing, etc.; asleep.

In addition, the four categories with an asterisk were combined into one called *all leisure activities*. Findings were reported separately for men and women, and for the average weekday, Saturday, Sunday, and the average day (i.e. the mean of all seven days).

The Opinion Research Corporation study (1962), the fourth listed in the summary table (Table IV), had respondents check off a list of activities that they engaged in "yesterday." The list consisted of the following twenty-one categories:

> watching television; visiting with friends or relatives; working around yard and in garden; reading magazines; reading books; going pleasure driving; listening to records; going to meetings or other organization activities; special hobbies; going out to dinner; participating in sports; playing cards, checkers, etc.; none of those listed; spending time at the drugstore, etc.; singing or playing musical instrument; going to see sports event; going to movies in regular theatre; going to drive-in movies; going to dances; going to play, concert, or opera; going to lectures or adult school.

Data were reported in terms of percent of respondents engaging in each of the activities, with subanalyses by age, sex, employment status, car ownership, rural-urban dichotomy, region, educational level, and family income.

The fifth study in the summary table (Table IV) was carried out by Robinson and Converse through the facilities of the Survey Research Center at the University of Michigan, during 1965-1966, using a diary method plus a follow up full-scale interview the ensuing day (*see also* Robinson, 1969). This study is of particular importance since it was designed as a benchmark survey for future comparative work, and its method of data collection, for example, has been used in the Multination Time-Budget Research Project (Szalai, 1966, 1972), a cross-national study involving twelve nations. Table V presents a shorthand version of the activity code used. It is obvious, again, that the suitability of this code will depend on the purpose of the particular study for which it is to be used. Perhaps the most valuable aspect of Table IV is the list of shortcomings of each of the studies, since these may reduce similar errors in future studies.

One question the designer of a time-budget study must face

TABLE V

SHORTHAND ACTIVITY CODE

0. Work Related	1. Housework	2. Child Care	3. Shopping	4. Personal Needs
009. Regular work	109. Preparing food	209. Baby care (under 5)	30*. Everyday needs	409. Washing & dressing
019. Working at home	119. Meal cleanup	219. Child care (over 5)	31*. Durable goods	419. Medicinal care
029. Overtime	129. Indoor chores	229. Helping homework	329. Personal care	429. Helping adults
03*. Travel at work	139. Outdoor chores	23*. Reading to	339. Medical care	439. Meals at home
04*. Waiting, delays	149. Laundry	249. Indoor entertaining	34*. Government services	449. Restaurant meals
059. Moonlighting	159. Mending	259. Outdoor entertaining	35*. Repair services	459. Night sleep
069. Meals at workplace	169. Other repairs	269. Medical care	36*. Waiting	469. Naps
079. Other	179. Animal/plant care	279. Other (babysitting)	37*. Other services	479. Resting
089. Coffee breaks	189. Heat/water upkeep	289. —	389. —	489. Private, other
09*. Travel to/from work	199. Other	29*. Related travel	39*. Related travel	49*. Related travel

5. Adult Education	6. Organizations	7. Social Entertainment	8. Active Leisure	9. Passive Leisure
509. Full-time classes	609. Organization work	709. Sports events	809. Playing sports	90*. Radio
519. Other classes	619. Work as officer	719. Nightclubs, fairs	819. Hunting, fishing	91*. T.V.
529. Special lectures	629. Other activity	72*. Movies	829. Taking a walk	929. Records
539. Polit/union courses	639. Volunteer work	73*. Theatre & concerts	839. Hobbies	93*. Reading books
54*. Homework & research	649. Religious clubs	749. Museums	849. Sewing, canning, etc.	94*. Reading magazines
55*. Technical reading	659. Religious services	759. Visits w/friends	859. Artistic work	95*. Reading newspapers
569. Other	669. Union-management	769. Parties w/meals	869. Making music	969. Talking (on phone)
579. —	679. PTA, VFW, etc.	779. Bars, tearooms	879. Games (cards, etc.)	979. Letters
589. —	689. Other	789. Other gatherings	889. Other leisure	989. Relaxing, thinking
59*. Related travel	69*. Related travel	79*. Related travel	89*. Related travel	99*. Related travel

*Activities with an * in the third column have further auxiliary codes.

Reproduced from the Study on Americans Use of Time, Project 491, Survey Research Center, The University of Michigan. Also in Szalai, A. (Ed.): *The Use of Time.* The Hague, Mouton, 1972, pp. 562-564.

whether a time diary is most appropriate or whether a recall questionnaire might suffice. The advantages and disadvantages of these two types of data collection have been investigated by Bishop, et al. (1975). The authors describe a recall questionnaire as one that

> typically asks the respondent to estimate (by recall) how often he or she has participated in each activity or the total time that he or she devoted to it over a long period, during which many activities have been interspersed (e.g. "How often do you go bowling?" or "How many hours do you watch TV during an typical week?"). The time diary, by contrast, asks the respondent to record the duration of each occurrence of the activity as — or immediately after — it occurs.

The authors conclude that "the use of time diaries might be an unnecessary expense and effort in some studies that are aimed at the collection of *summary* information about activity participation."

Robinson (1977), in an extensive report on the 1965-1966 Survey Research Center survey (Table IV, study 5) also deals with a comparison of diary versus estimate methods of obtaining activity data and reports a number of comparative studies. His conclusion is that

> estimate data do appear to provide a useful background of general life style, accurately distinguishing frequent from infrequent participants or nonparticipants in particular activities. Nonetheless, when one wants time-use figures that correspond fairly closely to how people actually spend their time, particularly if one wants to attach monetary values to such time figures, then the diary seems the most reasonable source of such data (Robinson, 1977, pp. 20-21).

We shall conclude this section by referring once more to the giant research effort conducted under the general leadership of Alexander Szalai (1972). This work is notable for at least three reasons. One, it thoroughly delineates problems and issues in time-budget methodology. Two, it presents a vast amount of meticulously collected research data. Three, it showed once again that "it can be done!" Twelve nations of varying political and economic systems, overcoming language and cultural barriers, actually got together, agreed on common research procedures, and established international cooperation. Diana Dunn

(1974) expresses the importance of this volume in her review of the *Use of Time*, as follows: "The work emerges as a classic. . . . Substantively and methodologically, it will be a resource for decades, and a bench mark for leisure researchers throughout the world." No attempt will be made here of a summary of the content of this voluminous work. Such a summary has been provided by Dunn (1975) in the just mentioned review. A brief discussion of methodological issues of time-budget research discussed in the light of this work may be found elsewhere (Neulinger, 1981).

Money-Budget Studies

When the accounting refers to money rather than time, a different set of categories becomes relevant. For example, de Grazia (1962) described one such study using the following categories of expenditures:

> All goods and services; food, beverages, and tobacco; clothing and accessories; medical and personal care; home operation and improvement; home furnishings and equipment; automotive; other goods and services; recreation and recreation equipment.

Findings were reported according to a breakdown of households, as follows:

> by annual household income; by level of education attained by household head; by occupation of household head; by age of household head; by household stage in the *life cycle*; by market and geographic location.

The abitrariness of categories or data breakdowns seems even more striking than it is in the case of time-budget studies. Perhaps it is fairer to say that the purpose of a study will be more obviously reflected in the categories chosen. If research were done by a beer manufacturer, food, beverages, and tobacco would not be lumped into one category. Or if the interest lies in recreation and recreation equipment, a more detailed analysis would be indicated, as, for example, a consumer expenditure report shows, also quoted by de Grazia (1962):

> *Theaters and entertainments:* motion picture theaters; legitimate theaters, opera, etc.; spectator sports; clubs and fraternal organizations

Participant recreation: commercial participant amusements; parimutuel net receipts; reading; gardening

Radios, Television, and musical instruments: radio and television receivers, records and musical instruments; radio and television repair

Sports equipment: nondurable toys and sports supplies; wheel goods, durable toys, sports equipment, boats and pleasure aircraft; other

It is clear that even this detailed system will only satisfy a specific need. The optimal method would be to use a tremendously large number of categories and let the computer group the data, after the fact, according to particular demands. Unfortunately, there are some very real limits in the number of categories one can use until data collection becomes impossible, and thus, a compromise must be worked out.

Free-Time Activities Surveys

Frequently a researcher simply wishes to obtain information about the type of free time activities in which a person engages. Examples are the well known Gallop Polls in which cross sections of the population are asked specific questions. Kaplan (1960a) reports results of one such 1959 poll, in which the following inquiry was made: "Which of the activities listed on the card have you, yourself, participated in during the last twelve months?" Activities were dichotomized into those concerned with recreational participation, and those concerned with recreational spectatorship. This frequently used distinction, similar to the active-passive categorization of leisure, is quite ambiguous and seems to be harder and harder to make. Is one participating in a lecture or is one observing it? Is one observing a Fisher-Spassky chess game on TV or is one participating by anticipating each move? The trend toward audience participation in theatre performances (*living theater, liquid theatre*, etc.), in rock concerts, and, last not least, in the many variations of encounter groups makes this distinction particularly difficult.

Kaplan (1960a) points out one of the main shortcomings of presenting respondents with a list of activities to check off: Leisure is defined for the respondent by the interviewer, and activities that the respondent might have viewed as leisure are not ascertained.

Another example of this type of survey is a study by The Group for the Advancement of Psychiatry (1958), reporting data for a random sample of 1,660 individuals. This was obviously no small effort. Yet, one wonders what the value of data reporting is when we are told that, for example, 62 percent of the respondents consider *radio, TV, or going to the movies* as one of the main things they do in their spare time; or that 25 percent consider *arts and handicrafts* in that manner. For one, the categories used are too broad to be meaningful. Second, leaving the choice of number of things to be checked off to the respondent invites a tremendous variation in what is considered a *main thing*. Differences obtained may reflect variations not in behavior but in judgments of what is important.

If one does use a list of activities, one might better specify a specific number of activities or else have all activities ranked, unless, of course, one is interested in the number of activities checked per se. The number listed then becomes a variable of interest, in addition to the nature of the activities listed.

Work-Related Information

For the person operating under the assumptions of a residual leisure definition, the amount of time spent at work is necessarily of critical importance. Problems and trends in obtaining work data are discussed by Zeisel (1958), in an article entitled "The Workweek in American Industry 1850-1956." The author traces the continuing long-term decline in the workweek in industry, for the years stated, and points out that sources of data were quite rare prior to World War II. The United States Department of Labor's Bureau of Labor Statistics published data for manufacturing industries, starting in 1919, and for some other industries at later dates. Only in 1941 did the Census Bureau start collecting data on hours of work for all employed persons, through household sample surveys. The Bureau of Labor Statistics collects data from payroll records of a relatively large sample of establishments. The latter data, thus, tend to be fairly precise estimates of average hours worked by industry, while census data have broader coverage and provide estimates of all hours worked by individuals, not only those employed by industry.

This type of data collection is not without its problems. One is that of dual jobs; if industry average working hours turn out to be less than those reported by census data, the difference could be due to second job holders. The amount of paid vacations, holidays, and sick leave granted to the working person also does not become evident from this type of data. It may become necessary to compute and report hours worked per year, rather than per week, to obtain comparable statements for different industries or even different individuals. Data on various aspects of work and leisure time, primarily hours of work, paid vacations, and paid holidays, covering the period of 1940 to 1960, are presented by Henle (1963).

Work patterns have seen some significant developments starting somewhat before 1970. A major change has been the introduction of the four-day workweek by a sizable number of establishments throughout the country. While the number of hours worked per week may remain constant (usually forty hours), these hours are compressed into four days. For a description of experiences by companies having adopted such a schedule, see Riva Poor's *4 days, 40 hours* (1970) and the *Four-Day Workweek: Fad or Future?* (Wilson & Byham, 1973); for an assessment of its effects on leisure participation, see Conner and Bultena (1979). Whether this trend will catch on, as did the five-day workweek some decades ago, is still a controversial issue although some feel convinced that it will. Others already project a three-day workweek.

Another change is the increase in the flexibility of work hours. We find not only staggered work hours, permanent part-time, and job sharing, but also so-called *flextime*. The latter refers to an arrangement whereby all employees must be present during some core time, but may choose flexible time around this core period (Fiss, 1976). The potentials and implications of all these developments are certainly tremendous, particularly if viewed in

51

combination with the changing vacation and retirement patterns.

The Meaning of Leisure

As pointed out previously, there are relatively few studies that address themselves to the meaning of leisure per se. In a theoretical article, entitled "Methods for Study of Meaning in Use of Time," Foote (1961) discussed methodological issues of time-budget studies, particularly problems related to data-gathering, respondent cooperation, sampling, and analyses of data. He stressed the advantages of obtaining data through diaries kept by the respondents and recorded "today," rather than through recall of what happened "yesterday." He also emphasized the microscopic level of analysis, that is, individual behavior acts rather than broader macroscopic levels that while leading to artificially high reliabilities and similarities in reported behavior, lose most qualitative aspects of the behavior studied.

> When certain authors group all leisure activities into less than ten catagories, the surprise they express over the remarkable similarity and stability of the proportions of time devoted to these categories by all kinds of persons seems gratuitous (p. 170).

To get at the meaning of activities, Foote suggests the use of five dichotomous evaluations of each episode reported: like — dislike; work — play; routine — special; wish more of — wish less of; and self-initiated — other-initiated.

An empirical attempt to get at what is most important in life and whether this involves work (or leisure by default) is a study by Dubin (1956) who investigated whether workers considered work and the workplace as their central life interest, as one might expect according to the tenets of the Protestant Ethic. Dubin defined *central life interest* as "the expressed preference for a given locale or situation in carrying out an activity" (p. 58). Contrary to expectations, respondents tended to choose the nonwork situation as the preferred locale, given the choice of carrying out certain activities relevant to either work or nonwork situations.

The Central Life Interest questionnaire consisted of forty questions, each dealing with an activity choice that could refer to either the job or workplace or to some aspect of the community outside of work. A third, neutral, or indifferent response, was available for each question. Following are two examples of the type of questions asked:*

I would most hate . . .
— missing a day's work
— missing a meeting of an organization I belong to
— missing almost anything I usually do
I would rather take my vacation . . .
— with my family
— with some friends from work
— by myself

Considerable work has been carried out on the concept of central life interest. For example, Orzack (1963) showed that for professionals work is more likely to be a central life interest than for industrial workers. Parker (1971) deals with the concept extensively, and refers to many others with similar interests (e.g. Lafitte, 1958; Kornhauser, 1965; Friedlander, 1966; Odaka, 1966; Dumazedier, 1967).

Another line of attack on the meaning of leisure is represented by the work of Havighurst and his colleagues (e.g. Havighurst, 1961). We shall discuss some of his studies, however, in the next chapter when listing some findings in regard to the meaning of leisure.

In concluding this section we present two more attempts to provide conceptual frameworks for the categorization of activities and, at the same time, get at the meaning of leisure. One is the ambitious work of Hanhart (1964), an investigation of the free time activities of the workers of Zurich, Switzerland, carried out by means of 875 interviews. In the theoretical introduction of his work, the author develops a typology of free-time ac-

---

*Reprinted from Dubin, Robert: "Industrial Workers' Worlds: A Study of the Central Life Interests of Industrial Workers," *Social Problems*, Vol. 3, no. 3, pp. 134, 135, 1956, by permission from THE SOCIETY FOR THE STUDY OF SOCIAL PROBLEMS.

tivities, using five methods of organization (*Ordnungsprinzipien*) as follows:

According to place and time (*nach Ort und Zeit*)
According to functional interrelationships (*nach der funktionellen Gebundenheit*)
According to purpose/orientation/ (*nach der Sinnerfuellung/ Orientierung/*)
According to mental or physical activities (*nach der geistigen und koerperlichen Aktivitaet*)
According to its reference (*nach der Abhaengigkeit*)

The author's stated intention is not to be exhaustive of all possible ways of characterizing free-time activities, but to work out several useful dimensions along which every activity can be considered. He stresses that his system applies to the adult working male only, and that such groups as adolescents, the retired, and women, working or not, will require special considerations.

Let us briefly look at these five methods of organization.

ACCORDING TO PLACE AND TIME. A distinguishing characteristic of free-time activities, in contrast to work, tends to be their freedom in regard to location. The most general classifications in this respect are *at or around the home* and *away from home*. Within these two major categories, the author introduces subcategories of temporal considerations, namely activities that are *always possible* and those that are *not always possible*. Finally, he distinguishes between *ubiquitous and nonubiquitous* activities, in the sense that certain activities may be carried out within the immediate environment while others can not. See Table VI for examples of this paradigm.

ACCORDING TO FUNCTIONAL INTERRELATIONSHIPS. Activities are seen either as bound to certain relationships or as independent of such relationships. A functionally bound activity requires for its realization the participation of a certain number of others, for example, one other in the case of playing chess or quite a few others in the case of viewing a movie. An activity like taking a walk can be carried out by oneself or with others.

ACCORDING TO PURPOSE OR ORIENTATION. When engaged in object-oriented or *resultant (resultativ)* activities, one is involved or occupied with something, one forms or changes something, one works towards a goal, a final result, a product. *Intrinsic* (?) (*immanent*) activities may also involve an object, but the emphasis is on the activity ; the doing, the activity, is the important aspect, rather than the product that might result. The distinction is often difficult to make since it depends primarily on the perception of the individual involved rather than the activity itself. As examples of object-oriented activities the author lists moonlighting, productive hobbies like carpentry or farming, adult education, and others. As intrinsic activities are listed primarily play and hobbies that are basically nonproductive.

ACCORDING TO MENTAL OR PHYSICAL ACTIVITIES. The author states a preference for a dichotomy of activities into *mental* and *physical* rather than the much used *active* and *passive*; however, he stresses that this dichotomy is a matter of degree, again depending on the individual's perception of the situation.

ACCORDING TO ITS REFERENCE. So-called free-time activities are never totally free, but still dependent on or formed by some external context. The author lists six such contexts or dependencies: work dependent; survival dependent; status dependent; family dependent; group dependent; and person dependent.

The reader will find examples of each of these categories in Table VI. A fuller discussion of this scheme is unfortuntely not possible here.

While Hanhart's approach to formulating a typology of free time activities may be viewed as a rational or *armchair* technique, Kenyon (1968; 1970) pursued a similar goal for a more restricted domain, namely physical activities of the nonutilitarian kind (specifically activities such as games, sports, calisthenics, and dance), using an empirical approach in addition to formal and intuitive methods. Kenyon's method of organization is the perceived instrumental value the activity has for the individual. Through sophisticated methods of statistical item analyses he derived six dimensions of physical activity: *social experience, health and fitness, the pursuit of vertigo, aesthetic experience, catharsis,* and

55

TABLE VI
EXAMPLES FROM A TYPOLOGY OF FREE TIME ACTIVITIES
METHOD OF ORGANIZATION

Free Time Activity:/	Place & Time	Functional Inter-relationship	Purpose or Orientation	Activity	Context
Chamber (house) music	at home; inside; always possible	group-dependent	intrinsic (hobby/play)	mental	person-dependent
Read the newspaper	at home; inside; always possible	solitary	intrinsic (resting)	mental	survival & group-dependent
Go to the movie	not at home; inside; ubiquitous; not always possible	secondary group-dependent	intrinsic or resultant	mental	person-dependent
"Hobbies"	at home; inside; always possible	independent	intrinsic or resultant	mental and physical	person-dependent
Skiing	not at home; outside; not ubiquitous; always possible	independent	intrinsic	mental and physical	survival & person-dependent
Listening to the radio	at home; inside; always possible	independent	intrinsic or resultant	mental	survival & person-dependent
Help the wife	at home; inside; "all day"; always possible	independent	resultant	physical	family-dependent

Source: Hanhart (1964), p. 61.

ascetic experience. Attitude scales were developed for each of these dimensions, but the author recommended at the time that their use be restricted to research purposes (Kenyon, 1970).

There is much evidence, by now, that free-time activities do cluster along underlying meanings, shared *press*, or common outcomes (e.g. Bishop, 1970; Witt, 1971; Burton, 1971a; McKechnie, 1974; Ditton, et al., 1975; Ritchie, 1975; Hautaluoma and Brown, 1978; Tinsley and Kass, 1978). The original impetus for many of these empirical studies have no doubt been the recognition that activities, per se, do not provide a very meaningful clue to useful categorization; one must look for underlying dimensions to bring order into the tremendous amount of potential activities available to any individual. An outcome of this trend in research, as well as an incentive for futher work, has been the introduction of the concept of "leisure activity substitutability." This concept refers to "the interchangeability of recreation activities in satisfying participants' motives, needs and preferences" (Hendee and Burdge, 1974). The practical implications of such substitutability for recreation planners seems obvious but must be carried out with caution based on the "necessity to distinguish between clustering of activities as carried out using factor analysis, and clustering of individuals on the basis of the activities in which they participate" (Beaman, 1975).

The advent of the computer and with it, highly sophisticated "packaged" statistical programs that everyone may use but hardly anyone understands fully, has provided us with many examples of

> The Rule of the Tool: Give a child a hammer and he will hammer everything he can find; give a researcher a statistic and he will analyze everything he can find (Smith and Haley, 1979).

The above quote is from an article that attempts to throw light on the important tool of factor analysis for leisure research; similar intents are evident in two other *Journal of Leisure Research* articles of the same issue (1979, *11*, No 2), one also concerned with factor analysis (Kass and Tinsley, 1979) and the other with cluster analysis (Romesburg, 1979). The reader concerned with such research will find these articles most useful.

This concludes our presentation of examples of research approaches to the measurement of various aspects of leisure. We shall next discuss the development of an instrument designed to measure not leisure, but rather attitudes toward leisure.

MEASURING LEISURE ATTITUDES

An attitude is generally defined as a disposition toward an object or event. The disposition is assumed to have cognitive, affective, and connotative components (e.g. Katz and Stotland, 1959). We define a person's attitude toward leisure as one's particular way of thinking about, feeling about, and acting toward or as regards leisure.

We do not feel the need to have to justify our considerable attention to the measurement of attitudes, at this point. Attitudes are a well-established construct of social psychology and have been instrumental in many efforts toward the understanding of human behavior. Our concern with the psychological aspects of leisure and any humanistic approach to leisure make the study of leisure attitudes an imperative task.

A CASE STUDY: DEVELOPING A LEISURE ATTITUDE QUESTIONNAIRE

We shall briefly outline various steps, assumptions, and considerations that went into the construction of the leisure attitude questionnaire, *A Study of Leisure*, Form 0769, (Appendix A). We feel that somebody who may be approaching a similar task for the first time may find this rather detailed account useful.

Preliminary Considerations and Questionnaires

The original intent was to develop a questionnaire that would enable us to deal meaningfully and quantitatively with various aspects of leisure, including specifically leisure attitudes. The assumption was that the multitude and diversity of questions relating to the leisure domain could be reduced to a relatively small number of basic leisure dimensions. As a first step, two preliminary forms were developed.

58

FORM 667-1: A SURVEY ON LEISURE (Neulinger, 1967a). The primary purpose of this questionnaire was to gain information about problems in writing questions in the leisure domain. Several open-ended items were included and respondents were encouraged to offer criticisms and make comments. The sample used and some results were described in the previous chapter (Neulinger, 1967a). Since the sample was very small we shall refrain from reporting further findings, except those for one item that we feel is of considerable interest.

Respondents were asked the following question: "If you did not have to earn your living would you work anyway?" If the answer to the question was yes, they were further asked to state the reason why. The majority (88%) said that they would work anyway and the reasons given were of two major types. One was for intellectual stimulation and satisfaction or, conversely, the need to escape boredom. The emphasis was on personal satisfaction. Examples of this type of response are as follows:

> I would work because I find it monotonous staying home every day.
> Because one needs to be stimulated and occupied.
> For the satisfaction I get from it and to avoid intellectual deterioration.
> To keep my mind active.

The second reason had a different flavor. It stressed the feeling of responsiblity, the need to find meaning in work. The emphasis was on fulfilling a social obligation rather than a personal need.

> To prove myself and to get feeling of being useful.
> Even if I was well off financially, I would feel guilty if I did not do something to contribute to the advancement of mankind.
> Because it is the most meaningful activity which a peacetime society offers.
> Because there are too many places where people are needed either as volunteers or paid workers.
> Work can be and should be a satisfaction. It is necessary for man's ego to achieve and do things.

Noteworthy are also a number of responses that seem to reflect a moral judgment:

> It is better for a person's mind and body to have some sort of employ-
> ment.
> It is good for your body, mind, and soul.
> Because there is nothing gained by idleness.
> Man and woman must produce and they must progress.
> Inactivity leads to introversion, self-love, selfishness.

FORM 1067-2: THE RANKING OF LEISURE ACTIVITIES (Neulinger, 1968). This study dealt with the question of how many categories a person might want to use when asked to sort leisure activities according to his personal preference. Might he prefer to use only two categories: activities he likes and those he dislikes; or might he prefer to use three, four, or more? Results of a small sample indicated that the preferred number of categories were either two or four, and that a ranking procedure probably ought not involve more than ten steps.

FORM 0368: A STUDY OF LEISURE — 1ST DRAFT (Neulinger, 1968). On the basis of the experience gained through the two previous questionnaires, using theoretical considerations, intuition, and sometimes mere curiosity, a third and rather lengthy questionnaire was developed. Space limitations do not permit a complete presentation of the questionnaire; we shall briefly describe a few of the items; some findings from this study are presented in the next chapter.

One set of items dealt with the idea of *self-actualization*. By this term was meant a force basic to the nature of man, "normative for the whole species rather than for particular times and places, i.e. . . less culturally relative (Maslow, 1962, p. iii). This need was also seen as similar to the "essential, inborn nature" of man, as described by Fromm (1955). (For findings, see next chapter.)

A number of items probed the area of self-definition, either through work or through leisure. Others explored cognitive, affective, and connotative aspects of leisure attitudes. Questions dealing with desired work load and amount of vacation were included. One section dealt with an estimated time budget for an average workday, another for an average Sunday; both used categories from the Activity Code of The Study on American Use of Time, Project 491 (*see* Table IV).

Since leisure activities are viewed by us as potential need satis-fiers, nine free-time activities were phrased in terms of Murray's (1938) *press* variables, and respondents were asked to rank these in terms of their personal preferences. "The *press* of an object is what it can *do to the subject* or *for the subject*, the power that it has to affect the well-being of the subject in one way or another" (Mur-ray, 1938, p. 121). The following *press* were included: *order, ag-gression, acquisition, play, affiliation, activity, blame-avoidance, achievement,* and *sentience.*

Another set of items elicited opinions regarding the advisabil-ity that society either encourage or discourage certain free-time activities. The questions dealt with the issue of society's responsi-bility for what people do in their free time. A further set of items dealt with the person's potential guilt feelings about leisure. One section elicited respondents' preferences for general and specific free-time activities (*see* next chapter for some of these findings). Finally, several miscellaneous items were included, one of which inquired about respondents' feeling toward an an-nual guaranteed income (*see also* next chapter). The last page of the questionnaire was devoted to standard background data.

The questionnaire consisted of a total of 150 items. Sixty-eight of these were used to derive basic leisure attitude dimensions via a factor analysis. This procedure has been fully described elsewhere (Neulinger and Breit, 1969), and we shall merely state here that seven factors were identified and labelled as follows: *amount of work or vacation desired; society's role in leisure planning; self-definition through work or leisure; amount of perceived leisure; au-tonomous versus passive leisure pursuits; affinity to leisure; importance of public approval.*

A Study of Leisure — Form 0769 (Appendix A)

A new form of the questionnaire was developed with the fol-lowing purposes in mind. First, the stability of five of the previ-ously identified factor dimensions was to be investigated. Two of the dimensions, *autonomous versus passive leisure pursuits* and *im-portance of public approval,* were deemed too weak to be signific-ant. Thirty-two items were included for the purpose of replication; twenty-seven of these were identical to the highest loading items in each of the previously identified five leisure dimensions. Five of the items were new and had been written to get at the *essence* of these factors.

Also included were the previously used *press* variables, except that *press aggression, acquisition, play* and *blame-avoidance* were dropped and instead *press autonomy, understanding, sex,* and *nurturance* were added. The final list, then, consisted of the following *press* in this order: *order, autonomy, sentience, understanding, achievement, sex, affiliation, nurturance,* and *activity* (*see* Appendix A, item 14, pp. 254, 255).

To explore differences in the meaning of leisure and work a *semantic differential* type section was included, using sixteen adjective pairs. Another section included five general questions abut sex. Since we consider leisure attitudes to be part of the person's broader value system, an investigation into the relationship of leisure and sex attitudes seemed appropriate. Finally, standard background variables were included similar to those asked in the previous questionnaire. A complete copy of the questionnaire is reproduced in Appendix A.

The replication study has been described elsewhere (Neulinger and Breit, 1971), but we shall report some of the material here since it is relevant, not only for the leisure attitude dimensions but also for some other findings to be reported later. From here on we shall refer to the sample used for this study as the *Norm* group.

> *Subjects* (The *Norm* Group). The sample consisted of 335 adults working full time, 198 males and 137 females, ranging in age from eighteen to sixty-eight, with a mean age of thirty-five. Thirty-six percent of the respondents were Jewish, 26 percent Catholic, 15 percent Protestant. Eighteen percent reported no religious preference. Respondents were predominantly white (90%), the majority married, and their educational level quite high (median category *some college*), although all levels were presented. Reported average family income was equally high: in the $11,000 to $13,000 bracket. Eighty-nine percent of the respondents were born in the United States. The spectrum of occupations was very broad and included the professions, business, industry, and the trades.
>
> *Procedure.* Data were collected in the Spring of 1970, in and around

New York City. Respondents were obtained through the cooperation of The City College students. Great emphasis was placed on appealing to the respondents' cooperation and honesty, and they were assured complete anonymity.

A factor analysis of the thirty-two relevant items yielded five factors which were in very good agreement with the original study (Table VII). As before, only those items were used to define factors that had loadings of at least .30, and .10 larger on the respective factor than on any other factor. Following are descriptions of the five factors, as offered previously (Neulinger and Breit, 1969, 1971):

Affinity for Leisure (I). This factor addresses itself to the person's liking of leisure as well as his perceived capacity for it. It may relate to the Protestant Ethic in terms of the person's desire for leisure, expressed for himself and for his children, but also in terms of his perceived guilt about having leisure time. It may identify the person who feels that leisure must be earned to be enjoyed, those who feel that man has an obligation to work, that, while work is a moral deed, leisure is, at best, neutral and unimportant, if not outright immoral.

Involved in this factor may also be the person's self-evaluation of his capacity for leisure. Thus, he may have, not only moral qualms about too much leisure, but he may feel also that he is incapable of handling too much free time.

Society's Role in Leisure Planning (II). This factor deals with a wide range of potential free-time activities and the position that society should take regarding these activities. There is relative overall agreement on which activities are desirable and which are not. The factor seems to deal with the person's general attitude toward society's control, regulation, support of, or interference with, men's free time.

Self-definition through Leisure or Work (III). This factor relates to the relative importance of work and leisure in a person's life, and more particularly, the degree to which he defines himself either through his work or his leisure. It is the factor of greatest theoretical interest since it may help to measure the degree to which the modern job has lost its potential as a foundation for self-definition.

Amount of Leisure Perceived (IV). This factor not only indicates the amount of a person's perceived leisure, but also his satisfaction with the amount he has or his need for more. On the one hand, it probably identifies the person who feels that he has enough free time, does not know what to do with it, and thus feels bored; on the other hand, it shows the person who never has enough time, who always has more

TABLE VII

LEISURE ATTITUDE FACTORS DERIVED FROM A FACTOR ANALYSIS
OF 32 ITEMS, BASED ON A SAMPLE OF 335 FULL-TIME WORKING
ADULTS AND INCLUDING FACTOR LOADINGS OF ORIGINAL STUDY[a]

Item	I	II	III	IV	V	Commu-nality	Original Loading
			Factor				
I: *Affinity for leisure*							
How long could you stand a life of leisure	.81	.—	.—	.—	.—	.72	.84
How much would you like to lead such a life	.75	.—	.—	.—	.—	.71	.77
Would you like your children to lead such a life	.68	.—	.—	.—	.—	.58	.66
Free time versus work time allocation[b]	.58	.—	.—	.—	−.32	.52	.—
Doing nothing, being idle, . . .	.39	.—	.—	.—	.—	.29	
Taking of habit forming drugs	.33	.—	.—	.—	.—	.18	
Would you feel guilty about living a life of leisure	−.57	.—	.—	.—	.—	.34	−.55
II: *Society's role in leisure planning*							
Productive efforts, such as certain hobbies	.—	.70	.—	.—	.—	.50	.67
Creative and/or artistic efforts, . . .	.—	.63	.—	.—	.—	.41	.52
Social affairs, such as volunteer work, . . .	.—	.57	.—	.—	.—	.36	.55
Physical exercise, such as sports, . . .	.—	.54	.—	.—	.—	.32	.45
Mental endeavors such as studying, . . .	.—	.47	.—	.—	.—	.23	.45
III. *Self-definition through leisure or work*							
Leisure activities express talents better than does my job	.—	.—	.69	.—	.—	.50	.73
Leisure activities are more satisfying than work	.—	.—	.67	.—	.—	.50	.66
Self-description through free time or work activities[b]	.—	.—	.66	.—	.—	.44	—
More important to be good at free time activities than work activities	.—	.—	.50	.—	.—	.29	.51
Prefer fame for job rather than free time activity	.—	.—	−.40	.—	.—	.20	−.52
Ambitions more realized on job than free time	.—	.—	−.64	.—	.—	.45	−.55

TABLE VII (Continued)

Item	I	II	Factor III	IV	V	Commu-nality	Original Loading
IV: *Amount of perceived leisure*							
I have enough leisure	.—	.—	.—	.61	.—	.46	.60
Leisure time felt to be boring[b]	.—	.—	.—	.41	.—	.19	—
How much of free time as "killing time"	.—	.—	.—	.40	.—	.20	.50
Little of my free time is actually leisure	.—	—	.—	−.41	.—	.21	−.48
Like more free time than I have now	.—	.—	.—	−.55	.—	.46	−.50
Always more things to do than time for	.—	.—	—	−.61	.—	.38	−.62
V: *Amount of work or vacation desired*							
How many weeks of vacation would you like to have	.—	.—	.—	.—	−.78	.67	−.63
Given the most ideal conditions, how many weeks of vacation should a person have	—	.—	.—	.—	−.73	.57	−.62
Given the present state of our society, how many days per week should be spent working	—	.—	—	.—	.46	.31	.66
Days per week you want to work for a living	−.30	.—	.—	.—	.67	.60	.72
Sum of squared factor loadings	3.25	1.98	2.82	1.75	2.38	12.18	
Percent of total variance	10	6	9	5	8	38	

[a] Three items were excluded as factor definers because they had highest loadings of less than .30 and one item because it was tied on two factors by a difference of less than .10. For the sake of clarity factor loadings of less than .30 have been omitted from this table.

[b] These were the new items written to get at the essence of the factor.

Source: Neulinger, J. and Breit, M.: *Journal of Leisure Research*, 1971, *3*,109-110.

things to do than he has time for and therefore would be very glad to have more free time. We would expect this factor to be related to the creative aspects of personality: autonomy, spontaneousness, a general curiosity about the universe and a desire to learn. On the negative side, this factor should reflect a person's apathy and disinterest in life. *Amount of Work or Vacation Desired* (V). The interpretation of this factor is direct: how much of a person's life should be spent at work as opposed to vacation or, in a broader sense, free time. It deals with a person's work ethics in a very practical manner. Note that both affective and conative as well as quasi factual components are touched on. The factor relates not only to how much a person likes to work but also to how much he thinks one ought to work and how much, in fact, he actually works. The same aspects are involved in the questions relating to vacation.

It might be interesting to investigate whether people who work more really like to work more or whether their attitudes developed as ego-defensive structures. Given that some people are forced to work longer hours for reasons beyond their control, do they compensate by developing more positive attitudes toward work?

The factors just described represent relatively stable and independent attitude dimensions in the leisure domain. The meaning of each factor, as inferred from the manifest item content, can be extended and made more explicit through factor correlates. Some findings relative to these dimensions will be presented in the next chapter and quite a few are available elsewhere (e.g. Neulinger and Breit, 1971; Neulinger, 1971; Neulinger and Raps, 1972; Jackson, 1971, 1973; Spreitzer and Snyder, 1974; Berg and Neulinger, 1976; Kleiber, 1979). Note that coding, scoring, and computing information as regards factor scores is provided in Appendix B.[3]

The appropriateness of the attitude questionnaire for subjects beyond the limits of the population on the basis of which it was constructed was tested in two separate studies. The original sample had consisted of adults with a mean age of thirty-five working full time. A replication of the study with a sample of first-year university students indicated that "the use of the instrument is appropriate for a student population and will lead to the measurement of leisure attitude dimensions similar to those in an adult population" (Neulinger, et al., 1976).

A study that examined the appropriateness of the questionnaire for an elderly population (ages 58 to 84, with a mean age of 71) yielded five factors also that were "in very good agreement

---

[3]The questionnaire *A Study of Leisure* has been translated into German, Japanese, and Spanish.

with the findings of Neulinger and Breit (1969, 1971)" and maintained the same labels for the factors as given by us (Teaff, Ernst, and Ernst, 1975). The authors recommended that usage of the questionnaire be restricted to "better educated older subjects," a recommendation with which we fully agree.

Further Leisure Attitude Measures

The work on leisure attitudes has recently been reviewed by Crandall and Slivken (1980). Particular emphasis is placed on "leisure ethic scales," by which is meant attitude scales "that concentrate specifically on assessing the degree of positive or negative affect associated with leisure" (p. 269). References to and information about the following measures are provided: a leisure orientation scale (Burdge, 1961a; Yoesting and Burdge, 1976); a five-item leisure ethic factor (Bryan and Alsikafi, 1975); part of a twenty-two – item attitude scale also measuring a Protestant work ethic factor and a work-leisure fulfillment factor; and an eight-item leisure ethic factor (Buchholz, 1978), embedded in a scale also measuring four work dimensions, described as "work as humanistic, Marxist-related statements, group-oriented work, and work ethic items" (Crandall and Slivken, 1980, p. 271). The authors also present their own ten-item "Leisure Ethic Scale" (Slivken, 1976; Crandall and Slivken, 1978). Median item-total score correlations are reported as in the .40s, thus supporting the notion that the ten items are measuring a single dimension. The authors, however, also refer to a factor analysis of the scale that indicated that one might view this scale as tapping three distinct though overlapping factors: *liking leisure, desire for leisure time,* and *positive spontaneity.*

Crandall and Slivken (1980, p. 265) refer to *A Study of Leisure* (Neulinger and Breit, 1971) as "the most widely used measure of leisure attitudes," but also raise a number of criticisms. Content validity is one: "we have no idea how important these five factors are among possible leisure attitudes" (p. 267). We agree with this reservation and anticipated this problem in our original work (Neulinger and Breit, 1969):

Obviously, we do not claim these dimensions to be exhaustive in describing leisure, or that we could not have arrived at 5, 6, or possibly 15 such dimensions. As every one knows, the items included in any factor analysis determine to a large extent the outcome.

The exploration of further leisure attitude dimensions and their relationship to ours, however, will throw light on this issue. Crandall and Slivken (1980, p. 275) provide such intercorrelations between two of our dimensions (*affinity for leisure* /N-I/ and *society's role in leisure planning* /N-II/) and their Leisure Ethic Scale, the Leisure Orientation Scale (Burdge, 1961) and a single-item leisure satisfaction measure. Unfortunately, as the authors point out, the analyses are based "on very small samples of from ten to twenty and, so, must be considered exploratory" (p. 274). Our (N-II) dimension does not relate significantly with any of the other scales, thus indicating "discriminant validity — that the scales do not correlate with just anything concerning leisure, but they reflect a specific type of leisure attitudes" (p. 274). That our (N-I) dimension showed relatively high correlations with the Leisure Ethic Scale (.58 and .45), as well as the Leisure Orientation Scale (.82 and .56), but not the leisure satisfaction measure, is perfectly in line with our description of this dimension as referring to the person's liking of leisure and as relating to the Protestant Ethic. Thus, these findings add support to the construct validity of our dimensions.

Another problem ascribed to *A Study of Leisure* is that "different items are answered on many formats and scales and are thus awkward to score" (p. 267). Such a procedure, indeed, does make scoring somewhat more difficult but attempts to avoid spuriously high correlations between items brought about by method similarities rather than by content similarities (Campbell and Fiske, 1959). Yet, another criticism that "it is somewhat clumsy to work with five separate dimensions" (p. 267), leaves us somewhat puzzled as to what we were supposed to do. That the leisure domain contains *at least* five relatively distinct dimensions, as indicated by our scale, has been confirmed by factor analyses replications of our own and others, and thus, we can only be left deploring that God created such a clumsy world!

Another recent treatment of the topic of leisure attitudes is that by Iso-Ahola (1980). He defines a leisure attitude as "the expressed amount of affect toward a given leisure-related object" (p. 251). He follows an approach developed by Fishbein and Ajzen (1975), whose conceptual scheme leads from *antecedents*, through *beliefs*, *attitudes*, and *intentions*, to *behavior*. Note that attitudes are distinguished from beliefs and intentions, but that all of them are highly consequential in determining any specific behavior. In that sense, the traditional three components of an attitude (cognitive, affective, and conative; e.g. Triandis, 1971, p. 3) are still taken into account. Iso-Ahola (1980), quite cavalierly, dismisses studies carried out with *A Study of Leisure* as not dealing with leisure attitudes, at least "in the sense in which they were discussed earlier in this chapter" (p. 269). We would like to reassure researchers who have used this questionnaire in the belief that they were studying leisure attitudes that they were. We find it hard to address ourselves to the kind of criticism raised by Iso-Ahola. For example, "How long could you stand a life of leisure," one of our items and the only one specifically mentioned, quite clearly refers to the conative component of an attitude. Yet, it is somehow seen as irrelevant without giving an explanation as to why. Other (nonspecified) items lead to the statement "In such a mixed package with a little bit of everything, it is difficult to tell from the attitudinal standpoint what these studies have accomplished" (Iso-Ahola, 1980, p. 269). Iso-Ahola ignores that this mixed package with a little bit of everything led, through thorough and replicated analyses, to five very distinct and meaningful dimensions; I fail to understand what "telling from the attitudinal standpoint" means.

In another instance, I was glad to see that Iso-Ahola, in criticizing me, agrees with me that "it should not be forgotten that the 'dimensions' emerging from the factor analysis depend on the kinds of opinion statements fed into the computer in the first place" (p. 270). The reader will remember that we just referred to a similar statement we had made in describing the limitations of our scale.

We find it unfortunate that we have to engage in what might

69

seem as an excessively negative review of somebody else's work. But, when our model (of the formation of leisure attitudes) is referred to as "not entirely misleading" (Iso-Ahola, 1980, p. 258), we owe it to those who work with our model to speak up. Iso-Ahola summarizes our speculations about five developmental stages and the formation of leisure attitudes, and then follows this with a paragraph that is, once again, presented *as if* it were *his* criticism of my theorizing. Thus, Iso-Ahola (1980, p. 257) says:

> First, while there is some evidence for the existence of five phases, the ages attributed to each stage have been chosen very arbitrarily. Even if everyone goes through the above stages in the same order, the time when a person reaches each stage varies from individual to individual. Furthermore, the phases are not separate and distinct from each other. . . .

These, however, were the very limitations that I originally ascribed to the *approximate* time table I had presented:

> Such a schedule is difficult to establish and must be interpreted very loosely, since there are great individual differences in these respects and because the aspects of the various phases may overlap in a given individual (Neulinger, 1974a, 120).

Additional criticism relates to the fact that I speculated about the relevance of each of five developmental stages, as described by Maier (1965) and based on the work of H. Erikson, Jean Piaget, and Robert R. Sears, and the development of leisure attitudes. "Following this line of reasoning, one would say that each day is critical in a person's life, with respect to later leisure attitudes" (Iso-Ahola, 1980, p. 257). I must confess that I am not able to follow this line of reasoning.

Rather than attempting further rebuttals of criticisms that I fail to understand, let me illustrate the tone and "clarity" of Iso-Ahola's writing through another quote (Iso-Ahola, 1980, p. 270):

> The real determinants of leisure choices and behavior are human social cognitions. In an effort to understand leisure behavior, one can learn little from variables like occupation and income. Unfortunately, researchers who have utilized these variables have assumed that occu-

pation, income, and other variables actually influence people's decision making about their leisure involvement.

Should we then assume that occupation, income, and other variables actually *do not* influence people's decision making about their leisure involvement? Are these variables irrelevant to my decision whether I shall go swimming at the fashionable country club or the local city pool, dine at the Ritz Hotel or at McDonald's, or take a vacation in Europe or on my front steps?

A TYPOLOGICAL APPROACH TO LEISURE

The previous section dealt with various approaches to the study of leisure, and specifically, the measurement of leisure attitudes. Presently, attention will be directed toward a different way of dealing with the same subject matter. This is not the place for a lengthy discussion of differences between or advantages or disadvantages of the trait versus the type approach in the study of personality. However, a few words are indicated to clarify some of the issues involved.

One way to look at differences between a trait approach and a type approach is to consider the units studied. In the trait approach the researcher centers his investigation on such entities as *aggressiveness, need for achievement, desire for stimulation* or perhaps a specific attitude toward an aspect of leisure. This so-called trait (need, desire, want, or attitude) is identified, isolated, measured etc., and people who *possess* this trait to various degreees are studied in terms of their respective differential behavior. The emphasis is on the particular trait and the effect it has on behavior.

The emphasis in the type approach is not on a particular trait, but on the whole person. The unit of measurement is the person. An attempt is made to classify people in terms of similarities and differences, using as many variables as possible, the more the better.[4] The advantage of such a multivariate typological system

---

[4]The term typology has been used for classification systems that use only a single variable and dichotomize subjects into those either high or low on the respective dimension. Such dichotomization may have their usefulness, but such classifications do not deserve the label *typology*.

is that it gives us a comprehensive picture of the individual. It describes the individual in terms of many dimensions, and most importantly, it permits the identification of interaction effects. For example, two people may be equally high in *need-achievement*, but they may respond quite differently in a given situation, if one of them is also high in *need-aggression*, while the other is low on that dimension. A typological approach has the potential of taking such interactions into account.

The issues involved in the justification and methodologies of typologies are many and quite complex. Let it suffice to say that we accept typologies, not only as a valid tool of classification, but as the most promising one (Stein & Neulinger, 1965; Neulinger, 1967b).

Turning now specifically to the leisure domain, the attempt is to establish *leisure types*, that is, to group people who share certain beliefs and attitudes about leisure and who are thus, as a group, different from other people, who may share different beliefs and attitudes with others. The assumption underlying this attempt has been stated by Kluckhohn and Murray (1962) as follows: "Every man is in certain respects (a) like all other men, (b) like some other men, (c) like no other man" (p. 53). We are trying to identify (b), the degree to which some people are like some other people. Furthermore, it is assumed that group members (*types*) will also be more similar to each other than nongroup members on variables not directly expressed in the leisure domain. This assumption simply reflects a widely accepted belief in psychology that basic attitudes are part of a total value structure or syndrome that is anchored deeply within the personality system.

In the following pages a number of attempts at formulating such types are described. These attempts were explorations; they lay no claim for methodological soundness. They may, however, serve as catalyzers for more research in this area and hopefully stimulate others to do a better and more thorough job.

Two Types of Self-actualizers

As an introductory example, two types are presented that

72

were derived from data of questionnaire Form 0368, *A Study of Leisure*, as described in this and the next chapter. Types were based on variables that correlated significantly (p <.01) with either of two criterion variables: a preference for the *acquisition of knowledge and/or skills, (Intellectual Self-actualizer)*, or a preference for *making or being with friends and/or coming closer to the community (Social Self-actualizer)*. Following are hypothetical descriptions of such types.

> *The Intellectual Self-actualizer*: These people enjoy tackling difficult tasks and achieving high standards in their leisure activities (.21); their primary concern is not with relaxation or play (—.17). Their work-day and Sunday is in part devoted to adult education or occupational training (.22 and .21). Their preferred free time activities are music and reading (.24), and engaging in volunteer work (.20). Of arts and crafts, they prefer writing (.16) to cabinet making (—.16), and their musical taste runs to opera (.26) rather than musicals (—.17). They prefer to attend a lecture (.27) or opera (.18) rather than a musical (—.27), the circus (—.23), or the movie (—.16). When watching television, they are likely to view political discussions (.36) and news (.27) rather than comedy shows (—.16) or sports events (—.17).
>
> *The Social Self-actualizer*: These people enjoy being with people and cooperating in common activities with them during their leisure (.23). They place little emphasis on tackling difficult tasks or gaining recognition for their accomplishments (—.16); they do not engage in activities for the enjoyment of aesthetic feelings and sensuous impressions (—.21). Their workday and Sunday is devoted to social entertainment and other social life (.23 and .33). They feel that society should encourage activities emphasizing social interactions (.30). Engaging in sports is not one of their preferred free-time activities (—.19), nor is arts and crafts (—.19). Given the choice of stretching out and doing nothing under various conditions, they are least likely to choose doing so in a gently drifting boat (—.16). Their preferred type of music is musicals (.20), and this is also the most likely event they would attend (.17).

The example given demonstrates the broad picture, the feeling of depth one gets in a typological approach. One actually sees the person come alive. It would be easy to formulate all kinds of hypotheses about other characteristics such a type should possess or how he/she might behave in various situations. Such formulations would lead to testable predictions, and this is how science progresses. Unfortunately, the above examples must not be taken seriously. They represent an intellectual game of playing with data, in which the leisure researcher especially should be given the right to engage. The method used was not a methodologically sound way of arriving at types. The main shortcomings were: one, a dichotomization on one variable was the basis of the types; and two, correlations between a set of variables and a criterion variable do not imply that the same subjects are involved in bringing about these correlations, particularly if the correlations are as low as they are in this case.

Having hopefully whetted the reader's appetite for the typological approach, a more serious attempt to develop leisure types will be described next.

Three Leisure Types — (Breit, 1969)

Miranda Breit (1969) investigated the possiblity of using items from *A Study of Leisure*, Form 0368, as the basis of a leisure typology. The fifty-eight items used included the nine *press* variables designed to tap the functions of free-time activities, and seven variables designed to elicit preferences among general types of free-time activities, and the forty-two variables designed to elicit preferences among specific types of free-time activities (*see* Table XI, p. 104). Data used were from the sample described in the next chapter, in relation to *A Study of Leisure*, Form 0368 findings.

Several steps were taken in developing leisure types (for a fuller description of the procedure, see Breit, 1969). First, a subgroup of 160 subjects was selected from the total of 335 subjects. This group was further divided into two subgroups of eighty subjects each and, following a suggestion by Armstrong and Soelberg (1968), identical Q-factor analyses were carried out on each group. In a Q-factor analysis, subjects are treated as variables and variables are treated as subjects. In each of the separate analyses, three types emerged that were judged to be similar enough to be considered the same. A third Q-factor analysis was then carried out on 129 subjects selected from the two subgroups (the total being determined by computer limitations). This analysis resulted in the identification of five fairly strong types, three of which were similar to the previously identified ones. A description of these three types is offered here, based on the items that defined the types.

THE ACTION ORIENTED TYPE: A member of this type prefers leisure activities that allow him to relax and amuse himself through fun and entertainment, joking, and being merry. He enjoys activities that relieve the feeling of listlessness by requiring his full attention and giving him a chance to be on the go. This type's activities are not the kind that require order and forethought or involve precision and neatness. He is not concerned with struggling for what he wants or with overcoming opposition forcefully.

This type's activities revolve around sports: engaging in sports, especially golf, attending sports events, and watching sports on television. He is least likely to engage in volunteer work, sit around and do nothing, or engage in arts and crafts. He chooses jazz and musicals as his favorite music, prefers movie-making and attending movies and musicals, and doing nothing in the outdoors, either in a drifting boat or under a shady tree.

THE SOCIAL-INTELLECTUALLY ORIENTED TYPE: A member of this type prefers leisure activities that allow him/her to relax, joke, and be merry through fun and entertainment. He/she engages in activities that provide for the enjoyment of aesthetic feelings, sensuous impressions, and colorful experiences as well as activities that involve meeting new people and engaging with them in common activities. He/she is least likely to participate in activities that involve overcoming opposition forcefully, and struggling for what he/she wants, or in those activities that enable him/her to achieve high standards offering recognition for his/her accomplishments.

He/she is characterized by his/her preference for listening to music, such as folk, musicals, and classical, or reading, and engaging in arts and crafts such as painting, photography, or playing an instrument. A member of this type is not likely to engage in sports or attend sports events. He/she prefers boating, doing nothing in a drifting boat, lying under a shady tree, or on the beach, attending movies, and watching news and political discussions on television.

THE SOCIAL-ENTERTAINMENT ORIENTED TYPE: A member of this type engages in activities that allow her to relax, amuse herself through fun and entertainment, joking, and being merry. She engages in activities that involve meeting new people and engaging with them in common activities that require cooperation. She is least concerned with a colorful vivid experience directed at her aesthetic feelings or with activities requiring precision, neatness, order, and forethought.

She is characterized by her preference for watching television, especially comedies and variety shows, and for listening to music or reading. She is least likely to attend or engage in sports events. She prefers boating and tennis, doing nothing on a soft bed or couch, engaging in photography or writing, listening to musicals and folk music, and attending movies.

An analysis of the background variables of subjects who belonged to these types revealed that the *Action Oriented Type* was predominantly male, with relatively high education. The *Social-Entertainment Oriented Type* was predominantly female, with somewhat lower education, and the *Social-Intellectually Oriented Type* was a mixed type, that is, with males and females with a median level of education about equally represented.

The results of this study were deemed promising, but we are not suggesting a replication or continuation of this work in its present form. The main shortcoming seemed to have been that the items used in the typology were not meaningful, precise, or basic enough. Only a relatively small number of subjects, out of the total number analyzed, could be placed unambiguously into one of the three types. The use of the now-developed leisure attitude dimensions in a typological approach, combined with other meaningful and relevant variables, should prove more successful.

More Q-Types

Duncan (1978) carried out a Q-type factor analysis in search of people who have similar patterns of leisure behavior. He surveyed a random sample of 984 households in Idaho, acquiring information about participation in 1972 in "21 indoor and home-based leisure activities, and 38 outdoor and sports activities." Drawing several subsamples from his data base, Duncan identified five leisure types for the general population, as well as five male and five female leisure types. Unfortunately, "none of the replicated factors extracted in the analysis of males show any obvious similarities to the factors extracted in the analyses of the general population." In general, "analysis of male and female samples produced different results from those found with general population data."

This is not the place for a detailed review of this very worthwhile article. We would like to make a few comments, however, so that the reader who might be discouraged by the somewhat inconsistent results will not turn away from this line of approach. First, there is good reason to expect different types emerging from a male or female sample. After all, our society still is very much sex-role oriented. But then, why do the respective male and female types not appear in the general population?

We are facing here a difficult issue: are we to follow mathematical dicta in a blind manner, or are we to let theoretical and *intentional* considerations influence our approach? For example, the author states

> Examples given in Kerlinger (1973) indicate that using about twice as many variables as people would be appropriate in "Q" analyses. The factor analyses in this study involved 58 leisure variables, the number of people included in the analyses ranged from 27 to 34 (Duncan, 1978).

Let us look at this for a minute. Given fifty-eight variables, the number of potential Q-types is practically infinite, certainly far beyond what might be a useful number. But, who is to say what that number should be. Certainly not some mathematical rule, but rather the social-psychological importance of any given constellation of combinations of activities. Perhaps there are five hundred distinct types each of which involves specific correlates of behavior and experience; perhaps there are only five (although common sense would speak against that). The point is that we do not know and will not know until we have explored any given population for any set of given variables in a most thorough way. Furthermore, whatever the number of types may be in a population, there is no reason whatsoever to expect that the proportion of individual types in the population should follow any particular distribution, normal or otherwise. The nature of such a distribution is precisely one of the facts we wish to discover through our analyses.

77

Given the unknown distribution of types in the population, their unknown but probably large number, and further, that this number will also be very much a function of our desire or need for the specificity of any given type, the likelihood that we shall be able to identify types in sample sizes of about thirty is indeed minimal.

Should we, therefore, drop our search for types? The answer to this question obviously depends on one's belief about the values of the type concept. I have made my bias in favor of that concept quite explicit and shall thus conclude with another quote from Duncan (1978): "The "Q" technique of defining leisure types appears to have a great deal of promise, and further research using the technique on different samples of people and leisure activities should be profitable."

MEASURING THE LEISURE EXPERIENCE

Leisure may be viewed as a state of mind. An attitude is usually defined as a state of mind (i.e., a predisposition to respond toward a given object). *Ergo*: leisure is an attitude. This obvious fallacy, unfortunately, does not seem to be so obvious to many, and we find that "leisure is sometimes referred to as an *attitude*, when intending to refer to it as a state of mind" (Neulinger, 1978a). This confusion can be particularly destructive if it takes place among professionals in the domain of leisure education and counseling. This concern is echoed by Mannell (1979) in his attempt to distinguish between leisure attitudes and transient experiences: "Terms such as state of mind, attitude, ethic, value and experience have been used interchangeably by many writers."

Let it be stated, then, for the record that the just discussed instrument, *A Study of Leisure*, is not intended to measure the leisure experience but is intended to measure attitudes toward leisue or related to leisure. My attitude toward leisure is distinct and distinguishable from my leisure!

We have on the other hand, developed an instrument that is specifically designed to measure (among other things) the leisure experience, or to put it more precisely, the conditions from

78

which we can infer the leisure experience. In Mannell's (1979) terms, we are dealing with the "causal influences on the leisure experience affecting its quality and duration." The instrument "A self-exploration: *WHAT AM I DOING?" (WAID)* has been more fully described elsewhere (Neulinger, 1981) but is referred to here to encourage its use for research purposes.

The WAID is basically a time-budget instrument. It is designed to collect information about the activities in which a person has engaged over a twenty-four hour period, using thirty minutes as the time unit. Information is collected about the nature of the activity, its duration, frequency, timing, sequential order, location, and social nature. In addition, however, the instrument also ascertains information about variables assumed to be critical to the leisure experience: perceived freedom (*choice*), intrinsic-extrinsic motivation (*reason*) and affect (*F/T*). Finally, respondents also are asked to describe in their own words both the need satisfied and the feeling experienced.

The instrument is designed with two distinct purposes in mind. First, we think of it as a research instrument; second, it may be used in a leisure education and/or counseling process.

The potential research applications of the instrument are large. First of all, norm data need to be established. How much perceived freedom, how much intrinsic motivation does a person experience during an average day? Is it possible to get a meaningful measure of these variables? What are individual differences in this respect? What between group differences? How do these variables relate to standard background variables? Once we have obtained data on these factors, we might go on to check differences across particular activities, for example, do males and females differ in terms of these variables given the identical activity?

The instrument can also be used to examine the validity of the leisure paradigm that is based on the variables perceived freedom and intrinsic/extrinsic motivation. How does affect relate to these variables? Are there people who experience lower affect with higher freedom? Are there specific activities for which this may be the case? If so, might this relate to mental health, addiction problems, life-styles, and so on.

The WAID instrument may be used in leisure education and/or counseling on a one-time basis, or we might administer it repeatedly over time. In the latter case, one would most likely intersperse some intervention technique between administrations, and data gathered would not only be helpful to the clients but could also serve for evaluation purposes. In general, the instrument is seen as promoting self-awareness and the clarification of one's motivations and needs, and goals and directions. Completing the questionnaire requires skill that might well be compared to that required for learning a new language — talking with oneself and recognizing what one is doing and where one is going. It is not an easy task and is one that actually may require some training.

CHAPTER 3

SOME LEISURE FACTS:
A SAMPLING OF RESEARCH FINDINGS

THE PREVIOUS CHAPTER stressed the methodology some representative studies employed in arriving at leisure findings. We shall now consider the content of some of these as well as other studies, including some of our own.

The amount of information available in this area is tremendous, and it is growing at an accelerating rate. Unfortunately, this information is scattered in widely different areas due to the interdisciplinary nature of leisure. We shall more or less follow the outline of the last chapter in selecting certain research findings and will frequently have to refer the reader to other sources. We are using the term leisure *facts* quite liberally; we hate to think of how many times so-called research findings turned out to be not quite so factual after all.

What, then, are the facts of leisure? What better place to look than the encyclopedic work of Berelson and Steiner (1964), *Human Behavior, An Inventory of Scientific Findings*. Checking the subject index, however, we find only one entry under *leisure* (and none under *recreation* or *free time*): "Leisure, class differences in."

C21 Classes differ in their use of leisure and in their tastes: the upper classes, being better educated, are interested in a wider range of life; and by virtue of being upper, they become the arbiters of the "proper" use of money, physical appearance and dress, etiquette, language, and aesthetic taste (p.488).

The authors further point to recreational differences and quote a study by Lazarsfeld (1959) relating to aesthetic differences among social classes.

This rather meager treatment of leisure reflects less the absence of leisure *facts* in the literature, than the limited importance given the subject by social scientists in general. This absence of interest is particularly evident in regard to the psychological literature. For example, the *Annual Review of Psychology*(Rosenzweig and Porter, Eds.), Vols. 18-31, 1967 through 1980, has only one entry under leisure; Volume 22 (1971) has two paragraphs on *leisure time*, in a chapter on mass communication. Sociologists and recreation professionals have contributed the largest amount of literature in the field, but there also has been considerable input from sources such as economics, political science, philosophy, counseling, and others.

In the following pages we present miscellaneous findings from various studies and sources in the leisure domain, or we indicate where the reader may find more complete information about a given topic.

The Boundaries of Free Time: Hours Worked

No matter what leisure conceptualization one adopts, free time will always be of special interest to the leisure theoretician. Even if one does not equate free time with leisure, the potential for a leisure experience during free time ought to be greater than during non-free time.

The major factor determining the amount of free time a person has in our society is the job, that is, the hours one needs to spend at work. Primary sources of information in regard to average hours of work for various groups of the population are The United States Department of Labor's Bureau of Labor Statistics as well as the Census Bureau and the Chamber of Commerce of the United States, Economic Research Department. Many secondary sources present summary tables of trends both across time and across various sections of the population (e.g. de Grazia, 1962; Ennis, 1968; Henle, 1963; Kaplan, 1960a; Scheuch, 1972a; Wilensky, 1961; Wolfbein, 1958; Zeisel, 1958). For example, Zeisel (1958) presents data on the continuing long-term decline in the workweek in industry. "From an average of about sixty-six hours worked in 1850, the equivalent of eleven hours a day, six days a week, the workweek in nonagricultural industries declined to nearly forty hours in 1956, generally eight hours a day, five days a week." A similar sharp reduction in hours worked occurred on farms. The workweek for the overall economy declined from about seventy hours in 1850 to forty-four hours in 1940. Hours of work dropped in all of the major nonagricultural industries during the depression, to different degree in different industries, but rose again after 1938, with highs reached during World War II, and levelling off during the fifties at about forty hours or less. We may well say that at present, "the forty-hour workweek is the norm in the United States, sanctioned by union contracts, by law, and by apparent usage" (Kahn, 1972, p. 160). This relative stability in average weekly hours of work since 1950 in the United States is not shared, however, by many of the major industrial countries. For example, "average weekly hours worked in manufacturing jobs declined by only about 2 percent in the United States between 1950 and 1974, as compared with declines of about 20 percent over the same period in West Germany, Italy, and Sweden (*Social Indicators, 1976*, 1977, 324).

Another way of looking at the dramatic difference between the seventy-hour workweek of 1850, and the forty-hour workweek of 1950 is to realize that the amount of free time available to the individual rose from an estimated 2.18 hours per day in 1850 to 7.48 hours in 1960 (Kaplan, 1960a).

Before we become too impressed, however, by this seeming progress, let us take note of Wilensky's (1961) observation that the average person's gain in leisure has been exaggerated. Viewed over several centuries, time at work actually increased before it decreased, and the present level of time spent on the job is equal to that of a person of the thirteenth century. Moreover, increases in free time have been unequally distributed by industry and occupational category, with professionals, executives, and managers working the longest hours. While the fraction of the total life span worked has remained about the same since 1900, the average labor force member in 1900 could expect only three retirement years; in 1950 this number had risen to six; and it is expected to increase more and more. To look at this from a different angle, "the population group aged sixty-five years and over increased from 3.1 million in 1900 to over 20 million in 1971, and by the year 2000 it will number about 25 million" (Martin, 1971).

Detailed information on gains in leisure time by various sections of the population during the years 1948 through 1960 is contained in Henle's (1963) article, with particular reference to paid vacations. For example, in 1940 most of two million organized wage earners were entitled to only one week of paid vacation. In 1957, 91 percent of workers covered by collective bargaining agreements were eligible for paid vacations, with 84 percent entitled to a maximum of at least three weeks. *Social Indicators, 1976* (1977,388) reports on paid vacations of plant and office workers, showing for example, that 27 percent of plant workers (38 percent of office workers) in 1959 received three weeks or more after ten years of service, while that number reached 75 percent (87%) in 1974. Respective figures for four weeks or more after fifteen years of service are 2 percent of plant workers (3% of office workers) in 1959 and 29 percent (and 29%) in 1974.

There are those who feel that leisure is not increasing. Two arguments are advanced in this respect (Godbey, 1971):

> First, that careful attention has not been paid to less obvious work and work-related activities such as time spent in commuting, overtime, dual job holding, etc.; and second, that time not spent in formal employment is not being successfully converted into leisure (p. 34).

The first argument had been raised by de Grazia (1962) in pointing out that the length of reported average workweek does not take into account second jobs people hold; it does not take into account the approximately 8½ hours a week spent in travelling to and from the job, nor hours spent by men and women working around the house. Taking all such additional factors into account, "the difference between 1850 and 1960 comes down to a few hours" (p. 79).

The second argument states that many of the things we are doing in our leisure are done under some degree of compulsion and often in close relation to the demands of work. Godbey (1971) quotes studies that show that we often read for profit, party for contacts, or do any number of things that will increase our chances for advancement on the job.

It should be apparent to the reader that much of the disagreement stems from a confusion of *leisure* with *free time*. Hours spent on the job or in job-related activities may determine the amount of free time, but they do not allow a direct translation into experienced leisure.

How We Spend Our Days: Time Budgets

As our one example of time-budget data we have chosen a summary table, as prepared by Ennis (1968), of the Lundberg et al. (1934), and Robinson and Converse (1965/66) studies (Table VIII). Robinson and Converse (1972), who analyzed differences between the two studies quite thoroughly (in a three-page category by category comparison with possible explanation of the differences), summarized the data as follows:

> . . . we could conclude that if the Lundberg data are not drastically distorted by uncontrolled day-of-week differences, Americans are now spending noticeably less time sleeping, eating, reading, frequenting places of entertainment (especially movies), playing sports, listening to the radio, motoring, playing cards, dancing, and going to church services. Many of these decreases seem attributable directly to the arrival of television. On the other hand, Americans are spending much more time traveling, taking care of home and family (especially true of American women), and perhaps working. Contrary to stereotypes, the largest increases have occurred in the nonleisure areas with the result that Americans in the national sample of 1965-66 had up to two hours less leisure time than the selected residents of Westchester County in 1931-33 (p. 79).

The data speak for themselves, and there is not much we could add to the above summary. Some of the problems in making comparisons between the two studies are also discussed by Ennis (1968), who points to factors such as differences in sampling, the Depression of 1934 that may have affected work and sleep hours, and the introduction of television.

Robinson and Converse (1972) further compare the

85

TABLE VIII

COMPARISON OF BUDGET AVERAGE FOR VARIOUS GROUPS IN 1934 LUNDBERG STUDY WITH SIMILAR GROUPS OF THE 1965-1966 STUDY (IN PARENTHESES)

Activity	Men			Employed women			
	Executives and professionals	White-collar	Labor	White-collar	Labor	Housewives	Overall
Nonleisure (Hours per day)							
Sleep	8.2 (7.7)	8.3 (7.6)	9.0 (7.4)	8.2 (7.6)	8.3 (7.4)	8.6 (7.5)	8.4 (7.5)
Work for pay	6.2 (6.8)	6.4 (7.2)	5.9 (7.5)	5.9 (5.4)	6.7 (3.9)	0.1 (0.2)	4.5 (4.5)
Care of self	0.7 (0.9)	0.7 (1.0)	0.8 (1.3)	1.0 (1.3)	1.0 (1.3)	1.0 (1.3)	0.9 (1.2)
Transportation	1.2 (1.6)	0.8 (1.5)	0.9 (1.3)	1.1 (1.3)	1.0 (1.3)	0.8 (1.0)	1.0 (1.3)
Household and children	0.9 (0.7)	0.5 (0.6)	0.6 (0.3)	1.2 (2.9)	1.4 (2.9)	4.2 (6.2)	1.9 (2.8)
Total	17.2 (17.7)	16.7 (18.1)	17.2 (17.8)	17.4 (18.5)	18.4 (16.8)	14.7 (16.2)	16.7 (17.3)
Shopping	— (0.4)	— (0.3)	— (0.2)	— (0.5)	— (0.7)	— (0.7)	— (0.5)
Leisure (Minutes per day)							
Eating	106 (78)	114 (73)	101 (76)	116 (59)	109 (52)	106 (79)	108 (71)
Visiting	79 (68)	81 (74)	94 (39)	94 (74)	74 (132)	151 (138)	103 (95)
Reading	74 (50)	61 (36)	95 (24)	43 (29)	38 (23)	84 (40)	68 (35)
Entertainment	15 (11)	45 (13)	35 (13)	48 (14)	29 (16)	44 (10)	37 (12)
Sports	40 (10)	34 (12)	35 (5)	19 (5)	20 (0)	16 (2)	47 (10)
Radio	22 (5)	34 (4)	32 (10)	18 (5)	45 (7)	29 (2)	30 (5)
Motoring	15 (2)	20 (2)	12 (1)	25 (4)	13 (1)	10 (3)	15 (2)
Clubs	10 (5)	8 (8)	0 (5)	3 (7)	0 (5)	61 (12)	20 (8)

Television	— (80)	— (75)	— (159)	— (58)	— (102)	— (75)	— (89)
Miscellaneous	40 (51)	35 (51)	5 (24)	33 (61)	8 (64)	50 (65)	32 (54)
Total leisure minutes	401 (360)	438 (348)	409 (366)	399 (306)	336 (402)	551 (426)	470 (381)
Total leisure hours	6.7 (6.0)	7.3 (5.8)	6.8 (6.1)	6.6 (5.1)	5.6 (6.7)	9.2 (7.1)	7.6 (6.3)
Total	*23.9(24.1)*	*24.0(24.2)*	*24.0(24.1)*	*24.0(24.1)*	*24.0(24.2)*	*23.9(24.0)*	*24.3(24.1)*

Sources: 1934 data from Lundberg, F., M. Komarovsky, and E. McInerny, *Leisure: A Suburban Study,* Columbia University Press, New York, 1934; 1965–1966 data from Robinson, John R., "Social Change as Measured by Time Budgets," paper presented at American Sociological Association meetings, San Francisco, 1967.

Source: Table 5, Chapter 10, of INDICATORS OF SOCIAL CHANGE, Edited by Eleanor Bernert Sheldon and Wilbert E. Moore, © 1968 by Russell Sage Foundation, New York.

Lundberg data with those of Sorokin and Berger (1939) and the J.A. Ward — Mutual Broadcasting Company (1954). The reader interested in time-budget data is encouraged to look into these quite thorough analyses. In addition, the reader will find there some very interesting cross-cultural, time-budget data, namely "Time expenditures for twenty-seven activity categories across the thirteen survey sites in the multination time-budget research project" (p. 30, 31). Data from this cross-cultural study (Szalai, 1966) are now available in a volume entitled *The Use of Time*, edited by Szalai (1972).

The Use of Time is a monumental work. Its 868 pages contain a wealth of data about the twelve nations studied; a detailed account of methodology; a series of essays and studies, theoretical and applied, related to the time-budget techniques and data; and several bibliographies. It is required reading for anyone considering getting involved in similar work, and no attempt will be made here to summarize this volume.

Further analyses and presentations of the American component of these data may be found in *How Americans Use Time: A Social-Psychological Analysis of Everyday Behavior* (Robinson, 1977). These data are not only important for the information they give us about everyday events of life but because "they also form a solid benchmark from which it will be possible to gauge clearly and accurately how daily life in the United States will change in future generations" (p. 190). An attempt was also made to get meanings attached to everyday activities, by either having respondents rate certain facets of their everyday life on a five-point satisfaction scale or by asking them to isolate the highlights and the low points of a particular day. While one may be somewhat skeptical about these findings in terms of their validity, particularly how they might have been influenced by social desirability, they are still of great interest in terms of *what people say* and how they differ in terms of what they say about the things that satisfy them. For example, men and women tend to rate marriage and their children as giving the greatest satisfaction, while clubs they belong to are seen as among the facets of life providing the lowest degree of satisfaction. In relation to these findings the author points to the correspondence between satisfaction and time use. People seem to arrange their lives in such a way as to spend maximum time on those activities that bring them the greatest satisfaction. Or could it be, the author speculates, that people derive the greatest satisfactions from the activities on which they have to spend most time, an explanation that would be in line with a cognitive dissonance theory approach (Festinger, 1957). The author further sees these data as giving strong support to the view that people's attitudes and their behavior are highly interdependent.

One other finding is notable. Work is mentioned as the least enjoyable daily activity more frequently than as the most enjoyable one. "This stands in marked contrast to the traditional survey finding that workers overwhelmingly rate themselves as satisfied with their jobs" (p. 125).

The findings mentioned are just token examples of the rich data provided. Again, we must refer the interested reader to the original source for further explorations.

One other study deserves mention in this context, a time-budget survey that included subjective as well as objective dimensions of leisure behavior (Levy, 1975). In addition to temporal, environmental, activity, and social dimensions (i.e. the objective circumstances), Levy also included thirteen need dimensions that represented subjective components of leisure behavior. It is encouraging to see that the need to include psychological components into time-budget studies is gaining more and more recognition. Our own previously mentioned time-budget instrument (WAID) is another example of this trend.

How We Spend Our Income: Money Budgets

How we spend our money for leisure or any other purpose is of interest to a great many people. Therefore, there is much information available on this matter, mostly through business or economic institutions or publications. There are basically two ways of getting at the amount of money spent on leisure, that is for events or goods related to the so-called leisure activities. One is to gather data from the receiver of the money spent. For example, the *Survey of Current Business,* published by the U.S. Department of Commerce on a regular basis since 1929, reports aggregates of all consumer expenditures, obtained on a national scale. The other method is similar to that of time budgets; one obtains information from the individual person or household who is spending the money; one collects money-budget data. Is one method better that the other? Ennis (1968) shows that a case can be made for either, but he reports interesting differences as a result of method used. One such comparison by Taylor (1967) indicated that the individual budget method was nearly $20 billion lower than the aggregate one, with the largest discrepancy, $6 billion, for alcoholic beverages. Taylor suggests a *Puritan* effect as responsible for this discrepancy!

The amount of money spent on recreation or leisure is a function of both income and education. Ennis (1968) shows that at the lowest income and educational levels, the percentage of income (money after taxes) spent in this manner is only about 2 percent; as income and education rise, there is a steady increase in this figure until at an income level of $15,000, it is between 5 and 6 percent for all educational levels. Note that there is not only an absolute, but a relative difference in the amount of money spent in this manner.

How is this vast amount of money distributed across the various leisure goods and activities? Summary tables of aggregate expenditures give us this information, but these data are obviously not meant to be applied to the individual. One such table, for example, shows how we spend our leisure money, using data from *Business Week* for the years 1929, 1939, and 1952 (Kaplan, 1960a, p. 6). Thus, in 1952, spectator amusements represented 13.5 percent of all recreational expenditures; participation amusements 3.8 percent; individual recreation 72.2 percent; gambling 3.6 percent; and other 6.9 percent. The three largest categories within individual recreation were magazines, newspapers, etc., 12.5 percent; radio, TV, records, musical instruments, 19.8 percent; and nondurable toys, 11.0 percent.

Such data are of great value to the economist, the recreation resource planner, the business person, etc., but they tell us relatively little about the spending habits of a particular individual. Such information can be better inferred from tables like that presented by de Grazia (1962, pp. 426-432), titled "Percentage distribution of expenditures," and "Average expenditures of households with different characteristics, by type of expenditure, 1956." According to these tables, recreation and recreation equipment expenditures ranged between 4 and 7 percent of money spent on all goods and services, 5 percent being the average of all households. The highest income group ($10,000 and over) reported 6 percent, but so did the $4,000 to $4,999 group. All other income groups reported 5 percent. All educational groups reported 5 percent, except the highest one, which gave 6 percent as their proportion. Age showed a linear trend: under thirty-nine years reported 6 percent; forty to sixty-four years, 5 percent; and sixty-five and over, 4 percent. The highest recreational expenditures, 7 percent, were reported by respondents who were heads of households, under forty, and without children.

By breaking the data into a large number of categories we tend to get closer to the individual. Unfortunately, in any one instance the individual is still only defined by one variable at a time, that is, by income, by age, or by education, rather than by a combination of several variables. Another way of getting closer to the individual is to look at relatively homogeneous subgroups of the population. For example, Kaplan (1960a, p. 78) reports "Recreational Expenditures by Regions and Community Types", "Recreational Expenditures by Negroes — Family Size and Education of Family Head" (p. 95), and "White and Negro Family Expenditures for Total Recreation, TV, Instruments, and Admissions" (pp. 96, 97).

In thus looking at leisure behaviors of specific subgroups of the population we identify differences that are due not just to one variable but to all those that characterize the particular group or groups involved. This has both advantages and disadvantages. The advantages of this type of analysis are that it takes into account, not only the effects of the individual variables, but also their interaction; thus, it is similar to a type approach. The disadvantages are that we do not know exactly which variables may be the critical ones, and that eventually, a single variable analysis may be necessary.

The kind of data reported and discussed in this section all take as their premise a residual definition of leisure. The questions we might ask within the framework of a subjective conceptualization of leisure would be quite different. For example, we might be concerned with the relationship between money expenditures and satisfactions gained within a given type of activity, as well as across activities. We may need to weight expenditures as some function of the individual's total income for our analytical purposes, to obtain some idea of the perceived importance of the money spent. We might even inquire into leisure experiences as a source of income rather than an expenditure, given that a considerable number of people do gain leisure from and through their work. If we wish to adopt a radical position, such a measure could be viewed as an index of our closeness to a leisure society. These examples should suffice to indicate the difference in approach dictated by one's conceptualization of leisure.

How We Spend Our Free Time: Activity
Participation and Preferences

There are two ways in which to obtain information about what people do in their free time. One is to ask individuals what they do or what their preferences are. The second way is to get this information from records kept by recreational organizations, clubs, federal or private agencies, etc. Ennis (1968) lists two useful sources of the latter kind, the *Outdoor Recreation Research, a Reference Catalog*, Washington, D.C., U.S. Department of Interior, Bureau of Outdoor Recreation, in cooperation with the Science Information Exchange of the Smithsonian Institution, and *Tourism and Recreation, a State of the Art Study*, Office of Regional Development Planning, U.S. Department of Commerce, Economic Development Administration, Washington, D.C.

Other sources of information are the periodic *Gallup Polls*. Kaplan (1960a, p. 10) reports an example of such a poll for 1959, showing data for recreational participation and spectatorships. From these tables we learn, among other things, that the three most popular recreational activities were swimming (33 million) fishing (32 million), and dancing (32 million),[1] while the most popular spectator sports were baseball (28 million), football (23 million), and basketball (18 million). As was the case with money expenditures, data of this kind may be of great interest to people who build baseball stadiums or swimming pools, but they tell us relatively little about the behavior of individuals.

Participation rates in recreational activities obviously vary a great deal as a function of time of year. Some reports take this fact into account, as for example Cicchetti's (1972) "A Review of the Empirical Analyses That Have Been Based Upon the National Recreation Surveys." The table reproduced here from this study (Table IX) contains principle results of the 1960 and 1965 National Recreation Surveys, based on samples that approximate U.S. Bureau of the Census data.

Data as presented in Table IX become much more meaningful when broken down according to respondents' characteristics. For example, de Grazia (1962, pp. 441-443) presents such a table, showing the percent of population that engaged in various leisure activities "yesterday." Thus, we find out, not only that 57 percent of the respondents watched television "yesterday," but how this figure varies as a function of age, sex, employment status, educational level of respondents, and four other characteristics.

The question, to what degree and how does recreational participation vary as a function of social class and/or occupation, is often raised. Surprisingly, there seems to be a controversy about whether it does vary. Clarke (1956), using a five-point occupational prestige scale, found that modal frequency rates of recreational participation varied systematically with prestige levels.

---

[1]Numbers represent total number of participants, with a participant being defined as having participated once or more.

TABLE IX
SUMMARY OF THE PARTICIPATION RATES IN THE 1960 AND 1965 NATIONAL RECREATION SURVEYS.

	Percent Participating						Days Per Participant					
	1960				1965		1960				1965	
Activity Name	Summer (%)	Fall (%)	Winter (%)	Spring (%)	Summer (%)	Annual (%)	Summer (Days)	Fall (Days)	Winter (Days)	Spring (Days)	Summer (Days)	Annual (Days)
Fishing	29	16	9	21	30	33	6.8	4.6	4.1	5.2	7.6	N.A. ⟶
Canoeing	2	1	#	1	3	4	3.0	1.9	•	2.6	4.5	
Sailing	2	1	#	#	3	3	3.0	3.9	•	•	6.2	
Other Boating	22	9	3	8	24	26	5.5	4.0	4.6	3.2	6.5	
Swimming	45	12	3	11	48	49	11.5	5.2	5.6	4.6	14.3	
Water Skiing	6	2	#	1	6	7	5.1	2.8	•	3.8	6.6	
Camping	8	5	2	4	10	14	5.7	4.2	3.7	3.6	6.9	
Hunting	3	13	11	3	4	13	5.6	5.6	7.1	5.0	N.A.	
Bicycling	9	7	6	8	16	19	19.4	13.2	14.2	20.1	20.6	
Horseback Riding	6	4	3	5	8	10	7.5	5.5	6.5	8.7	6.8	
Playing Outdoor Games or Sports	30	22	15	27	38	41	12.3	12.6	16.9	14.0	17.3	
Picnics	53	24	8	27	57	60	4.0	2.6	2.5	2.1	5.6	
Walking for Pleasure	33	35	36	33	48	51	13.1	11.9	13.6	13.5	15.2	
Driving for Pleasure	52	50	51	51	55	59	12.7	8.6	9.1	9.8	12.1	
Sightseeing	42	31	24	27	49	54	5.2	4.4	4.9	4.4	6.6	
Attending Outdoor Sports	24	29	11	18	30	42	5.5	4.3	4.2	4.2	5.8	
Attending Outdoor Concerts	9	4	1	3	11	14	2.4	2.2	2.9	2.2	3.0	
Mountain Climbing	1	#	#	#	1	1	3.7	•	•	•	3.1	

Hiking	6	2	2	2	7	9	4.4	2.9	2.7	2.4	5.1
Nature Walks	14	16	10	12	14	16	5.2	4.3	6.3	5.5	5.9
Ice Skating	N.A.	N.A.	7	1	N.A.	9	N.A.	N.A.	7.5	3.3	N.A.
Snow Skiing	N.A.	N.A.	2	#	N.A.	4	N.A.	N.A.	3.6	•	N.A.
Sledding	N.A.	N.A.	9	2	N.A.	13	N.A.	N.A.	4.9	4.0	N.A.
Bird Watching	N.A.	N.A.	N.A.	N.A.	5	6	N.A.	N.A.	N.A.	N.A.	15.9
Wildlife and Bird Photography	N.A.	N.A.	N.A.	N.A.	2	2	N.A.	N.A.	N.A.	N.A.	5.9

N.A. Not available.

Less than .5%.

• Insufficient sample size.

Source: Cicchetti, C. J.: A review of the empirical analyses that have been based upon the National Recreation Surveys. *Journal of Leisure Research*, 4: 1972, pp. 98-99.

For example, those in the lowest prestige level (level V) participated most frequently in watching television, fishing, playing
poker, attending drive-in movies, spending time in a tavern or
zoo, and attending baseball games, while those in the highest
level (level I) were more likely to attend theatrical plays, concerts
or lectures, visit museums, play bridge, etc.[2] On the other hand,
Burdge (1969) found that "persons in the highest occupational
prestige level were the most active in all major types of structured leisure." Some prestige level differences were found, but
these were not substantial, and the author concluded that "the
concept that various forms of leisure or free-time activity are associated with specific social classes should be reexamined."
Similarly, Cunningham, Montoye, Metzner, and Keller (1970),
studying free-time activities of 1,648 working men, stated that
"little or no relationship was found between participation in active leisure activities and occupational grouping." Bishop (1971)
took strong exceptions to Cunningham, et al.'s findings, saying
that these "should be accepted only with great caution," giving as
reasons methodological weaknesses of the study and substantial
contradictory evidence. Zuzanek (1978) sees the controversy as
predominantly a methodological one.

> Much of the discussion on leisure differences, their size and direction
> of change suffered from insufficient awareness of the multidimen-
> sionality of leisure phenomena, a lack of operational consensus, and,
> as a result, considerable differences in the quantification of leisure in-
> equalities. The author then reports an analysis in which he investi-
> gates separately rates of leisure participation, the allocation of leisure
> spending, and the allocation of leisure time.

Perhaps at this point some common sense is indicated. The
scientist is not supposed to be influenced by it; however, when a
finding goes that strongly against common sense, a bit of skepti-
cism and a thorough reexamination of methodologies involved
is indicated. The author is reminded of the twenty-year controversy in attitude measurement as to whether a highly pre-
judiced person can objectively judge an attitude item in the area
of his prejudice domain. Common sense tells one, no. However,

---

[2]See also White (1955), "social class differences in the uses of leisure."

several studies, all involving the same methodological error (e.g. Thurstone and Chave, 1929; Hinckley, 1932), established the opposite view, and it took twenty years before the error was discovered (Hovland and Sherif, 1952). Social class differences in free-time behavior are guaranteed by the very way we usually define social class, namely by using income as a component of the definition. Very few people with income of $16,000 or less (about 50% of the population) will engage in yachting, and very few people with incomes of $30,000 or more will be seen spending their free time sitting on the front steps of their slum-located apartment houses. A hot summer in Harlem is still different from a hot summer in East Hampton!

An obviously related topic is race differences in recreational activities. Kraus (1970) studied "Negro Patterns of Participation in Recreation Activity" in twenty-four suburban municipal recreation departments in New York, New Jersey and Connecticut, and in the five boroughs of New York City. Summarizing his major findings he stated that "particularly within the area of sports, there is a striking contrast between the reported recreational involvement of Negro and white participants." Blacks were overrepresented in the areas of track and field, use of swimming facilities, basketball, and several forms of combative activity, especially boxing, while they were underrepresented in areas such as tennis, golf, archery, and bocce. Team sports like baseball, softball, and football were said to fall within a middle range. The author also noted that blacks made much use of recreation facilities for picnicking, fishing, and biking, but little of facilities for boating, skiing, and riflery.

What Does It All Mean and Why Are We Doing It?

Myersohn (1969) found few studies dealing with the meaning of leisure. According to Meyersohn, the best methodological effort in this respect was the work of Foote (1961), described in the previous chapter. Meyersohn (1972), as another example of a study getting at the meaning of leisure, describes a study by Donald and Havighurst (1959), based on a sample of adults in New Zealand and Kansas City. Respondents were asked to apply twelve meaning statements to their two favorite leisure activities. Meanings that topped the list were "just for the pleasure of it," "welcome change from work," "gives new experience," "contact with friends," and "chance to achieve something," approximately in that order, although there were some inversions between the Kansas City and the New Zealand sample and between males and females. Lowest on the list were "makes me popular," "gives me more standing with others," and "self-respect for doing it." Havighurst found few significant relationships between the rating of the meaning of leisure activities and sex, age, or social class and concluded that "the meanings people find in their favorite leisure activities are more dependent on their personality than on age, sex or social class" (Havighurst, 1961).

In comparing the meanings of work and leisure, Havighurst states a general principle of the *equivalence of work and play:* "to a considerable extent people can get the same satisfactions from leisure as from work" (p. 320). He also recognizes that "responses to a check-list of possible meanings are likely to be inadequate for expressing fully the values they find" (p, 320). To improve the procedure he used a method of judging what people said in a two-hour interview, along fourteen rating scales, as follows:

    Autonomy versus other-directed
    Creativity (new solution, novel behavior)
    Enjoyment versus time-killer
    Development of talent
    Instrumental versus expressive
    Physical energy input
    Relation of leisure to work (complimentary-competitive)
    Gregarious versus solitary
    Service versus pleasure
    Status, prestige
    Relaxation from anxiety-arousing tensions
    Ego-integration versus role-diffusion
    Vitality versus apathy
    Expansion versus constriction of interests and activities

Using this procedure in the Kansas City Study of Adult Life (Havighurst, 1957a) with a sample of subjects aged forty to seventy, Havighurst found that "there was a high degree of relationship of the leisure values with personal adjustment, a moderate degree with social class, and a low degree with age and sex."

Havighurst further questioned whether these fourteen value variables would cluster into broader dimensions (Havighurst and Feigenbaum, 1960). A principal component analysis of the data revealed five dimensions, as follows:

I.   Challenging new experience versus apathy.
II. Solitary instrumental service versus gregarious expressive pleasure.
III. Solitary expressive pleasure versus gregarious instrumental service.
IV. Masculine active escape versus feminine passive home-centered.
V.   Upper-middle class active dutiful versus lower class passive pleasure.

Havighurst further enriched his conceptualizations by using the term *life-style*, "a characteristic way of distributing one's time, one's interest, and one's talent among the common social roles of adult life — those of worker, parent, spouse, homemaker, citizen, friend, club or association member, church member, and user of leisure time." Through pattern analysis he arrived at four principal life-styles: (1) balanced high; (2) home-centered high; (3) home-centered medium; and (4) low level (Havighurst, 1957b). While he found only minor differences between life-styles as a function of sex and age, there were considerable differences between social class groupings. For example, the "balanced high" life-style was more frequent in the upper and upper-middle class, while the "home-centered medium" style was most frequent in the lower-middle and upper-lower classes.

Havighurst's work represents a challenging attempt to cope with the complexity of the issues involved and certainly deserves to be pursued most vigorously. Another line of attack, already discussed in the last chapter, are the studies concerned with *Central Life Interests*. These studies may be of particular interest in relation to the function that leisure fulfills for the individual. For example, Dubin (1963) reported that while work and the work-place were not central life interests for almost three out of every four industrial workers studied, Orzack (1963) found that they were central life interests for four out of five nurses studied. (*see also* Dubin and Goldman, 1972). These findings support the hypothesis that the type of work may determine the function of leisure.

As was pointed out before, an inquiry into the meaning of leisure also leads to an investigation of the motivation for leisure. Two approaches can be distinguished. In one, the motivation for a specific free-time activity is explored. Much of marketing research that ascertains why a person buys a particular leisure-related product or engages in a so-called leisure activity falls into this class. We could also include here studies that investigate motivation for drinking (e.g. Riley, Marden and Lifshitz, 1958; Roebuck and Kessler, 1972; McClelland, Davis, Kalin, and Wanner, 1972) or for drug use (e.g. Ausubel, 1961; Walton, 1960; Fort, 1972). The second approach is of a more general nature. Rather than being concerned with one or several specific leisure activities, the emphasis is on the person and his whole repertoire of leisure behavior. An attempt is made to derive this from his personality structure or dynamics. Once we establish the person's motivational profile, we can then predict his leisure behavior from the potential need-satisfaction power (*press*) of any given free-time activity.

One section of the questionnaire "A Study of Leisure" (Appendix A, p. 254) provides for such an approach. Respondents are asked to rank nine *press* paragraphs (as described in the previous chapter) and profiles of either individuals or groups may be obtained, indication what the respondent (s) is (are) looking for in his/her (their) free-time activities. Table X presents such data for two groups, a sample of the *Mensa* society and a *norm* group (Neulinger and Raps, 1972). *Mensa* is an organization whose only membership criterion is a score on an intelligence test higher than that of 98 percent of the general population. The *norm* group consisted of adults working full time in or around New York City (fully described in the previous chapter).

100

The data indicate, for example, that *Mensa* members rank activities involving *understanding* highest (3.8), while for the *norm* group the preferred activity involves *affiliation* (4.3). The findings seem remarkable in the sense that even though there are obviously tremendous individual differences in each group (especially since the *norm* group was intended to be as heterogeneous as possible), the average rankings still show quite significant differences. Further evidence for the meaningfulness of these rankings were significant correlations with the respondents' leisure attitudes, indication that these responses do reflect basic value structures.

SELECTED FINDINGS FROM "A STUDY OF LEISURE"

In the previous chapter the identification of five leisure attitude dimensions through the development of the "A Study of Leisure" questionnaire was described. No data, however, were presented, nor were all of the items involved in the five leisure dimensions. Presently, we shall report some of the more interesting findings. In reflecting on these, the reader should keep in mind the composition of the respective samples.

Form 0368 — "A study of Leisure"

Data for this study were collected during the spring of 1968 in and around New York City. The subjects were described as follows (Neulinger and Breit, 1969):

> *Subjects.* The sample consisted of 320 adults working full time, 171 males and 149 females, ranging in age from twenty to sixty-five, with a mean age of thirty-eight. About one-third of the respondents were Jewish, one-quarter Catholic, and one-fifth Protestant. Respondents were predominantly white, the majority were married, and their educational level was quite high, although all levels were represented. Reported average family income was equally high: 45 percent of the respondents reported incomes of more than $13,000. Eighty-one percent of the respondents were born in the United States. The spectrum of occupations was very broad and included the professions, business, industry, and the arts.

AREAS OF SELF-ACTUALIZATION. Respondents were asked to distribute one hundred hours of unexpected free time among

101

TABLE X
MEAN RANKS OF THE PRESS OF NINE FREE TIME ACTIVITIES

Press Variables	Mensa (N = 343)	Norm (N = 335)	t
Understanding: This activity involves reflection, thinking, analyzing and asking questions. It involves seeking scientific and philosophic truth and an understanding of life.	3.8	4.7	5.13[b]
Sentience: This activity provides for the enjoyment of aesthetic feelings and of sensuous impressions. It may involve the enjoyment of one or more of the arts, and indulging in sensory pleasures and feelings.	4.0	4.6	2.86[a]
Autonomy: This activity allows you to do as you please regardless of rules or conventions. It provides for adventure, change and independence, involving a minimum of rules.	4.5	4.9	1.85
Achievement: This activity enables you to tackle a difficult task and to achieve high standards. It offers recognition for your accomplishments. It involves determination and the will to succeed.	4.6	4.8	1.08
Sex: This activity involves forming and furthering sexual relationships. It involves the enjoyment of feelings of love. It provides the opportunity for attracting others and flirting.	5.1	5.4	1.62
Affiliation: This activity gives you a chance to be with others and meet new people. It provides the opportunity for cooperation with others and engaging with them in common activities.	5.3	4.3	5.74[b]
Order: This activity gives you a chance to organize and arrange things. It demands precision and neatness. It requires a sense of planning, order and forethought.	5.6	5.8	1.09
Nurturance: This activity gives you an opportunity to help others who are in need and to protect and support them. It may involve being with children or taking care of animals.	6.1	5.1	5.79[b]
Activity: This activity gives you a chance to be "on the go." It relieves the feeling of listlessness and provides for action. It keeps your mind off things because it requires your full attention.	6.1	5.4	3.42[b]

[a]p < .01
[b]p < .001

Source: Neulinger, J. and Raps, C.S.: *Journal of Leisure Research*, 1972, *4*, 201.

five areas in any way they wished. Findings showed the following distribution of average hours allotted to five potential areas of self-actualization: 25.8 hours for the acquisition of knowledge and/or skills; 21.5 hours for affiliative activities; 21.0 hours for health care and physical well-being; 16.4 hours for creative or self-expressive activities; 15.1 hours for mere activity. Respondents also indicated that they would like to have spent 16.5 hours in areas other than those listed. This is a relatively small figure and indicates that we had pretty well covered potential areas of activity. The most striking finding seems to be that no one area predominates as a choice. That there is diversity in the group, as as whole, does not imply that the choices made were not meaningful for the individual. A detailed analysis of two of these alternatives (described in the previous chapter in the section on typologies) revealed that one's choice of area of self-actualization indeed relates to one's overall view of the leisure domain and, it is probably safe to assume, way beyond that.

GUARANTEED ANNUAL INCOME. A remark by one of a growing number of American academic, business, and financial leaders who have come to believe in some form of a universal guaranteed income, "The only ones really against it are the people," seems to be at least half true (Dale, Jr., 1968). One hundred sixty-three (53.6%) of 304 respondents replying to a question about a guaranteed annual income were not in favor of it. The median guaranteed income suggested by those who were in favor of the idea was close to $5,000, with twenty respondents suggesting $3,000 or less, and forty-one $8,000 or more.

These data indicate that we are still far from being able to accept the idea of a leisure state for whatever reason. There is a substantial minority, however, with a different view, and it might be interesting to investigate this group in detail.

PREFERRED FREE-TIME ACTIVITIES. Preferences for seven general areas of free-time activity as well as specific activities within some of these areas were elicited from the respondents. These data reflect what the person would like to do rather than what he actually does. Our interest lies in the possible use of this information for diagnostic and predictive purposes rather than in its veridicality. (*See also* the section on typologies in the previous chapter, for an application of these data.)

Findings are presented in Table XI. For example, in this group the least preferred area of free-time activity is "stretch out and do nothing." Within this category, however, the most preferred place to do nothing is "on the beach," the second most preferred, "under a shady tree," and the least preferred, "in the bathtub." It is clear that such data have very limited *descriptive* value unless they are based on a random or representational sample or stem from relatively homogeneous subgroups. Their use for diagnostic purposes, however, seems challenging and awaits further exploration.

TABLE XI
RANKING OF SEVEN AREAS OF FREE TIME ACTIVITY,
AND SEVEN SPECIFIC ACTIVITIES WITHIN AREAS
(N = 310)

Rank	Area of Free Time Activity	Specific Activity (listed in rank order from 1 to 7)
1	listen to music or read	classical—musicals—folk songs—jazz—opera—oriental—electronic
2	engage in sports	boating—tennis—golf—skiing—fishing—baseball—hunting
3	engage in arts and crafts	photography—paint—play a musical instrument—write—movie making—cabinet making—pottery
4	watch television	news—variety shows—comedy shows—political discussions—sports events—Westerns—quiz shows
5	attend a sports event	(not asked)
6	engage in volunteer work	(not asked)
7	stretch out and do nothing	on the beach—under a shady tree—in a gently drifting boat—in a hammock—in a soft bed—on the living room couch—in the bathtub
	Attend one of these*	movie—musical—concert—ballet—opera—lecture—circus

*Not included in ranking of areas.

104

Form 0769 — "A Study of Leisure" (Appendix A)

The sample used in this study, the *norm* group, was already described in the previous chapter. Two findings related to items not involved in the leisure attitude dimensions were also reported in previous sections. One was the ranking of free-time activities, expressed as *press,* and the other the leisure and work profiles, which we reported in chapter 1. Findings as regard items relating to beliefs and attitudes about sex will be discussed in the next chapter, when considering covariates of leisure attitudes.

FREE TIME — LEISURE DISTINCTION. Respondents were asked whether they distinguished between free time and leisure. Two hundred and three (61%) of the 335 respondents indicated that they did make such a distinction and that, on the average, they considered 33.5 percent of their free time to be leisure. An interesting follow-up would be to ask respondents what they do in that part of their free time that is not leisure as well as in that part that they do consider leisure. The need for a clearer distinction of these two concepts has been raised by Scheuch (1972b) who speaks of *Freizeit* (free time) and *arbeitsfreier Zeit* (time free from work), the latter being time during which the individual neither sleeps nor pursues his job. This, of course, represents a recognition that the objective or residual definition of leisure is inadequate when we start to consider psychological aspects of leisure. A similar point has been made as regards the concept of recreation (Burton, 1971b, p. 19).

LEISURE ATTITUDE DIMENSIONS. Factor scores are useful for measuring basic dimensions more reliably and parsimoniously than individual items, but they are void of meaning other than that contained in the items that make up each factor. Furthermore, factor scores tend to have a mean of zero as an arifact of the statistical procedure used in obtaining them. To interpret such a zero mean one must inspect the mean values of the individual items. For this reason, these are presented in Table XII, together with standard deviations and lowest and highest factor scores for each dimension. In future work, a positive factor score will imply a position above the mean of this *norm* group, and a negative factor score a position below.

Following is a brief summary of the *norm* group's position on these five leisure attitude dimensions. (The reader may wish to consult the original questionnaire, Form 0769, Appendix A, for a fuller description of each item.)

Affinity for leisure: People are uncertain whether they would like to lead a "life of leisure"; there is just a very slight tendency toward liking it. They feel they could stand it for more that one year, but not quite two years. They lean toward not wanting their children to lead such a life, and they are uncertain whether they would feel guilty themselves about living such a life. They tend to divide their days about equally between free time and work, with a hardly noticeable greater amount of free time.

Society's role in leisure planning: Society certainly is seen as having a role to play in leisure time planning. The strongest encouragement should be directed toward activities emphasizing mental endeavors and physical exercise. Somewhat less, but still positive, encouragement ought to be given to the promotion of creative and/or artistic efforts; to productive efforts like hobbies; and to an even lesser degree, to activities involving active participation in social affairs.

Self-definition through leisure or work: As one might expect, self-definition is oriented toward work rather than leisure. People feel that it is more important to be good at one's work rather than one's free-time activities and that one's talents are better expressed by one's job than one's leisure activities. They are undecided whether their work or their leisure activities are more satisfying. They are uncertain whether their personal ambitions can be more fully realized on the job than in their free time or whether they would prefer fame for something they had done on the job or in their free time; but in each case, there is a slight tendency to lean toward the work rather than the leisure side. Interestingly enough, however, in describing what is most important about themselves, they would talk about work and free time, with a tendency to talk more about free time than work.

TABLE XII
WEIGHTED z-SCORES AND MEANS AND STANDARD DEVIATIONS OF ITEMS IN EACH LEISURE DIMENSION
(Norm Group, N = 335)

	Mean	*SD*
Affinity for leisure (Range: — .96 to 1.38)	.00	.55
How long could you stand a life of leisure	26.2	21.8
How much would you like to lead such a life	22.5	16.7
Would you like your children to lead such a life	17.6	16.9
Free time versus work time allocation	16.9	5.4
Would you feel guilty living a life of leisure	19.6	16.6
Society's role in leisure planning (Range: —1.44 to .89)	.00	.41
Productive efforts, such as certain hobbies	5.4	1.0
Creative and/or artistic efforts, . . .	5.6	1.0
Social affairs, such as volunteer work, . . .	5.3	.9
Physical exercise, such as sports, . . .	5.8	1.0
Mental endeavors such as studying, . . .	5.8	1.0
Self-definition through leisure or work (Range: — .89 to 1.17)	.00	.42
Leisure activities express talents better than does my job	3.6	1.9
Leisure activities are more satisfying than work	4.0	1.7
Self-description through free time or work	33.1	11.9
More important to be good at free time activities than work activities	2.9	1.5
Prefer fame for job rather than free time activity	4.2	1.8
Ambitions more realized on job than free time	4.1	1.8
Amount of perceived leisure (Range: — .56 to 1.07)	—.06	.28
I have enough leisure	3.0	1.7
Leisure time felt to be boring	2.2	1.0
How much of free time is "killing time"	19.9	18.7
Little of my free time is actually leisure	4.6	1.8
Like more free time than I have now	5.5	1.5
Always more things to do than time for	5.2	1.7
Amount of work or vacation desired (Range: —3.01 to 1.01)	.00	.53
How many weeks of vacation would you like to have	7.7	8.6
Given the most ideal conditions, how many weeks of vacation should a person have	7.4	8.0
Given the present state of our society, how many days per week should be spent working	4.4	.6
Days per week you want to work for a living	4.0	.9

107

Amount of perceived leisure: There is a moderate desire for more free time and a recognition of not enough leisure. There always seems to be more things to do than there is time for, and if there is free time, it may not really be leisure. Only about one-fifth of free time may be considered that, and the rest is just "killing time." It is rare that people do not know what to do in their free time; usually they have no trouble finding things to do to keep them busy.

Amount of work or vacation desired: Work is the dominant orientation for this group. The desired number of weeks of vacation per year is less than eight (7.7), and even under the most ideal conditions and having been employed by a company for ten years, the person is still seen as deserving only slightly more than seven weeks (7.4) of vacation. Given our present society, a work week of 4.4 days is considered optimal, although people would like to work only 4.0 days themselves.

These, then, are the average attitudes of our *norm* group. It must be kept in mind that such average attitudes do not necessarily exist in any one person. They are useful, however, to make comparisons among subgroups delineated from the total group or for comparisons with future samples.

THE SYSTEMATIC COLLECTION OF LEISURE FACTS

It is quite evident that there has been a considerable amount of research on leisure activities and time and money budgets, but has there been any systematic approach to the overall problem of leisure? Riesman (1967) commented in his introduction to Dumazedier's book *Toward a Society of Leisure*, as follows:

> ... we do not study or collect figures on the overall problems of leisure, for it is somehow still not serious with us, in the sense of having a bureau or department of its own, or even a section meeting at the American Soiciological Assoication annual meetings.[3]

Smigel (1963), in the introduction to *Work and Leisure,* makes a similar point:

> Hard facts about leisure are not easy to come by. Information concerning the interrelationship between work and leisure is even more difficult to find. Among the many reasons for this scarcity, possibly

the most important is the Calvinist feeling in American Culture that work alone is good — that a preoccupation with leisure borders on an endorsement of sin.

And here is a third relevant voice from the 1960s, to round off this rather pessimistic view: "... There is very little research on the attitudes of the American people about leisure activities" (Brightbill, 1964).

It is quite customary to look at the sixties as a distinct and specific period, quite different from the following seventies. We tend to characterize those years by student unrests; the youth cult; awareness movements; a turning inward; and overall, a discontent with existing norms, including a rejection of the GNP (Gross National Product) as the ultimate criterion of the success of a society. There is little question that new values were born (or perhaps old or repressed values were merely reborn) and that they fermented during those years. It is my guess that one of the strongest impacts of those years was on our leisure attitudes and our understanding of the meaning of leisure. The seventies bear witness to developments that clearly reflect the direction of these changes.

For example, not only does our government concern itself now with the happiness of our nation (it theoretically did so all the time), but it is becoming officially involved in the measurement of this happiness. Yes, we may not be far away from the day when a "Council of Social Advisers turns over to the President an annual reading on the national happiness in the way the Council of Economic Advisers now reports on the national income" (Campbell, 1972, p. 464). That such a report would not delve heavily into the leisure domain is unthinkable, and it would obviously require a solid empirical foundation. To achieve this, "periodic surveys on leisure are clearly necessary to clarify and refine the intuitions that will have to suffice until there is a

---

[3]The American Psychological Association had its first symposium devoted specifically to the problem of leisure at its 1973 annual meeting in Montreal, Canada, titled "Into Leisure with Dignity" (Neulinger, 1974b). A number of other leisure symposia have since been held both at the American Psychological and the American Sociological Association meetings.

stronger empirical basis for decision" (Ennis, 1968, p. 532). The previously mentioned work by Robinson (1977) is a step in that direction, and so, of course, is the *social indicator movement* that has sprung up in response to this need. We are devoting a separate chapter to this development.

Another most telling sign of the times is the appearance of leisure studies departments or inclusion of the term *leisure* into department titles at colleges and universities throughout the United States and Canada. It can be shown quite convincingly by 1980 that there are, indeed, systematic efforts underway to collect data on the overall issues of leisure. The problem seems to become one of making the growing volume of information readily available to researchers and potential users. Since no single documentation center is any longer capable of collecting and disseminating all available information, an international leisure Information Network (LINK) has recently been set up, designed to link existing information centers and provide comprehensive services to potential users.[4]

Yet another example of the current trend is the introduction of agology, or more specifically the agology of leisure, at the universities of Brussels and Ghent in 1971. Dr. Willy Fache has described agology as a fully recognized branch of the social sciences in Dutch and Belgian universities, as a discipline formally on a par with psychology, sociology, and political science. Topics are said to include: community development; information systems to make people more aware of what helping, educational, and recreation institutes can do for them; emancipation strategies for women; the improvement of social planning on governmental and municipal levels; organization change; citizen participation; collective decision making; youth work; adult education; architectural influences on life style; and the like.[5]

Leisure, within the broader frame of a psychological defini-

---

[4]The first LINK conference was held at the Vrye University in Brussels, January, 1980 and was attended by leisure and recreation professionals from nine countries. For information and proceedings of the conference, contact the World Leisure and Recreation Association, 345 East 46th Street, New York, NY 10017.

tion, is indeed linked with all of these topics, or generally speaking, with the improvement of the quality of life. It is this tie that provides the leisure professional with a true challenge. Whether this development will come to fruition will depend largely on the degree to which a psychological conception of leisure will prevail. Leisure studies has the potential of becoming an important component in any systematic effort to improve the quality of life and, perhaps, even to become the leader in this movement. This, however, will be possible only if leisure is perceived in a broader context than it traditionally has been. Twardzik (1980), in outlining new goals for the recreation profession, states this point quite succinctly:

> We could retain our present goal of improving the quality of *leisure time*.
>
> There is, however, another road open to us. We may choose instead to improve the *quality of life*. This choice represents a radical not-so-simple departure from the historic and current professional goal, broadening as it does our range of endeavor *far beyond leisure time* (*italics added*).

---

[5]Abstracted from a paper by Dr. Willy Fache, of the University of Ghent, "Improving leisure policy at organizational and community levels by action research," presented at the International Colloquium of Popular Culture in the 20th Century, University of Quebec at Three Rivers, Three Rivers, Quebec, Canada, April 1980.

CHAPTER 4

LEISURE IN
THE SOCIAL-PSYCHOLOGICAL
CONTEXT

LEISURE, NO MATTER HOW DEFINED, is part of the person's total life experience. It is subject to all of the forces, personal or environmental, impinging on the individual, and in turn, it leaves its mark on the individual's life-style. In this chapter we are dealing with variables that have been shown to relate to leisure behavior and attitudes or that one might expect to be related on the basis of theory or common sense. Most studies on leisure include information on such correlates, but few attempts are made to provide theoretical links for these relationships or to use them as evidence for or against a theory of leisure.

> ... the sociology of leisure today is little else than a reporting of survey data on what selected samples of individuals do with the time in which they are not working and in the correlation of these data with conventional demographic variables (Berger, 1963).

This state of our science is, however, beginning to change. Serious empirically based attempts at theory building and verification are becoming more frequent (e.g. Burch, 1969; Bull, 1971; Kelly, 1976; Iso-Ahola, 1979a,b).

We shall examine variables for their relevance to the leisure domain, in general, and to leisure attitude dimensions we have identified, in particular. Our emphasis is on the implications of these variables for leisure and on the problems that the investigation of them may pose rather than on a listing of findings.

SOCIOECONOMIC-STATUS VARIABLES

We begin by looking at the standard socioeconomic-status vari-

113

ables that have traditionally been included in survey research. There is hardly a need to justify their inclusion in this context, since they are obviously related to most aspects of life, and we certainly may expect differences in leisure behavior and attitudes as a function of these variables.

Very often such relationships may seem self-evident or predictable by *common sense*. Thus, if we find that men are more likely to engage in football than women, or that women show a greater interest in ballet than men, we might be tempted to say: "Well, I could have told you so." Nevertheless, such findings may still be of interest. For one, the degree of correlation or difference may be the information sought rather than the mere fact of a relationship. Two, some obvious findings may turn out to be not so obvious after all. Common sense or folk wisdom is often quite contradictory. Thus, while it is *true* that one is never too old to learn, it is also *true* that you can't teach an old dog new tricks. And while absence makes the heart grow fonder, it is also *true* that out of sight is out of mind (Krech, Crutchfield, and Ballachey, 1962).[1]

Sex: Separate But Unequal

There is no questions that our society still draws a sharp delineation between the roles of men and women, particularly in the area of work. The man is still the primary breadwinner, and the woman is still tied to child rearing and housekeeping. There are exceptions, and they may become more frequent; but they are still only exceptions. These different roles imply different work patterns and, in turn, result in different free-time allocations. They also can be expected to affect both the meaning and function of leisure. Just to keep track of these ever-changing sex role patterns becomes a challenging task for the social scientist.

An example of such an effort is the previously discussed study by Robinson (1969), who compared male and female time budgets of a cross section of American adults during 1954 and 1956-1966. His findings confirm that work (i.e. the job) consumes a much greater proportion of the males' time than the females'; yet there are only small differences between the total leisure activity hours listed by males and females. The categories used in describing these activities are unfortunately so broad that they may well have covered up some meaningful distinctions. And time-budget studies are not generally designed to get at the meaning or function of leisure activities. Thus, even if the total number of leisure hours is the same for males and females, the nature and quality of that leisure is bound to be to be different. Robinson (1977, p.29) reports that sex "was associated with greater differences in time use than any other variable . . . except the day of the week."

There is also the methodological question whether there may be a sex bias in responses to participation surveys. Stephen Smith (1979) investigated this issue and concluded that "the basic form of the sex bias in response to open-ended questions is that an individual of a given sex tends to under-report participation in activities dominated by members of the opposite sex." He offered a weighting formula to adjust for this bias.

The role of sex becomes less obvious when dealing with leisure attitudes rather than behavior. For example, should we expect the female to have more *affinity for leisure* (i.e. experience less guilt about a life of leisure) since the work role is associated with being male? Or should we expect her to have less affinity for leisure since she is unused to free time (i.e. household work is never done!) and has less experience with many leisure activities (like sports)? What should be sex differences in regard to *self-definition through leisure or work?* Parsons (1949), in his analysis of sex roles, states that "only in very exceptional cases can an adult man be genuinely self-respecting and enjoy a respected status in the eyes of others if he does not 'earn a living' in an approved occupational role." Parsons contrasts to this the radically different female role showing woman's fundamental status to be that of her husband's wife and the mother of his children. Thus we might expect that men would be more likely to define themselves

---

[1]For a similar discussion of the same issue see Jones and Gerard, 1967, pp. 33-35.

in terms of their work rather than their leisure. We could argue that, if a woman does hold a job, she might even be more likely than a man to identify herself with that job since it is still an atypical experience.

The above considerations imply that a simple breakdown of data by sex may not be enough. Some very significant sex differences could be lost by such an analysis. The investigator must try to spot, perhaps at this point by intuition, those variables that might interact with sex and then carry out an analysis that will bring that interaction into the open. In the hypothetical example described in the previous paragraph of self-definition through leisure or work, it would not be enough to analyze data separately for males and females, but both males and females ought to be broken down further into those who hold a job and those who do not.

A further question that may be raised is whether it is sex (the male-female distinction, a demographic variable) or one's sex role (the degree of masculinity-femininity, a personality variable) that is more influential in one's leisure attitudes and behavior. The reader is referred to a study by Gentry and Doering (1979) for a detailed examination of this issue. The authors conclude that sex explained more in the differences in attitudes toward free-time activities and free-time use than did the personality variable, masculinity-femininity. They add, however, that "the fact that the concept of androgyny was helpful in predicting participation in certain activities is indicative of the impact of changing sex-roles to date."

For each of the variables discussed in this section findings from the *norm* group (described in chapter 2) will be presented, if available. An analysis of sex differences for the five leisure attitude dimensions revealed only one significant difference ($p <$ .01) for dimension IV, *amount of perceived leisure*. Males were more satisfied than females with the amount of leisure they had, or conversely, females had a greater desire for more leisure than did males. The females in this sample were all working full time. Under those conditions, free time may well be particularly precious to females in our society.

To repeat the rather obvious, sex is a variable that ought to be taken into account when designing and analyzing leisure research. Analyses should be routinely carried out separately for males and females and include relevant variables that might lead to interaction effects. Data for males and females should be combined only after extensive analyses have shown neither main nor interaction effects.[2]

Age: It Is Not How Old You Are

Age, like sex, will have some rather obvious effects on leisure behavior. We do not expect to see too many octogenarians racing down a ski slope, nor would we think of teenagers generally spending their free time in rocking chairs. Between these extremes, however, there is a relatively large area of undefined territory, and the trend seems to go in the direction of lessening age restrictions. Note, for example, the recent "promotion," advocacy or general approval of sexual activities, not only for ever-younger age levels, but also for the "older generation" (e.g., Rubin, I. 1970; Scheingold and Wagner, 1974).

Note further in the above paragaraph that we, too, have fallen into the trap of referring to leisure as if it implied activities only. It is the age variable that brings out better than anything the need for a clear conceptualization of leisure. Reflect that leisure, as defined by the residual definition, loses its meaning at both ends of the age continuum. What does leisure, in that sense, mean for the one-year-old, the five-year-old, or the teenager? What does it mean to the person who is retired or who is convalescing in an old age home? It is obvious that a job-based definition of leisure is inappropriate for these instances; but more importantly, any objective definition will be inadequate and, at

---

[2]This admonition seems to be contrary to Tinsley and Kass's (1978) statement that "the inclusion of sex as an independent variable in future research is not necessary, although it may still be desirable," and that "leisure activities differ in the needs they satisfy and that sex is not a moderator of this process." Carefully note, however, the authors' warning that "these results should not be interpreted, however, as suggesting that males and females do not differ in their psychological needs." They may simply agree in their perception of the needs a given activity might satisfy.

times, incapable of dealing with the many social-psychological issues that are so relevant to these age groups. We are devoting a special chapter to leisure and gerontology and shall restrict ourselves here to some general points regarding age correlates.

Age effects may be of two kinds. One reflects people's life histories, time and place of their growing up, their particular developments and the state of their physical and mental well-being. The other relates to external factors that are imposed upon people and about which they have little control. Examples of the latter type are the legal drinking age, age limitations for driver's licenses, hunting licenses, mandatory retirement ages, etc. Since the second type of age effects are based on chronological age alone, they may have quite different consequences for people with different life histories.

Opinions about age-dependency of leisure-time activities vary. Bergler (1966) speaks of three types of interdependencies: a decrease of activity with age (e.g. visiting theaters and concerts, reading books); an increase of activity with age (e.g. reading newspapers or gardening); fluctuating activities (e.g. reading magazines). Schmitz-Scherzer and Strödel (1971) feel that "chronological age is not necessarily the key variable with regard to leisure-time activities. Rather, social variables, personality traits, and health status seem to influence greatly the use of leisure time."

Age is like time, an ever-present factor. Yet, it is not age per se that tends to bring about relationships to certain conditions, behaviors, or events, but rather it is that certain conditions, behaviors, or events are frequently, though not necessarily, associated with specific age periods. But we will discuss more of that later, too.

Judging from our *norm* group the younger generation feels a greater *affinity for leisure* than does the older (r= −.18, p < .01). There is no way of knowing whether this reflects changing values in our society or a true age factor. Only a longitudinal study could furnish the answer to this question. The younger generation also identified more with leisure (Dimension III, r = −.12, p

< .05), and showed less desire for work (Dimension V, r = .12, p < .05). Perhaps the only surprising aspect of these findings is that these relationships are not stronger.

Educational Level: It Is Whom You Know ...

Number of years of education is likely to determine significantly the nature of both one's work and free-time activities. Certain avenues of both work and free time remain closed to those with little formal education. Thus, not only is a college degree required for many positions in government, industry, and education itself, but equally, a college background is necessary to give people access to certain social circles that in turn determine their total life-style. Even though our present educational system does not yet provide formal leisure education, it is likely that people with more education will have a greater potential for leisure, since they are better equipped to do what they want to do on their job and during free time.

Educational level is also of interest as the variable that "has traditionally been used as an indicator of social class" (Brim, Glass, Neulinger, and Firestone, 1969). When interpreting findings related to this variable, one must keep in mind that differences found may be social class rather than educational discrepancies. Similar caution, of course, is indicated when dealing with income or occupational variables.

The *norm* data indicated that the more educated person showed a greater desire for vacations than did the less educated one (Dimension V, r = − .23, p < .01). One may wonder to what degree this simply reflects the fact that the more educated person tends to have a longer vacation. Note, however, that the more educated person also showed a higher *affinity for leisure* (r = .20, p < .01). Such a person tended to identify more with work than did the less educated one (Dimension III, = − .19, p < .01), which may reflect the greater meaningfulness of the job held.

Income: The One-Eyed Is King Among the Blind

There are problems both in the collection and interpretation of income-related findings. In terms of data collection, it is well

119

known that people are hesitant to report their incomes, and if they do, they may be either overstating or understating it for any number of reasons. There is also the difference between gross and net income that can be considerable, depending on income range and particular circumstances. Then there is the problem of family income: Does the respondent report only the money he/she makes or do they add their spouse's earnings? Should they add the money their father-in-law makes, who lives with them part of the year? What about income from a second job? Or even that money one gets from an occasional odd job, which is not much but can make a big difference in terms of what one can afford to spend during one's free time.

Assuming that one has managed to deal with the above problems in data collection, there are next the problems of data interpretation. What does a given income mean to a particular person? How should one take family size into account? How does one adjust for unavoidable expenses, such as medical care, that vary tremendously and can distort gross income to the point of being meaningless.

Finally there is another variable, the persons's frame of reference, which tends to be totally neglected, and which is very difficult to take into account in considering a person's income, but which can make a tremendous difference in the subjective perception of one's income. For someone with well-off friends and neighbors living in the rich part of town, a given income may seem pitifully small. The same income may appear plentiful to the person living in a poverty-striken neighborhood where demands and aspirations are much lower. In addition, the same income may have different implications at different stages of a person's life. At the start of one's career, a person generally expects to earn little. As one progresses in age and in one's career, the person expects to make more; and when the day arrives when one realizes that one is never going to make any more, things may suddenly be seen in a different light. Yesterday's satisfactory income may become today's hopeless subsistence pay. An income that may have seemed relatively small while working may be experienced as sufficient and generous at retirement.

It follows that in evaluating income data a great deal of caution is required. It is usually impossible to take the above factors explicitly into account since necessary relevant data are hard to collect. Since money, however, is such an important variable in our society, one hopes that some relationships will become evident in spite of all the noise in the data.

Keeping the above limitations in mind we note that only *self-definition through leisure or work* showed a significant relationship with income in our *norm* group. The higher the respondents' income, the less likely were they to identify themselves through leisure ($r = -.15$, $p < .01$). An explanation for this finding may be one similar to that offered for educational level: the person with a well-paying job (i.e. the better educated one) is also the one who has a job that allows ego satisfaction. Since the *norm* group contained a relatively large number of professionals with high incomes such a relationship may well be expected.

Occupation: A Rose Is Not a Rose ...

The link between occupation and leisure has traditionally been considered a very strong one, probably because occupation is a major factor in determining social class, and social class, in turn, is intrinsically related to leisure behavior. To the degree that occupation is correlated with income and education, occupational variations in leisure behavior may, indeed, be viewed as social class differences. Many scales of social class combine these three variables into an index of social class (e.g. Hollingshead and Redlich, 1958).

A prime reason why occupation has been of traditional interest in the study of leisure is that the person's work is the major determining factor of the nature and amount of one's free time. In addition, there have been suggestions all along that the quality of one's work behavior will effect the quality of one's free-time behavior (e.g. Wilensky, 1960). Thus, avocational guidance always has to take into account the person's vocational interests and activities even if one is not concerned with a complete life-style counseling.

The major problem facing the person who wants to use occupation as an independent variable is to find a satisfactory system of classification. The distinction between many jobs is becoming increasingly diffuse, and simplified systems, such as *blue-collar* versus *white-collar* workers, are losing their usefulness. There are detailed systems of classification available (e.g. the Dictionary of Occupational Titles, U.S. Department of Labor, 1949), but these may not reflect the interests of the researcher. For one type of study one might be concerned with the status aspects of an occupation; a classification reflecting this variable would then be indicated. For another type of study, the concern may be with the creative potential of an occupation, and a totally different categorization may be relevant. It is clear that the purpose of the research must dictate the nature of the classification system to be used, and one might well consider the use of several systems in one study, if different aspects of leisure behavior are under investigation.

The effect of social class on leisure behavior has been extensively studied (e.g. Clarke, 1956; Dowell, 1967; Kaplan, 1960b; Kenyon, 1964; Reismann, 1954; Sutton-Smith, 1963; White, 1955; Zborowski and Eyde, 1962), and we discussed a controversy about this effect in the last chapter (e.g. Cunningham, Montoye, Metzner and Keller, 1970; Burdge, 1969; Bishop, 1971).

Let us once again add that other point that is nearly always neglected in establishing the relationship between social class and leisure behavior. The quality of the free-time activity and its context, mode, and subjective experience is not taken into account. Swimming is coded in the same category whether it takes place on a crowded city beach or at an exclusive private one. Going out for dinner at McDonald's is equated with going out for dinner at the fanciest restaurant, and traveling on the crowded Long Island Railroad commuter train is taken to be the same as going by parlor car. One cannot find differences that one does not include in one's coding system!

In the analyses of the *norm* group the following broad classification of occupations was used: *professional, business-sales, business-service, public service, clerical, tradesman,* and *miscellaneous.* Both professionals and people in business-sales identified themselves more with work than leisure compared to people in clerical jobs, tradesmen, and to a lesser degree, people in business-service and public service (Dimension III, $F = 7.11$, $p < .01$). Professionals also expressed the highest *affinity for leisure* compared to all others, but particularly tradesmen, clerical, and business-sales ($F = 3.20$, $p < .01$). Professionals were also clearly more vacation-oriented than all other groups (Dimension V, $F = 5.91$, $p < .01$). Finally, there is a distinction between professionals and business-sales people: the latter perceive themselves as having enough leisure while the former would prefer to have more. These findings support the theory that the nature of the job may determine whether it can serve as the basis of self-definition, but also that the broader educated person has a greater potential for the uses of leisure.

Religion: Cause or Effect

A good argument can be made that religion ought to be the variable that is most intimately related to work and leisure attitudes. One might even say that, for some, work and perhaps, for others, leisure, *is* their religion. We speak here of religion, not in the formal sense, but as a basic belief that determines one's life-style. Even if we think of religion in a narrower sense, it is certainly true that religious dogma had a great impact on work and free-time habits throughout the centuries. In Western culture it is probably the Protestant Ethic (Weber, 1952) that had the greatest influence on our present day thinking as regards matters of work and leisure. This orientation, springing from the Protestant teachings of the Reformation, "emphasized work *per se* as desirable and idleness, or lack of work, as undesirable. The only types of leisure activity this orientation condoned were those that contributed directly to increasing an individual's work output"(Burdge, 1961b). Work was not only desirable, but "for those responding to Luther, work, of no matter what nature, became a religious duty" (Macarov, 1970). Since wealth, or the fruits of labor, were viewed as a sign of Salvation, a negative attitude toward poverty and the poor became morally justified. It is easy to see a link between these beliefs and frequently expressed attitudes toward welfare. The poor are accused of not wanting to work, of being lazy, of preferring to be on welfare rather than earning an "honest" dollar, etc. There is little evidence, however, for the assumption that not wanting to work is the prerogative of the poor. On the contrary, a study that addressed itself specifically to the question, "Do the poor want to work?," found that poor people "identify their self-esteem with work as strongly as do the nonpoor" (Goodwin, 1972). The study revealed no significant differences between poor and nonpoor in their desire to work or in their life goals. Work as *a good* permeates the American scene, from rich to poor.

In spite of the apparent importance of the Protestant Ethic for the formation of values in our society, very little empirical research has been carried out on this topic. Only quite late has a scale been developed to measure specifically the Protestant Ethic as a dispositional variable (Mirels and Garrett, 1971). One might wonder whether the attitude implied is still linked to a specific religion, or whether it has transcended religious boundaries. McDonald (1972), in a study of the correlates of this scale, found frequency of church attendance significantly though weakly related to scores on the Protestant Ethic Scale, but the relationship was higher and significant only for Catholic rather than Protestant subjects. The author did report slightly higher means on this scale for Protestants than for Catholics. Unfortunately, the author does not report findings for subjects who held no religious preference. In our own studies we have found the largest differences on variables related to the Protestant Ethic between those subjects who report any kind of religious preference and those who claim none.

In support of the contention that the Protestant Ethic leads to negative attitudes toward poverty and the poor, MacDonald (1972) reported significant correlations between scores on the Protestant Ethic Scale and a measure of attitudes toward the poor, i.e. MacDonald's Poverty Scale (MacDonald, 1971). The author further reported a negative correlation between the Protestant Ethic Scale and a measure of one's evaluation of an enjoyable, leisurely life, i.e. "pleasure."

Crandall and Slivken (1980), in line with their previously mentioned work on a Leisure Ethic scale, raise the question whether work and leisure ethic scales would be negatively correlated, as is generally assumed. From their own work and that of some others (Bryan and Alsikafi, 1975; Buchholz, 1978), they conclude that "the available data suggest that the leisure and work ethics are unrelated" (p. 276). They do indicate, however, that we might well find people for whom such a correlation is positive and others for whom it might be negative. A critical issue here is how people view a leisure ethic. Do they think in terms of a free-time conception of leisure, or do they relate to a state-of-mind orientation? In the latter case, we might expect a positive correlation; while in the former, a negative one is more likely.

The leisure attitude dimension that comes closest to measuring the Protestant Ethic, namely Dimension V, *amount of work versus vacation desired*, showed significant religious differences for the *norm* group, with Protestants showing the strongest work attitudes and *Other* and *None* the lowest (F = 12.90, p < .01). Catholics were relatively high in work attitudes also, but their position was not significantly different statistically from any of the others. There were also minor differences on Dimensions I and III, but no clear pattern emerged one way or another.

"Race?"[3]

Differences in leisure behavior and attitudes between groups that are identified by racial labels, particularly blacks and whites, certainly deserve detailed investigation. Consider the projection that by the year 2000, half or more of the population will be black in the following cities: Washington, D.C.; Cleveland, Ohio;

---

[3]The author considers the term *racial differences* an unfortunate and misleading one for describing differences between cultural subgroups; however, since no more appropriate term seems to be available and since it is still used in much of the ongoing research, it was also used in this discussion.

Newark, New Jersey; Baltimore, Maryland; Chicago, Illinois; New York City; Philadelphia, Pennsylvania; Detroit, Michigan; and St. Louis, Missouri (Kahn and Wiener, 1970). It becomes clear that race, indeed, could be a major factor in shaping leisure behavior, attitudes, and policies, if not now, then in the near future.

The question might be asked whether there are any theoretical reasons to expect major differences in leisure behavior and attitudes between blacks and whites. It should be stressed that when we talk about racial differences here, we do not imply that these differences might be accounted for by one person having black skin and the other white skin or that there are some genetic differences between blacks and whites that lead to differences in leisure behavior. The reason why we expect such differences lies in the different histories of blacks and whites. Leisure behavior is part of one's cultural heritage, and the American black certainly had a cultural background different from the "average" white American, even if we consider only the generations of blacks after their arrival in this country. Perhaps we should say, particularly if we consider how blacks were brought into this country and what conditions they had to endure before today when they are slowly given the opportunity to assimilate to the American way of life. American blacks literally stood at the opposite end of the classical Greek leisure continuum; their job was to make leisure possible for everyone but themselves. The very condition for leisure, namely freedom, was absent from their life, and they were thus denied the right to develop as human beings. Indeed, so it would be strange if such an experience would not have left an impact on the person's attitudes toward work and leisure. Beyond these historical determinants there must be added others that have kept American blacks in a special status: their generally low income that keeps them on the lower end of the social class scale; the generally low level of education as a result of their membership in the lower classes; their restriction to low status occupations; their restriction to certain areas of residence, such as the ghettoes of large cities or the other side (i.e. the wrong side) of the tracks in smaller towns. These factors, and many more, have contributed to shaping a black subculture that is bound to have its own values and idiosyncracies of behavior. Add to this a final factor, the movement toward black awareness and the struggle for identity and for political and economic power, and the issue really becomes complex. For a nation at war, leisure may lose its relevance; it might be viewed as an ultimate goal, but while the fighting goes on it may be considered dangerous, leading to a weakening of the moral fiber and to self-indulgence. A nation at war does not have the freedom to allow its citizens the luxury of leisure. Work for the sake of freedom, work for the sake of country, become the slogans, and the person preaching work for the sake of self becomes suspect of treason. We would expect, then, that the black militant movement promotes austerity, a turning away from pleasure, and a devotion to duty, which means work for the movement.

There is another reason why a black person may be hesitant to proclaim an affinity to leisure. Leisure, as pointed out before, still bears the connotation of relaxation, doing nothing, idleness, and laziness. This, however, is part of the very stereotype we have imposed on the black person for years (Katz and Braly, 1933; Gilbert, 1951). Coming out in favor of leisure, then, could be interpreted as a confirmation of such a stereotype if leisure is perceived in such a manner.

If differences in leisure behavior and attitudes exist between blacks and whites, it is important to make these known so that desirable changes may be brought about. An effort in this direction is the work of Nesbitt, Brown and Murphy (1970), as outlined in *Recreation and Leisure Services for the Disadvantaged*. The authors addressed themselves to understanding and alleviating urban recreation problems and are inevitably drawn into a consideration of racial problems. They document striking differences in patterns of participation in recreation activities between blacks and whites and stress the tremendous need for social action.

One of the major problems in studying so-called racial differences in leisure behavior, or any other area, is that of control. Given the unequal distribution of blacks in our social system, it is very difficult to separate social class factors from purely racial ones. The complexity of attempting to separate environmental and genetic factors has been highlighted in relation to the question of intelligence. Jensen's (1969) stress on hereditary aspects of intelligence has been argued by a number of experts (e.g. Light and Smith, 1969; Stinchcombe, 1969; Fehr, 1969; Cottle, 1969, Deutsch, 1969), and if anything is clear, it is that there is no clear-cut answer to the whole issue.

Without underestimating the importance of an understanding of the theoretical issues involved, let us be concerned with the practical implications without waiting for *the* final answer that may never come. Let us determine whether differences exist in leisure behavior and, particularly, in the potential to experience leisure between groups that are predominantly black or white. Let us be aware of such differences among minority groups, be they distinguished by racial or religious labels, nationality designations, sex role definition, class distinction, rural-urban location, and so on. Let us determine whether and to what degree such differences are imposed by society, by economic or other limitations or whether they may be self-chosen and perhaps a reflection of desired cultural differences. This is our task as scientists; as citizens and, perhaps, even as professionals, we may feel that we must do more than that *if* such differences are the result of constraints and impositions.

That various groups engage in different free-time activities may merely reflect the fact that there are a multitude of ways to achieve the leisure experience. The task of society is not to prescribe or guarantee the same activity for everyone (an impossible task, anyhow). The obligation is to provide an equitable potential for all to achieve the leisure experience by whatever way desired, as long as it is within socially acceptable channels. That everyone desires the leisure experience is, of course, the basic assumption of my leisure philosophy.[4]

---

[4]Some individuals are threatened by and have difficulties in coping with freedom. We shall address that issue later when dealing with leisure education and counseling.

OTHER BACKGROUND VARIABLES

There are obviously quite a number of other background variables that one might want to relate to leisure behavior and attitudes. The selection of a few for discussion must be relatively arbitrary, and there is no doubt that the reader could have suggested others equally deserving ones.

Country of Birth

To the degree that leisure behavior and attitudes are culture bound, country of birth represents a critical variable. Since the number of foreign-born in some sections of the United States is considerable, a control for this factor may be indicated. If a study is concerned with the development of leisure attitudes, the country of birth of the respondents' parents also should be taken into account.

A word of warning; if the immigrant respondent shows and attitude different from his American-born counterpart, refrain from generalizing about his native country. The immigrant's attitudes reflect the interaction of American and native values and cannot be taken as representative of his countrymen's attitudes. A sample from the Italian-American community in New York is not a sample of the population of Italians living in Italy.

Birth Order

"Few if any aspects of family structure have so intrigued psychologists and the general public as has birth order" (Clausen, 1966). In spite of much controversy in this area, a number of findings seem to stand the test of replication. The one of most interest to the leisure domain may be the consistent finding relating first-born children to greater achievement and eminence. Since these accomplishments are generally obtained in the area of work, it is only reasonable to assume that first-borns' work *and* leisure behavior and attitudes are different from those born later. There is also direct evidence of differences between those born first and those born later in the leisure domain. Nisbett (1968), for example, reported that first-borns were less likely than those born later to participate in dangerous sports. He attributes this to the first-borns' greater fear of physical harm.

It is likely that other alleged characteristics of first-borns, as their greater need for affiliation under stress conditions, will lead to free-time behavior patterns different from those of persons born later. The delineation of reliable differences in leisure behavior as a function of birth order could contribute not only to a better understanding of leisure dynamics but also to a solidification of the very birth-order phenomenon, which stands on very shaky theoretical legs.

Work Status

The person's work status will play a very different role depending on whether we operate within an objective (residual) framework of leisure or a subjective (psychological) one. In the former case, work status will tend to be a defining (independent) variable. Parker (1971), in discussing the problems of defining leisure, considers, in addition to the full-time and part-time employed, the following four groups of nonworkers: prisoners, housewives, the unemployed, and the idle rich. To this we may add groups such as students, the retired, and children. Presumably, the criterion variable of classification for these groups is "work status"; however, each of these categories carries connotations that go far beyond the context of this variable.

Work status does not present this type of problem when we operate within the subjective framework of leisure. Leisure, then, is defined independently of the concept of work (employment) or any of the categories of work status used. It may or it may not manifest itself within each of these categories, including full-time work and free time. The complexity of each of the categories is still there, but it is no longer confounded in the very definition of leisure. Leisure is likely to be the dependent variable, to be studied within the context of these various circumstances. We may, of course, decide to study how leisure (now as an independent variable) affects these various categories (as the dependent variables). For example, we could investigate how an increase in leisure experiences affects the behavior of prisoners or of housewives.

In whichever theoretical framework we operate, it is necessary to develop special techniques and instruments for use with each of these subcategories of work status. While we can and should demand that the leisure professional be clear as regards the denotation of the word leisure, we cannot expect that from the subjects from whom we elicit our data. This problem will haunt us when our subjects stem from different work status categories, and there is no easy solution to this issue. Spelling out different meanings of leisure to the subjects may influence the subjects' responses in ways we do not know. Not spelling out these meanings may result in responses the meaning of which we do not know. There is much room here for important methodological research.

Health

The potential effect of leisure behavior on physical and/or mental health is well recognized. Leisure as recreation emphasizes this relationship. Health is viewed as the dependent variable, and variations in health, i.e., physical or mental states, are sought as a function of leisure behavior. At this point, however, we want to look at health as the independent variable. How does leisure behavior or attitudes vary as a function of health?

Some relationships seem obvious. The person with a weak heart is not likely to engage in weight lifting, nor will the person suffering from emphysema spend much time with water sports. Nevertheless, certain physical handicaps may lead to the choice of activities because of their recreational value, as well as their impact on self-confidence and self-esteem.

The relationship of health to leisure attitudes is probably quite complex. Leisure may have functions for the disabled that it need not generally fulfill for the normal. The added importance may reflect itself, not only in the kind of attitude held but also in its intensity. There may be a need for overcompensation. In addition, certain physical or mental states may vary in their potential for experiencing leisure. Pieper (1963), for example, suggests that sleeplessness may imply an incapacity for leisure. One needs to be able to let go to experience leisure, just as one does for falling asleep.

131

The ability to sleep and to relax or to devote oneself with satisfaction and without interference to a desired task (i.e. to *leisure*) is often taken as an indication of one's state of mental health. The delineation of the leisure behavior and attitudes of people from different psychiatric diagnostic categories may thus be of considerable interest. Note in this context that the *Diagnostic and Statistical Manual of Mental Disorders*, DSM-III, (1978) refers to the "use of leisure time" as a criterion of level of adaptive functioning. Let us observe that we are dealing with an area in which the distinction between cause and effect becomes difficult. Does an "inappropriate" leisure attitude or the incapacity to leisure affect one's mental well-being, or does one's mental well-being affect one's leisure attitudes and capacity? An explicit theoretical link between leisure and mental health needs to be spelled out so that relevant hypotheses can be appropriately tested.

PERSONALITY VARIABLES

The previous sections dealt with socioeconomic status and background variables as potential determinants of leisure behavior and attitudes. Our interest is twofold. One, we need information about the degree to which leisure behavior changes as a function of these variables. For example, we may want to know the proportion of males and females engaging in certain free-time activities, or we may be interested in participation rates as a function of income level. We might want to investigate whether and how educational levels affect one's potential to experience leisure. This type of information is of value for planning purposes, policy determinations, and similar administrative functions. Two, we are interested in these relationships to further our understanding of the dynamics of leisure. For example, knowing that males rather than females have a particular leisure attitude may be linked with the function of this attitude and may lead to insights into sex-specific leisure behavior.

The usefulness of delineating relationships between personality variables and leisure behavior is primarily of the latter kind, namely better understanding. Such understanding, however, may, in turn, lead to better prediction of leisure behavior and

132

may also be useful for therapy and counseling.

We would also like to reiterate the statement made in the preface that leisure is an ideal place to investigate personality dynamics. While this may seem intuitively obvious, it has also been stated on theoretical grounds. For example, within the context of attribution theory Jones (1979) argues that "behavior under free-choice conditions is more diagnostic than behavior under constraint." At least we are more likely to make a dispositional rather than a situational attribution.

A word of caution. While the concept of personality trait and the idea of a consistent self is intuitively very appealing, its usefulness in predicting behavior has been seriously questioned (e.g. Hunt, 1965; Mischel, 1968, 1969). While correlations of .30 or higher are rare in personality research and are generally considered a respectable finding, they explain less than 10 percent of the relevant variance, a proportion that has little practical value. There are, however, at least two reasons why such low correlations have been the rule. One, most of these correlations relate to one independent variable only; there is still relatively little multivariate research going on, a state that is changing rapidly with increasing sophistication of researchers and availability of computers. Two, most personality psychologists have attempted to use personality models *in vacuo,* that is, without including the environmental context into their prediction equations. You cannot hope to predict accurately whether an aggresive person will behave aggressively tomorrow unless you know that person's situation tomorrow. The prediction problem must be treated within a person-environment interaction approach.

The social scientist who wants to use personality variables in research has a wide choice of tests and techniques available. It is obviously impossible to suggest certain tests as more appropriate than others, since their usefulness will depend on the nature of the problem, the subject pool involved, the resources available, etc. Our own bias lies with a method originated by Murray (1938) who employs a scheme of *needs* and *press* to categorize both the person and the environment. A study employing this approach was mentioned in the last chapter (*see* Table IX). The main problem in trying to predict leisure behavior from personality traits may be that any given activity may fulfill different needs for different people or even the same person at different times. Playing golf may fulfill the need for affiliation for one person, for achievement for another, and for aggression for yet another; and it can, of course, fulfill any combination of needs at the same time. As scientists, all we can hope for is that some activities tend to have certain primary psychological functions, and we need to identify these in a systematic manner (e.g. Kenyon, 1970).

Looking at the other side of the coin we might ask which areas of personality might be particularly relevant to research in the leisure domain. The answer seems equally difficult; one probably could make a good point for almost any personality variable or syndrome, and the choice will reflect strongly the researcher's orientation and the particular conceptualization of leisure used. In this spirit we shall mention just a few areas that might be particularly fruitful for future research. The perception of choice and implications thereof, as investigated through research on the internal-external control dimension (Rotter 1966) and attribution theory, seems one area of immediate relevance to the very conception of leisure. Another phenomenon that may well be related to the issues is that of alienation. A person without freedom, a person without choice, is a person without power. Then there is the matter of self-definition. What is the person's perception of work and leisure? How is self-esteem and level of aspiration related to leisure behavior? Finally, there are the many variables or states associated with mental health deviancies or disorders, such as rigidity, compulsivity, ennui, anxiety, depression, and so on. Research in these areas as regards leisure is barren because the prevalent conception of leisure as a residual does not relate to these concepts. By using a psychological, i.e. subjective definition of leisure, however, we are placing the issue in the midst of these phenomena. We are doing no less than making the ability *to leisure* a criterion of mental health.

LEISURE AND ATTITUDES TOWARD SEX

One of the few generally accepted dictums in social psychology is that the various attitudes a person holds tend to form an internally consistent pattern. There is a constant striving for a state of balance among one's cognitions (e.g. Heider, 1958; Festinger, 1957; Osgood and Tannenbaum, 1955). A person's attitude will influence not only one's behavior, but the attitudes one holds in other areas. Freud (Erikson, 1968, p. 136) spoke of two central spheres of life, love and work *(lieben und arbeiten)*, and there are few who would want to disparage the importance of these two areas of life. Since, however, they are that important, it follows that we are likely to strive for consistency in their respect. We shall attempt to bring our work, and concomitantly our leisure attitudes, in line with our attitudes toward sex.

What, however, does congruence mean in this instance? A look at the connotations of the terms *sex* and *leisure* may throw some light on this issue. What comes to mind when we think of sex? Pleasure, joy, delight? Or do we experience uneasiness, a feeling of shame and guilt? Or even worse, do we feel threatened? Do we think of sex as something to be avoided at all costs? Now, let us switch to leisure. What comes to mind when we think of leisure? Pleasure, joy, delight? Do we experience uneasiness, shame and guilt? Or do we feel threatened and are we doing everything we can to avoid leisure? There is a striking similarity in our feelings toward sex and leisure, and the reason is not hard to find. Our attitudes toward both topics were shaped by the same set of values, namely the Protestant Ethic. This view, as already pointed out, not only glorified work and denigrated leisure, but it also implied a stern position on sexuality. "The glorification of virginity led by inperceptible stages to the formulation of 'fornication' as a deadly sin, . . . " (Ellis, 1936), and even the love between husband and wife involved too much concupiscence and "could hardly be expressed at all without some measure of sin" (Bird and Bird, 1967). To the degree, then, that the Protestant Ethic permeates our culture, it is not surprising to find a common core in our leisure and sex attitudes.

An implication of all this may be that it is very difficult to do something about changing a person's work-leisure or sex attitudes, since both involve the person's core value system. It implies that if we do bring about a change in either one of the systems, the other one is likely to be affected also. Perhaps a therapist could take advantage of this by switching from one area to the other if either one is blocked by the patient's resistance.

Sex and Leisure Attitudes: Some Findings

"A Study of Leisure (Appendix A) included five items relating to sex attitudes. Below are previously unpublished data from the *norm* group (Neulinger and Breit, 1971), the *Mensa* group (Neulinger and Raps, 1972), and a pilot study of alcoholics in a Veterans Hospital treatment center (Neulinger, Berg and Weiss, 1972). The response distributions for the three samples show some rather striking differences (Table XIII). We shall not attempt to account for these here, since the subjects of these samples differed, not only in terms of their group membership but also in terms of religious affiliation, social class, and age (see also Berg and Neulinger, 1976).

The main interest, however, lies in the relationship between leisure and sex attitudes and these are investigated by means of analyses of variance in both the *norm* and the *Mensa* group. For ease of discussion, we shall call first-alternative respondents of each of the sex questions "conservative" (e.g. 'I feel that a person should engage in sexual relations only after he or she is married") and second-alternative respondents "liberals" (e.g. "I approve of premarital sex"). In the *norm* group, liberals differed significantly from the conservatives on leisure attitude dimensions I, III, and V, on each of the four questions analyzed.[5] Conservatives had a lower *affinity for leisure* score, identified less with leisure, and had a stronger work orientation than did liberals. Ten of these twelve analyses (four questions for each of three dimensions!) were replicated significantly in the *Mensa* group;

---

[5]Data for males and females were combined since preliminary analyses had shown no significant sex differences. No analyses of variance were carried out for question one because of the highly skewed response distribution.

TABLE XIII
RESPONSE DISTRIBUTIONS TO SEX RELATED ITEMS FOR THREE
GROUPS: THE *NORM* GROUP, THE *MENSA* GROUP AND A GROUP
OF ALCOHOLICS

Item:	NORM ($N = 335$)	MENSA ($N = 343$)	ALCOH'S ($N = 84$)
	P e r c e n t		
(1) I feel that the main reason for having sexual relations should be to have children	6	1	20
I feel that having sexual relations for pleasure only is fine	76	94	50
I prefer not to answer this question	17	5	30
(2) I feel that a person should engage in sexual relations only after he or she is married	25	17	24
I approve of premarital sex	61	72	66
I prefer not to answer this question	14	11	10
(3) I feel that children should not be aware of the fact that their parents engage in sexual relations until the parents feel it is necessary to introduce the subject	42	24	64
I feel that it is all right for children of any age to be aware of the fact that their parents engage in sexual relations	42	66	29
I prefer not to answer this question	16	10	7
(4) I feel that society should permit only heterosexual (male-female) relationships	32	16	47
I feel that society should be permissive of all types of sexual relationships	54	73	32
I prefer not to answer this question	15	11	21
(5) I feel that the institution of marriage, as we know it today, should be here to stay	68	59	74
I feel that the institution of marriage, as we know it today, should be abolished	12	18	11
I prefer not to answer this question	20	23	15

two were nonsignificant.

These data strongly support the contention that the person's value system is integrated and that somebody with conservative leisure attitudes will also tend to have conservative sex attitudes. One might argue that this relationship has some usefulness for the person as a means of coping with sexual anxieties. Inhibi-

137

tions in the sexual area may find an outlet in the work area with appropriate attitudinal support.

A look at the conative component of leisure attitudes involving sex, that is leisure preferences such as "engaging in sexual or affectional activities," was taken by Mancini and Orthner (1978), who found that "recreational sexuality preferences" differed for men and women and also differed among those at different stages of the life cycle. This research sparked a controversy as to whether sex is an appropriate topic in a survey of leisure activities. Opinions expressed in this respect may be found in an issue of the *Leisure Information Newsletter* (1979, Vol. 6, No. 2)[6], and range from "Sex is not leisure" (Edwards, 1979) or sex is certainly an appropriate topic for leisure research (Orthner, 1979), to seeing sex as perhaps the most suitable vehicle for *pure leisure,* at least in terms of joint (two person) activities (Neulinger, 1979a).

---

[6]The *Leisure Information Newsletter,* to 1980, Vol. 6 No. 4, was published by The Leisure Institute, 145 East 92nd Street, New York, N.Y. 10028; from 1980, Vol. 7, No. 1 on, it is published by the Department of Leisure Studies, New York University, 70 Press Annex, Washington Square, New York, N.Y. 10003.

CHAPTER 5

THE MEASUREMENT OF THE QUALITY OF LIFE: SOCIAL INDICATORS

We can only learn what we are predisposed to discover. Johnston, 1980

"The word (leisure) specifically denotes and commonly connotes free or discretionary time, . . ."; so writes a "member of that surviving subset of sociologists that seeks the highest possible level of generalization" (Moore, 1976). I am using this quote as a reminder that *leisure*, indeed, still means to many, if not most, *free time*. I am also using it as an anchor point against which to measure the tremendous shift this meaning is undergoing, both in denotation and connotation, and particularly among leisure professionals. The shift in denotation, which is the move from a concern with a time period (or an *institution,* as used by Cheek and Burch, 1976) to a concern with a state of mind, is the most relevant to this chapter.

It has been well recognized that a concern with the quality of life must include a concern with leisure, that is free time and recreational activities. We certainly would not want to contradict nor discourage that trend. Both *Social Indicators, 1973* (1973) and *Social Indicators, 1976* (1977) include chapters referring to leisure, but the treatment of the topic is based on the sociological perspective, the residual definition of leisure. The indicators presented tend to reflect this orientation; they are primarily time usage and activity participation measures.

Once we accept a psychological framework of leisure, once we start denoting by leisure a state of mind, two major developments are bound to take place. The first of these already has taken roots and shows itself in the increased concern with the psychological aspects of free time and free-time activities. Perceptions, feelings, satisfactions, and motivations related to these phenomena are gaining more and more attention.

The second development, however, is bound to be the really revolutionary one. Once we follow through (and this may take a long time!) on the implications of a state of mind conception of leisure, we are forced to give up the work-leisure dichotomy. We then find ourselves suddenly confronting not just a part of a person's day, a section of life, but all of it, the total sphere of human activities.

Such a development will change the role leisure plays within the context of the quality of life. At the moment, leisure is viewed as just one of many areas of concern and social indicators are being developed to measure it in much the same manner as other relevant areas. If it should come to pass that leisure, indeed, would be recognized as a criterion of the quality of life, it would assume a quite different and unique role. It would become a yardstick by which everything else is measured.

Our intention, in this chapter, is to suggest that possibility. We shall review issues related to the quality of life and its measurement, trace the historical development of this field of endeavor, and then devote some time to exploring implications derived from an acceptance of leisure as a criterion of the quality of life.

THE CRITERION PROBLEM

"There are as many quality of life definitions as there are people" (Liu, 1975, p. 10). This truism could be and has been taken as a reason to discourage many an attempt to measure the quality of life. Fortunately, it did not have that effect on the author of that statement, nor is there any real reason why it should. The reason that there are as many definitions of the quality of life as there are people is that people are unique individuals. This uniqueness, however, has not kept social scientists from viewing people as their proper subject matter. In addition to uniqueness, people also share common characteristics and ways of behaving, and it is those commonalities and only those, with which the scientist is concerned.[1] Similarly, as scientists, we shall

140

be concerned with those aspects of the quality of life on which people can agree. Furthermore, this diversity does not necessarily imply that everyone disagrees with everyone else. We may find subgroups who share common views, and this clustering may turn out to be a function not only of personality and environmental factors but may reflect a person-environment interaction.

The multitude of possible definitions of the quality of life does represent one of the difficulties in measuring it. This difficulty is closely intertwined with a second one. Definitions tend to include two components, an objective and a subjective one. The former may refer to the person's living standard as reflected by objective facts such as number of square feet per living quarter, amount of electrical energy consumption, money spent on consumer goods, and so on; the latter may relate to the person's perceived satisfaction of needs and wants or, even, to just a general feeling of well-being. Doubt about the possibility of measuring subjective states represents the second major obstacle to progress in quality of life research.[2] Such states, however, can be measured reliably and validly, and psychologists have developed appropriate methods ever since the days of Fechner (1860). Until very recently, psychologists have been guilty of neglecting the importance of the person-environment interaction. Yet, it is this aspect that is particularly relevant to subjective components of the quality of life. The popular saying, "one man's meat is another man's poison," expresses this person-environment interaction well; yet, it is only slowly being integrated into the thinking of social scientists and, particularly, personality theorists.

The importance of such an interaction effect has recently been demonstrated in a study by Gratton (1980). Individuals from three social class groups evaluated the importance of Maslow's

---

[1]The scientist is in search of general laws. What is unique is by definition not general, or even common. To the scientist, uniqueness is but error.

[2]Note, in this context, the article by Turner and Krauss (1978), "Fallible indicators of the subjective state of the nation."

141

(1954) five needs (ranging from physiological, through safety, belonging, and self-esteem, to self-actualization). Results indicated that

> some life domains and aspects of domains will be intrinsically more important than others. *And this difference in domain importance will vary across social class* (Gratton, 1980, italics added).

The author also refers to previous research by Strumpel (1976a) who showed that respondents differed, as a function of their background, about which they considered most important: a prosperous life, an important life, a secure life, or an exciting life. Respondents with a college degree or professionals, for example, rarely selected a prosperous life, while the black and managerial groups chose it most frequently. College degree respondents were more likely to be concerned with an important or exciting life.

These examples make it clear that it is not enough to specify a criterion of the quality of life; the specification must include the target population for which it is to be the criterion. This rule becomes the more important, the more specific we get. If we use an abstract term like *happiness* as an ultimate criterion, we might safely make the assumption that all strive for it.[3] The more concrete we get, however, the more we shall have to take into account individual persons, their respective environments, and the interaction between the two.

The Quality of Life: The Criterion

The previous discussions indicate that the measurement of the quality of life really involves two aspects, although their distinction becomes at times blurred. The first is a determination of what constitutes *the good life*. What are the domains of importance, and within each domain, what is the direction of improvement and what of decline. The second aspect involves measuring these domains or, rather, relevant variables within those domains. These measures are referred to as social indicators, and we shall turn to them shortly. First, some more about

---

[3]We would, no doubt, assign pathology to those who might question this criterion.

142

that which we refer to when speaking of the quality of life.

What is *the good life?* Theologians and philosophers have searched for the *summum bonum,* the supreme or highest good, ever since the dawn of human kind without reaching unanimity. Their aim seemed to have been the identification of a particular state of mind that would be associated with *the good life,* such as happiness, beatitude, contentment, or perhaps just pleasure. In modern, economic times we see a shift in approach; attempts are made to identify *the good life* through indicators based primarily on materialistic factors. The classical example is the use of the *GNP,* the gross national product, as the measure of the quality of life. The inadequacy of this measure for such a purpose is becoming, however, well recognized:

> As concern over the quality of the environment and social welfare mounts, the conventional measure of well-being, GNP, which has served for decades as a means of establishing goals and measuring achievement of the goals at the policy-making level, has been criticized — on the one hand — because it is not an appropriate index of welfare, and — on the other — because it does not include the important values of increased leisure, the services of housewives, the hidden rent, farmer's consumption of their own products, etc. (Liu, 1975, p. 6).

What is to take the place of the GNP? Should we return to a direct search for happiness? The previously made distinction between identifying *the good life* and measuring it, becomes relevant. The GNP refers to the latter aspect; it is an indicator of the good life, a measure of a means or potential condition for experiencing it. Happiness refers to the goal itself or rather to the state of mind one experiences when living the good life. Since a goal is always primary to any means of achieving it, is it not self-evident that establishing the goal must be our primary task?

The problem, however, is that specifying a goal in as abstract a term as happiness is just not enough. To be able to work with this concept, we must concretize it, we must operationalize it, and we tend to end up where we started, namely specifying the conditions that will bring about the concept, stating the means by which to measure it: social indicators. The issue becomes further complicated because there are always many different means to achieve a given goal, some sufficient ones, others only necessary but not sufficient.

Let us look briefly at two approaches to identifying the good life that attack the problems discussed, but from opposite directions. The first is exemplified by "A research approach to improving our quality of life" (Flanagan, 1978), an investigation carried out by the American Institutes for Research (AIR). The first issue tackled and the one we are interested in here, was

> to define the critical requirements of a person's quality of life in an empirical manner. To accomplish this, more than 6,500 critical incidents were collected from nearly 3,000 people of various ages, races, and backgrounds representing all regions of the country" (Flanagan, 1978).

These incidents referred primarily to events or experiences that were especially satisfying or dissatisfying to people. An eventual sorting led to fifteen quality-of-life components that were listed under five headings: physical and material well-being; relations with other people; social, community, and civic activities; personal development and fulfillment; and recreation. What we have here, then, is a comprehensive and well-organized list of "things" that are important to the good life. These things not only refer to activities or material goods but also to mental states such as safety, freedom from anxiety, sociability, self-knowledge, and so on. Yet, all of these are related to means rather than directly to the final goal, and they are obtained on a more or less a-theoretical basis. As the author states: "This first step in this program provided an *empirically derived criterion* defining the quality of life for Americans" (Flanagan, 1978, italics added).

The second way of identifying the good life starts from a theory or at least a basic assumption. For example, the approach I am suggesting is that we make the assumption that leisure is a state of mind that all desire, one so important that we may consider it at least as a first approximation to a criterion of the quality of life.[4] Leisure, as we have stated previously, is the state of mind emerging from the perception of freedom and involvement in intrinsically motivated activities. As I have pointed out elsewhere (Neulinger, 1979b), these are the conditions that lead one to perceive oneself as being an *origin* rather than a *pawn*, a desire that is overriding all other motives (deCharms, 1968); it involves behavior that makes a person feel competent and self-determined (White, 1959; Deci, 1975); they are necessary conditions to engage in the search for meaning, a core motivational propensity common to all (Maddi, 1970); they are essential to the perception of *flow* (Csikszentmihalyi, 1975). In short, these are the conditions underlying the need for and fulfillment of *being* rather than *having* (Fromm, 1976).

Once we have thus identified our final goal, our task becomes specifying the conditions that will lead toward that goal. If we accept *perceived freedom* and *intrinsic motivation* as the critical conditions for attaining the leisure experience, that means developing measures (social indicators) that will give information about these two variables, in all areas of human concern. That would not mean eliminating most of the present indicators, such as those related to housing, employment, and so on, but it would furnish us with a theoretical orientation in terms of which we could phrase our questions in a much more meaningful manner.

It goes without saying that the identification of a final goal, an ultimate criterion of the quality of life, involves a value judgment. It is precisely for that reason that the task is so important and should not be left to the whim of some powerful politician or government, nor to chance. It ought to be the expression of the will of the people. Translating this will into action is the challenge facing the social indicators movement.[5]

THE SOCIAL INDICATORS MOVEMENT

As Liu (1975, p. 9) points out, "the preamble to the United States Constitution includes as one statement of purpose, 'to

---

[4]Notwithstanding de Grazia's previously quoted view that leisure is desired by but few (*see* page 5).

[5]Some of the thoughts expressed here have also been elaborated on elsewhere (Neulinger, 1980).

promote the general welfare;' " and "quality of life" is just another more modern term for "general welfare" or "social well-being." It seems thus quite appropriate that the government is actively involved in promoting the quality of life. An actual *social indicators movement* did not materialize until the 1960s, but its roots can be traced much earlier. According to Wilcox, et al. (1972), the following dates and events are important precursors of this movement in the United States; later dates and events are added to bring these developments up to date.

1929: President Hoover commissioned a group of scientists to study the feasibility of a national survey of social trends, including an annual report on such trends.

1933: *Recent Social Trends* (1933) was the result of the work of the 1929 commission, containing twenty-nine chapters, including topics such as changing social attitudes and interests, rural life, the family, recreation and leisure time activities, crime and punishment, health and medical practice, and others. The importance of trend analyses to an understanding of social phenomena was recognized and the necessity for an interdisciplinary approach stressed. A National Advisory Council was proposed that eventually led to the National Council of Economic Advisers.

1937: "On measurement of relative national standards of living" (Bennett, 1937). Although primary emphasis shifted to economic conditions, there was continued interest in assessing qualitative social trends, as exemplified in Bennett's work. This project attempted to measure the national "standard of living" of fourteen countries over a ten year period. Five categories investigated were: food, clothing, shelter, transport and communication, and professional services.

1953: *Psychosis and Civilization: Studies in the Frequency of Mental Disease* (Goldhammer and Marshall, 1953). Trends in mental health and the quality of life are of common interest, whether one considers the two causally related or not. Could one speak of an improvement of the nation's quality of life, if its state of mental health were decreasing at the same time? Goldhammer and

146

Marshall attempted the difficult task of obtaining measures of mental health, by using first admission rates to mental hospitals as an indicator. Their conclusion was that there had been no long-term increase during the last century in the incidence of the psychoses of early and middle life.

Studies of mental health have remained of interest to students of the quality of life for two reasons. One, these studies tend to relate mental health to socioeconomic conditions and thus deal with variables with which quality-of-life studies are concerned (e.g., Faris and Dunham, 1939; Hollingshead and Redlich, 1958; Scrole, et al. 1962; Dohrenwend and Dohrenwend, 1969). Two, they tend to deal with questions of happiness and general satisfaction, issues that are obviously related to the quality of life (e.g., Gurin, Veroff, and Feld, 1960; Bradburn and Caplovitz, 1965; Cantril, 1965).

1960: REPORT OF THE PRESIDENT'S COMMISSION ON NATIONAL GOALS FOR AMERICANS: PROGRAMS FOR ACTION IN THE SIXTIES. A presidential commission, established by President Eisenhower, suggested guidelines for policy in terms of "Goals at Home" and "Goals Abroad." Areas of domestic concern included the individual, equality, education, arts and sciences, technological change, living conditions, health and welfare, and others. Six years later, Biderman (1966) attempted to identify indicators for eighty-one subgoals that were derived from the commission's more general goals. He was able to locate relevant indicators for only forty-eight. By that time the need for the evaluation of social policy and programs had been well recognized, and pointing to this lack of means of evaluation helped to spur progress toward the development of social indicators. This need was further emphasized in the final report of the National Commission on Technology, Automation and Economic Progress (1966).

1966: *Social Indicators* (Bauer, 1966). The author of this work is generally referred to as the *father* of the current social indicator movement. Raymond Bauer, a member of a committee of the National Aeronautics and Space Administration, suggested

147

the need for a comprehensive system of social indicators capable of assessing the social impacts of phenomena such as space exploration to aid in the development of social policy, and later brought together some well known social scientists to consider the ramifications of social indicators (Wilcox, et al., p. 5).

Publications by the American Academy of Political and Social Science (*Social Goals and Indicators for American Society: Vol. I & II*, 1967) and the American Academy of Arts and Sciences (*Toward the Year 2000: Work in Progress*, 1967) further strengthened the impetus of the social indicator movement.

1969: TOWARD A SOCIAL REPORT (U.S. Department of Health, Education and Welfare, 1969). This project, commissioned by President Johnson in 1966, dealt with the development of social indicators designed to measure progress toward societal goals and assess the social well-being of Americans. It was clearly intended to go beyond economic indicators.

At about that time the so-called Mondale Bills (sponsored by Senator Walter Mondale and others), the "Full Opportunity and Social Accounting Act" of 1967 and the "Social Accounting Act" of 1969, were introduced. These bills were to provide for

(1) an Annual Social Report of the President,
(2) a Council of Social Advisers to aid in preparing the report and (3) a Joint Committee on the Social Report to review and transmit the findings to Congress (Wilcox, et al., 1972, p. 6).

These bills, however, were never enacted into law.

1972: The establishment of the Center for Coordination of Research on Social Indicators (CCRSI) in Washington, D.C. in 1972 may be viewed as another important milestone in the social indicators movement. The purpose of this center was described as

to enhance the contribution of social science research to the development of a broad range of indicators of social change, in response to current and anticipated demands from both research and policy communities (Van Dusen, 1974, p. v).

CCRSI was established by the Social Science Research Council (SSRC), a private nonprofit organization formed for the purpose of advancing research in the social sciences. SSRC is publishing a most informative *Social Indicators Newsletter*.

1973: *Social Indicators, 1973* (1973) was published by the statistical policy division, Office of Management and Budget, United States Government. This book was organized around eight major social areas: health, public safety, education, employment, income, housing, leisure and recreation, and population. The following year, a symposium was held that considered the value and utility of this publication. Proceedings of this conference were published as *Social Indicators, 1973: a review symposium* (Van Dusen, 1974).

According to Natalie Ramsoy (1974), one of the symposium members, *Social Indicators, 1973* (1973) marks the beginning of a new era: the *second generation* of social indicators. The first consisted of such works as *Toward a Social Report* (1969) and *Indicators of Social Change* (Sheldon and Moore, 1968), with emphasis on textual discussions and the very problems of observing and measuring social phenomena. The second generation is said to consist of books such as the above mentioned *Social Indicators, 1973* and similar ones published in Great Britain, France, Sweden, and Norway. In these volumes, the idea of social indicators is already taken for granted; their need or feasibility is no longer an issue. The task is perceived as finding ways of improving them and making them more sensitive to social conditions and useful for policy decisions.

1977: The U.S. Department of Commerce published *Social Indicators, 1976* (1977). This volume covers eleven major social areas; the three added were family, social security and welfare, and social mobility and participation. This second report by the Federal Government of the United States is a much extended version of the 1973 study. Its intent is stated as providing "a factual basis for independent assessments of our current social conditions and the directions in which we appear to be evolving as a society."[6] A third social indicator report was published in 1980.

The social indicators movement is well on its way to becoming a permanent institution. A Social Indicators Office was estab-

---

[6]An issue of *The Annals* of the American Academy of Political and Social Science (Vol. 435, January 1978) featured papers related to *Social Indicators, 1976.*

lished at the Bureau of the Census in 1977.[7] We conclude this section by recommending to the reader an excellent introduction and overview of this area, the *Handbook of Social Indicators* (Rossi and Gilmartin, 1980).

LEISURE AND SOCIAL INDICATORS

There is still much disagreement in the field about what exactly the defining characteristics of a social indicator should be. Most researchers, however, would agree that such a measure must have at least the following characteristics. (1) It must be concerned with socially relevant issues; more specifically, it must be related to the welfare of the people. (2) It must furnish the basis for value judgments as regards this welfare; it must enable us to judge whether "things" are getting better or worse, whether people are better off now or whether they were better off in the past. (3) It must involve a longitudinal approach, that is, it must measure changes over time. This condition, of course, follows directly from the previous one.

Agreeing about these characteristics, however, still leaves the main questions unanswered. What is it we shall measure? What constitutes social welfare? In which direction do "things" have to change so that we can say they are getting better? In other words, we are once again back at the criterion problem.

Let us then briefly speculate about implications that could be derived were we to accept leisure as a criterion of the quality of life. Some of these would follow from the mere fact that we have accepted a criterion, no matter what its nature. Others would relate specifically to the fact that we chose leisure rather than some other criterion.

GENERAL IMPLICATIONS. Having a generally accepted criterion on hand would make it much easier to agree on variables as relevant social indicators. The problem would not be totally eliminated; it would be shifted from having to make such decisions as

---

[7]We also wish to bring to the attention of the reader *Social Indicators Research,* an international and interdisciplinary journal for quality-of-life measurement. It has been published since 1974 by D. Reidel Publishing Company, Dordrecht, Holland, and contains theoretical and research papers and book reviews.

regards innumerable variables, to heated disputes and extensive research as regards whatever was chosen as the criterion.

A second and related advantage would be that the criterion would also determine whether a measured socially relevant change is to be judged as positive or negative. For example, in the case of leisure as the criterion, the answer would be derived from an evaluation of whether a potential increase or decrease in *perceived freedom* and/or *intrinsic motivation* may be derived from the change measured.

A third general advantage of having a commonly accepted criterion of the quality of life would be a potential streamlining of policy decisions, the closer relevance of social indicators to such decisions, and their immediate relevance to the evaluation of social programs derived from these decisions.

A danger of such a commonly accepted criterion might be that this criterion was not so commonly accepted. As we pointed out before, it is quite likely that we shall find considerable disagreement about criteria of the quality of life, unless we use quite abstract concepts.

SPECIFIC IMPLICATIONS. The first and most obvious implication of accepting leisure as a criterion of the quality of life would be the development of adequate techniques to measure it. Such measures should furnish quantitative and eventually even qualitative information about leisure experienced by people. These measures should be in the form of "disaggregatable time series" (Rossie and Gilmartin, 1980, p. 15). That is, they should allow the identification of trends as well as breakdowns by variables such as background information, personality characteristics, or environmental factors. It will then be possible, for example, to specify the average amount of leisure experienced for the population as a whole; for subpopulations; for people, in general, engaging in certain activities; and for subpopulations engaging in certain activities.

Depending on the theory of leisure used to construct the measure, approaches to the measurement of leisure will differ. The instrument we have developed to serve as an indicator of the leisure experience, *What Am I doing: A Self-Exploration* (WAID), provides information about *perceived freedom* and *intrinsic motivation,* from which the experience of leisure can be inferred. It would also be very useful to have indicators that measure the leisure experience itself rather than the conditions for it (for example, as suggested by Mannell, 1979). One could then explore what circumstances lead to a leisure experience and what factors might inhibit it.

A second implication of accepting leisure as a criterion of the quality of life would be having a theoretical framework and orientation for selecting, developing, and evaluating social indicators. As elaborated throughout this volume and elsewhere (Neulinger, 1981), the attainment of leisure requires certain prerequisites, both personal and environmental. For example, I have pointed to the need of having developed a sense of basic trust for the optimal experience of leisure. Similarly, this experience will be easily attainable to the degree that existence and subsistence needs have been taken care of.

Having a leisure orientation in developing social indicators, then, implies focusing on those domains which are prerequisites for the leisure experience. As indicated before, this would not imply that most existing social indicators would become obsolete. They would merely take on new meaning or require some modifications.

For example, indicators presented in *Social Indicators, 1976* (1977) in chapters on housing; social security and welfare; health and nutrition; public safety; and income, wealth, and expenditures are clearly relevant as major factors in determining the *potential* for leisure. As another example, a measure "Relative importance of five selected job characteristics," in the chapter on work, has similar relevance to leisure through its question on meaning. Had it been constructed with an eye toward the importance of leisure during work, it might however have included more specific questions about *perceived freedom* and *intrinsic motivation.*

Let us conclude with a general implication that could be derived from having leisure as a criterion of the quality of life. Leisure, in this context, refers to a state of mind, which by itself could contribute greatly to the already existing trend of using more and more subjective measures of the quality of life. Strumpel (1976b, p. 1) in his discussion of social indicators of well-being and discontent, quotes the words of George A. Lundberg: "Poverty was once 'a state of the stomach,' but now has become, for most Americans, 'a state of mind.' " The industrial society, based on solid materialism, an objective view of the world, and an emphasis on production and consumption, may have needed a measure like the GNP as its yardstick of success. The postindustrial society, in the process of achieving the freedom to turn attention to nonmaterial aspects of life, will require a nonmaterial measure as its criterion of success, and perhaps leisure can serve that purpose best.

CHAPTER 6

THE FORMATION
OF LEISURE ATTITUDES

Nothing contributes more to the understanding of a phenomenon than a knowledge of its genesis. Much effort and research has gone into attempts to discover how people develop the attitudes and beliefs they hold. The literature in this area is voluminous and relevant studies can be found in fields such as child development, socialization processes, attitude theory, and many others. No attempt of a comprehensive review of the literature shall be made; the reader may find this elsewhere (e.g. Hoffman and Hoffman, 1964; Crain, 1980). Instead the major approaches to attitude formation will be highlighted in relation to their relevance to leisure attitudes.

First, a caveat; this chapter deals primarily with the formation of leisure attitudes, and not with the leisure experience per se. At times, however, the processes that will influence the formation of attitudes may also play a significant part in the development of the capacity for leisure or the ability *to leisure*. This is particularly true in the early stages of development. We may, then, make some references to the leisure experience. We shall more fully discuss, however, these developmental aspects in later chapters when discussing the syndrome *leisure lack*.

Perhaps it is best to start with a short history of the concept of *attitude*. Allport (1968) called it "probably the most distinctive and indispensable concept in contemporary American social psychology." Herbert Spencer (1862) introduced the concept into the psychological literature as an equivalent of *mental set*, and N. Lange (1888) used it to connote a motor set or a muscular preparation set. Attitude gained its acceptance into modern day psychology through the emphasis placed on it by Thomas and

Znaniecki (1918) who defined social psychology as "the scientific study of attitudes." In the sixties, most of the efforts in attitude research were devoted to two aspects: the measurement of attitudes and the problems of attitude change (e.g. Fishbein, 1967; Insko, 1967). In the seventies, the emphasis on attitude research seemed to have waned somewhat, but McGuire (1979) predicts a renewal of interest in attitudes during the eighties.

What is the meaning of the concept attitude? There is disagreement among psychologists as to the exact definition of the term, but most would agree with Allport's statement (1968) that " 'attitude' connotes *a neuropsychic state of readiness for mental and physical activity.*" Furthermore, it is generally agreed that this readiness expresses itself in three areas, although different theorists place varying emphasis on these. For example, Krech, Crutchfield, and Ballachey (1962) define attitude as follows:

> An attitude can be defined as an enduring system of three components centering about a single object: the beliefs about the object — the *cognitive component;* the affect connected with the object — the *feeling component;* and the disposition to take action with respect to the object — *action tendency component.* (Also referred to as *conative component*)

It should also be noted that an attitude always implies an object, something about which one has information, toward which one has feelings, and in regard to which one wants to act one way or another. In this sense, attitude differs from value in that the latter does not necessarily imply a specific object.

LEISURE ATTITUDES AND DEVELOPMENTAL THEORIES

Attitudes do not exist by themselves within the individual, as separate, independent or isolated units. They are part of an interdependent system, a dynamic whole that constitutes much of what is called personality. Developmental theories of personality thus become relevant to an explanation of the genesis of attitudes, and in turn, childhood becomes the focus of attention, as it is the primary formative period of the personality. Since it is difficult and quite arbitrary to decide when childhood ends and adolescence begins or, for that matter, when adolescence ends and adulthood begins, we have included adolescence in both this

156

and the next section.

Childhood and Adolescence

Most theorists agree that the person's development goes through certain stages, the most famous of which are probably Freud's (1905) psychosexual ones. More recently, H. W. Maier (1965) has attempted to synthesize the work of three well-known developmental theorists, Erik H. Erikson, Jean Piaget, and Robert R. Sears, by placing their ideas and some of his own within five developmental phases of child development: (1) establishing primary dependence, (2) establishing self-care, (3) establishing meaningful secondary relationships, (4) establishing secondary dependency, and (5) achieving balance between dependence and independence. Let us briefly look at each of these stages with an eye toward implications for the formation of leisure attitudes.

PHASE I: ESTABLISHING PRIMARY DEPENDENCE. During this first phase of the developmental process the crucial factor is the children's total dependence on the adult, whoever they may happen to be. Food, clothing, and shelter are matters of survival. Children must learn to accept their dependency and develop "a sense of basic trust." During this period children also acquire sensory and motor skills and much of their energy is devoted to this enterprise. One might speculate that this period is too early to be critical in terms of specific leisure attitudes. Nevertheless, it may be of crucial importance in the development of a basic attitude of openness, optimism, and confidence that allows one fully to experience leisure. To devote oneself totally to an activity and become wholly absorbed in one's actions may require a kind of relaxation that is based on the conviction that everything else will work out all right, will take care of itself, and that one need not be concerned with matters of survival.

PHASE II: ESTABLISHING SELF-CARE. In this period, children learn to break out of total dependency. They attempt to achieve a degree of autonomy. They try to gain mastery over the environment, still primarily the physical, but to some degree the social environment. This is the period when parental "training" is particulary difficult; it must not be too much and not too little, not too soon and not too late. It is also the time when play enters as a critical mode of experiencing new situations, of testing one's capacity, and of providing a permissive atmosphere for developing one's potentials (e.g. Singer, 1973). "Play constitutes a child's most reliable device for self-help" (H.W. Maier, 1965, p. 275).

The permissive atmosphere of play may, at times, distinguish it from leisure. Play, to be redundant, is playful; it is never totally serious, although to the child it may seem so. It is always viewed with an element of "it doesn't really matter." Leisure, however, can be very serious. People *leisuring* may be doing the most important thing in their lives. It strikes us as incongruous that people should risk their lives for their play, but we can accept the idea that some people put their lives on the line for their leisure pursuits. The picture comes to mind of the mountain climber, the explorer, or the person who tries to cross the ocean in the smallest of vessels.

To return to Phase II, what must children learn during this period? They must learn to channel their desires into adaptive actions. In doing so, they meet with frustrations with which they must be tolerant and cope. They must learn to express their feelings — when, to what degree, and in what manner? Speech becomes an important tool for this purpose. Their cognitive development enters a new phase: preparation for conceptual thoughts.

What might be the implications of all this for the formation of leisure attitudes? The critical aspect might be the realization that the outer world has some very real demands and the perceived scope of these demands. Children become aware that they have to devote much of their energy to coping with frustrations. Only a limited amount of energy is left for going beyond these frustrations to new and unexplored activities. This phase may be critical in terms of the amount of energy people might feel they have available for nonsurvival-related activities. To the degree that they view leisure as a non-essential luxury, this attitude will be reflected in the amount of time, energy, and perhaps money they feel free to devote to it, and how much they reserve for "more worthwhile and necessary" activities.

PHASE III: ESTABLISHING MEANINGFUL SECONDARY RELATIONSHIPS. In this period children go beyond their immediate environment, particularly beyond their immediate social environment. Peers take on an important role, and they have to learn to find their place among them, securely, dependent on others, and yet autonomous. Much of the child's energy is devoted to "becoming his own parent, that is, in developing his own superego" (H.W. Maier, 1965, p. 253). Their intellectual functioning is still quite primitive, their thought processes are still *concrete*. They do develop, however, a degree of initiative that expresses itself particularly well in their play. There they may act out fantasies and desires that reality does not permit them to do. Social play, that is, play initiated by or carried out with others, mostly their parents, becomes particularly important. Such play tends to emphasize different values and goals: exploration, winning, having fun, or just being together. One might speculate that this is the phase when children develop the attitudes that they will later express in, and that will determine in part, their choice of specific free-time activities. Will they be looking for activities that will allow them to be competitive, creative, sociable, or just pleasure seeking ? While the previous phase may have been more critical in terms of the quantitative aspects of leisure behavior, this phase may relate more to the qualitative aspects, that is, the type of specific activities a person seeks in his free time.

PHASE IV: ESTABLISHING SECONDARY DEPENDENCE. This period is also concerned with establishing children's independence, but this time not so much from their parents than from their peers. The role of others takes on a new clearly defined quality. Children are concerned with establishing their positions vis-à-vis their peers; they are busy working out regulations in games and dealing with rules. They are also concerned with their own development; they are in competition with themselves, they want to do better than they did before (H.W. Maier, 1965, p. 255). Yet, they are still children, and their way of thinking is still limited by their cognitive development.

This is the period when the concept of work first enters into the children's lives. They develop a "sense of industry." They are concerned with developing their skills, in perfecting themselves, and they are on their way to developing habits that may later express themselves in their attitudes toward work and leisure. They may now engage in activities, not because they offer intrinsic satisfaction, but because they have instrumental value or offer extrinsic reward. The activities may help them to "become a success," to ward off inferiority feelings, or they may simply pay off in terms of some desired reward. Perhaps this is the period that is most critical in determining what people will seek in their jobs: a means to an end or an end in itself. The implications for leisure are obvious and quite startling. People who view their job as a means will seek a truly significant activity outside their work area; their leisure will be nonwork-oriented. People who consider their job as an end in itself may turn their work into their leisure.

PHASE V: ACHIEVING BALANCE BETWEEN DEPENDENCE AND INDEPENDENCE. This is the period of adolescence, the time between childhood and adulthood, a period of great change. It involves the resolution of many problems, the primary one being that of identity: Who am I, or, as Erikson might say, Who am I becoming? During this stage children complete their intellectual development and arrive at intellectual maturity. "The individual's basic pattern of thinking and reasoning has been established" (H.W. Maier, 1965, p. 141).

This may be the phase during which environmental factors outside the family have their strongest effect on the developing leisure attitudes. The kind of peer group individuals associate with, the type of school they attend, the people they admire, important events that happen to occur during this period, all of these factors are bound to affect their attitudes, even though the basic quality of attitudes are already established. This is the time when people start to think seriously about a career choice, and such a choice is bound to be intimately related to their beliefs and attitudes about leisure. It is also a period of great flux, that is, people may go through various changes in attitude, testing out and trying to find the attitudes with which they will feel most comfortable. The attitudes that will eventually stabilize will, of course, have been determined by the interplay of the many factors involved in all of the five phases.

The reader would probably like to have a timetable to delimit these developmental phases. Such a schedule is difficult to establish and must be interpreted very loosely, since there are great individual differences in these respects and because the aspects of the various phases may overlap in a given individual. An approximate timetable might look as follows:

Year one and two:	Phase I	— establishing primary dependence
Year two, three and into four:	Phase II	— establishing self-care
Year four through eight:	Phase III	— establishing meaningful secondary relationships
Year eight through twelve:	Phase IV	— establishing secondary dependency
Year twelve through eighteen:	Phase V	— achieving balance between dependence and independence

Adolescence and Adulthood

The foregoing has dealt with developmental processes in childhood as they might relate to the formation of leisure attitudes. It is clear, however, that "the socialization experienced by a person in childhood cannot prepare him for all the roles he will be expected to fill in later years" (Brim, 1966). The task of socialization continues during adolescence and even adulthood, but it takes on a different quality. It's usual objective is

> to get one to practice a new combination of skills already acquired, to combine existing elements into new forms, to trim and polish existing material, rather than to learn wholly new complexes or responses, as in the case of the relatively untrained child, for whom the socialization effort starts with little more than initial intelligence and primary drives (Brim, 1966, p. 28).

161

In additon to a change in the task of adult socialization is a change in the role that the different agents of socialization play. The "Family of Orientation," parents and siblings, recedes into the background and the "Family of Procreation," spouse and children, takes over. Formal schooling is likely to diminish its impact as a socializing agent and eventually fade out entirely. Economic and political institutions take on important functions in forming the adult person.

One should not conclude, however, that economic and political factors did not have an influence on the socialization process during childhood. The occupational milieu, for example, to which individuals were exposed in their childhood may have had a considerable effect on their development. This consideration seems to be a neglected topic in many of the developmental theories of adolescence and the middle years. As Borow (1966) states:

> It does not seem to have been sufficiently appreciated that work and the characteristic work customs and values of particular subcultures profoundly affect socialization processes in pre-employed youth. Long before the individual reaches employment age, it is possible to examine with profit the processes by which he acquires concepts of work; the nature of his work concepts and fantasies; the social valence he attaches to the work functions; . . . (p. 374).

There are different approaches to the understanding of the development of adult values. Some theorists attempt to trace the factors that are related to specific occupational choices (e.g. Ginzberg, 1951; Roe, 1956), while others, like Havighurst (1953, 1964) are more concerned with the development of the general attitudes underlying one's position toward work and, concomitantly, toward leisure.

Havinghurst's scheme, reminiscent of and influenced by Erikson's conceptual paradigm, is presented in Table XIV (P. 163). The developmental stages in this scheme are fairly self-explanatory, as described in the table. Of particular interest are the last three stages that take over at approximately the time that the previously discussed phases of H. W. Maier leave off. They are closely related to Erikson's last three stages of *Intimacy*

TABLE XIV
VOCATIONAL DEVELOPMENT: A LIFELONG PROCESS

Stages of Vocational Development	Age
I. Identification with a Worker Father, mother, other significant persons. The concept of working becomes an essential part of the ego-ideal.	5-10
II. Acquiring the Basic Habits of Industry Learning to organize one's time and energy to get a piece of work done. School work, chores. Learning to put work ahead of play in appropriate situations.	10-15
III. Acquiring Identity as a Worker in the Occupational Structure Choosing and preparing for an occupation. Getting work experience as a basis for occupational choice and for assurance of economic independence.	15-25
IV. Becoming a Productive Person Mastering the skills of one's occupation. Moving up the ladder within one's occupation.	25-40
V. Maintaining a Productive Society Emphasis shifts toward the societal and away from the individual aspect of the worker's role. The individual sees himself as a responsible citizen in a productive society. He pays attention to the civic responsibility attached to his job. He is at the peak of his occupational career and has time and energy to adorn it with broader types of activity. He pays attention to inducting younger people into stage III and IV.	40-70
VI. Contemplating a Productive and Responsible Life This person is retired from his work or is in process of withdrawing from the worker's role. He looks back over his work life with satisfaction, sees that he has made his social contribution, and is pleased with it. While he may not have achieved all of his ambitions, he accepts his life and believes in himself as a productive person.	70+

Source: MAN IN A WORLD AT WORK, edited by Henry Borow. Copyright © 1964 by National Vocational Guidance Association. Reprinted by permission of Houghton Mifflin Company. (p. 216).

versus Isolation (young adult), *Generativity versus Self-Absorption* (adulthood), and *Integrity versus Despair* (mature age). The common theme which runs through both Erikson's and Havighurst's paradigm is the unquestioned assumption that true meaning in life must be obtained through one's work, which both authors equate with one's job. For example, Havighurst (1946), quoting Kenneth Keniston in describing the so called youth culture, implies that true involvement with life must come from the job rather than from leisure, and that the latter cannot be satisfying unless the former is also. Satisfactions "*should* inhere in work" (p. 231; italics added). It is our opinion that it is precisely this assumption that ought to be seriously questioned, particularly if technology keeps accelerating at the rate it has during the last decades.

It is clear that much research and education are needed to clarify the function and meaning of work and leisure for the developing adolescent and adult. Borow (1966) suggests that

> there is need for considerably more research to test the hypothesis that the vocational fantasies, choices, and conflicts of youth are linked to attempts to deal with such psychological need-states as belonging-ness, recognition, states, and self-esteem (p. 417).

There is no question that such research would be equally fruitful if it dealt with the avocational fantasies, choices, and conflicts of youth.

This concludes our rather brief discussion of leisure attitudes in the context of developmental theories. We have allowed ourselves to speculate rather freely and hope that some of our ideas might eventually be put to an empirical test. There are, of course, many other areas of leisure behavior that need to be investigated in a developmental context. For example, there is the development of sex roles in leisure behavior; there is the effect of hobbies and interests engaged in during childhood on leisure behavior in adulthood (e.g. Yoesting and Burkhead, 1973; Yoesting and Christensen, 1978). There is the development of the capacity for intimacy and the ability to experience *sex as leisure* (Neulinger, 1979a). One needs also to include later life de-

164

velopments, such as the likely change of leisure attitudes from before to after retirement (Yuskaitis, 1981) and from before children leave the home to after "the nest is empty." We need to consider the interrelationship of work, family, and leisure, and how these spheres of life interact and mutually affect each other throughout the life cycle (Rapoport and Rapoport, 1975). An extensive review of work related to leisure behavior and socialization throughout the life course, as well as directions for further research has been provided by Kleiber and Kelly (1980). While many of the above issues refer to leisure behavior rather than leisure attitudes, there is little doubt about their relevance for attitude formation: behavior shapes attitudes, just as attitudes shape behavior.

LEISURE ATTITUDES AND THEORIES OF ATTITUDE CHANGE

In the previous section the formation of leisure attitudes was treated within the context of developmental processes. The concern was with historical and long-range factors and how they affect the developing attitude system. This section deals with the influence of contemporaneous factors on leisure attitudes and the conditions that are likely to bring about attitude change. The topic of attitude change has occupied a great deal of attention in social psychology and has been treated primarily within the context of either a reinforcement related theory (e.g. Hovland, et al., 1949; Hovland, et al., 1953) or a balance type theory (e.g. Festinger, 1957; Heider, 1958; Osgood and Tannenbaum, 1955). Let us take a look at the latter approach. These theories deal with the inter-relationships of the cognitions a person holds, and the basic assumption of all of the theories is that inconsistent or incongruous cognitions result in a state of imbalance (incongruity, dissonance) that the organism seeks to balance (make congruous, reduce). The state of imbalance has motivational qualities; that is, it provides the energy needed to bring about a change in cognitions. To change one's cognitions is one way of bringing about balance. The model has obvious implications for attitude change. For example, if one wishes to manipulate a person's attitudes, one only needs to introduce an appropriate state of imbalance in the person's cognitive system and a change is very likely to occur.

People with relatively negative cognitions about leisure do not like to "waste a lot of time on leisure activities"; they feel that what one does in one's free time is not important. It is safe to assume that such people, like most, have positive cognitions about good health; they value being healthy. What happens if such people are exposed to information that shows that it is important for health to enjoy free-time activities, that people who cannot relax in their free time are more likely to get heart attacks, and so on?

The person is now faced with two incongruent cognitions: "I do not like leisure," and "Leisure is good for my health which I value." A state of dissonance is aroused that the person will seek to reduce.

There are several ways in which dissonance reduction can be brought about. An extremely common one is denial. Forget the information, forget about the news that leisure is good for one's health. Think of the millions of people who continue smoking in spite of the negative links between smoking and health having been clearly established, and one realizes how popular a mechanism denial is.

Another way of reducing dissonance is to change the cognition involved. For example, people in the previous example could change their cognition or feeling about health; they could convince themselves that health is not important. This, of course, is an unlikely solution since the importance of health is probably one of the most basic values in anybody's belief system. Thus, it is more likely that they may change their feeling about leisure; they may start to think more positively about relaxing and enjoying free-time activities, and their cognitions about leisure and health will now be in a state of balance.

There are many factors involved in the process of attitude change. Social psychologists tend to investigate these in terms of three aspects; the communicator, the person who attempts to

166

bring about an attitude change; the communication, the particular message or form that the communicator uses;and finally the audience, the characteristics of the persons whose attitudes are being manipulated (e.g. Jones and Gerard, 1967). This is not the place to consider each of these topics in detail; the literature in this area is vast (e.g. Insko, 1967; Fishbein, 1967; Kiesler, Collins and Miller, 1969; Rosenberg, Hovland, McGuire, Abelson and Brehm, 1960). The importance of this work for leisure research lies in three areas. *One,* theories and hypotheses developed in the area of attitude change may be used to explain differences in prevailing leisure attitudes. *Two,* methodologies of experimental manipulation of attitudes may be applied to the testing of leisure hypotheses. *Three,* and perhaps most importantly, principles of attitude change may be useful in bringing about desirable changes in leisure attitudes; they become an integral part of leisure education (Neulinger, 1976b).

In concluding this section let us look at an example of the use of dissonance theory to explain the dynamics of leisure attitudes. A finding showed that people who work more and who have shorter vacations also say that they want to work more than the average person and that they desire shorter vacations (Neulinger and Breit, 1969). The question was raised

> . . . whether people who work more really like to work more or whether their attitudes developed as ego-defensive structures. Given that some people are forced to work longer hours for reasons beyond their control, do they compensate by developing more positive attitudes toward work?

The implication is that the cognitions "I have to work long hours," and "I dislike work," are incongruent and create a state of dissonance. People who cannot change the conditions that make them work long hours cannot change their cognition about working long hours. They can change, however, their cognition about work. They can start to like work and thus reduce the state of dissonance.

An interesting prediction that is contrary to common sense, but could be derived from dissonance theory is the following:

People who have their working hours shortened should become more negative toward work, all other things being equal. The argument would be like this. The person has two cognitions: "I do the things I like a lot," and "I just cut down on my work which I like." These two cognitions are incongruent and produce dissonance. If the work reduction was imposed on the person, people would have no way of changing their cognitions about that aspect of the situation. But, if their liking of work decreased, their cutting down on that activity would be in line with their feelings about the things they like to do a lot.

The problem with the application of dissonance or similar type theories to real life situations is that "all other things" never are equal. Furthermore, it is very difficult to know which cognitions, among the many that a person holds, are the relevant ones that are supposed to create the dissonance. Finally, dissonance theory does not take into account individual differences, the possibility that for some people a state of incongruence is less disturbing if not desirable (Neulinger, 1965).

LEISURE ATTITUDES AND SOCIETY

We have considered attitude formation from a developmental standpoint, and we have looked at it in the light of immediate cognitive input. We shall now point to another major source of attitudinal differences, namely societal factors. We would want to become acquainted with such differences not only because leisure attitudes are a most revealing characteristic of any society but also because these differences may help us understand the dynamics of attitude formation.

Cultural Differences in Leisure Attitudes

It is quite conceivable that the strongest factor in the development of leisure attitudes is the person's cultural background. This may seem obvious when we compare such diverse cultures as, for example, the Japanese and the American. But one can trace differences in leisure and work attitudes even within the sphere of Western Civilization that are accounted for primarily by societal rather than psychological factors. For example,

168

McClelland (1961) has demonstrated striking differences in both the industrial development and work attitudes between Catholic and Protestant countries in Europe. While McClelland does postulate a psychological intervening variable, namely *need-achievement,* the primary determining factor remains a cultural one: the parent's religion and set of values associated with it.

Cross-cultural, time-budget studies, as those carried out by Szalai (1972), are most relevant in this context. While time-budget studies do not generally measure leisure attitudes per se, they are of help to attitude formation research in two ways. *One,* we may infer (although with considerable trepidation) attitudes from behavior and, in line with a functional approach to attitude formation (Katz and Stotland, 1959), formulate hypotheses about the different functions that free time fulfills in various countries. *Two,* the studies are bound to clarify and unify the meanings of the terms used in different cultures to describe leisure concepts.

For example, what German term is the equivalent for *leisure,* used to imply a state of mind? *Freizeit* (free time) is obviously inappropriate and the term *Musse* has its own unique connotations. The Japanese concept *yutori* is a term "describing the ideal state of mind for leisure" (Takeo Doi, 1979). Yet, there are certain very distinct characteristics associated with this concept that one would lose were one merely to equate those two terms. There is no question that a major difficulty in the study of leisure attitudes in various cultures is a linguistic one. The meanings of leisure terms are hard to define within any language, and to obtain cross-cultural equivalences is a truly Herculean task that waits to be undertaken.

One suggestion to anyone attempting to do cross-cultural research is to use the well-known method of double interpretation. Assume that you want to study leisure attitudes in the United States and Poland. First, have your questionnaire translated into Polish, and then have your Polish translation translated back into English, but by somebody else. Differences in meaning that become obvious through this method are often astounding.

An enormous amount of work remains to be done in this area, although some beginnings have been made (e.g., Jackson, 1973). Leisure attitudes, particularly in non-Western countries, might offer much to be studied, to be understood, and perhaps to be aspired to. It may not be possible to lift leisure attitudes out of the context of one culture and implant it into another. We have just shown how attitudes are part of the total value system of the person. Yet, this area seems so promising that every effort to at least understand other cultures' leisure attitudes should be strongly supported.

Subcultural Differences in Leisure Attitudes

Just as cultural factors are bound to be major determinants of leisure attitudes, so will be subcultural ones as, for example, social class belongingness or so-called race differences. That is not to say that one can necessarily predict a person's leisure attitudes from a knowledge of his social background. One son of an upper-class, suburban family may have very conservative, work-oriented leisure attitudes while his brother is the very opposite. Yet, *both* their attitudes cannot be fully understood without taking into account their family's position in society. Even in their differences they may reveal a common denominator that distinguishes them from others with a different social background.

The potential effects of various background variables have already been discussed in a previous chapter (Chapter 4). At this point, the emphasis is not on individual variables but on social groups that have distinct characteristics and that transmit their values and attitudes through the usual socialization processes. There is ample evidence, for example, that social class has a strong determining effect on trends in infant care and child training. It might be very rewarding to parallel Bronfenbrenner's (1958) classical study, "Socialization and Social Class Through Time and Space," a survey and reanalysis of studies covering twenty-five years (1932-1957), with one placing special emphasis on behavior and attitudes relevant to leisure. Such a systematic effort might reveal trends that any individual study cannot hope to discover.

Aside from social-class groupings there are other subcultures that might be of particular interest for studying the formation of leisure attitudes. The most obvious such group is that of the so called Hippies. One of the most characterizing aspects of this group is its rejection of the Protestant Ethic and acceptance, instead, of a value system that has been referred to as a "hang loose" ethic (Simmons and Winograd, 1966):

> One of the fundamental characteristics of the hang-loose ethic is that it is irreverent. It repudiates, or at least questions, such cornerstones of conventional society as Christianity, "my country right or wrong," the sanctity of marriage and premarital chastity, civil disobedience, the accumulation of wealth, the right and even competence of parents, the schools, and the government to head and make decisions for everyone — in sum, the Establishment.

One would expect that a child reared within the context of such values would develop leisure attitudes that are radically different from those of the so-called middle class, but it is not so clear what these attitudes would be like.

Closely related areas of study are the many communes that are springing up all over the country. The question of free time, how to allot it, how to use it, how and whether to control it, and many similar questions are of critical importance to the very survival of the commune. The answers to these questions must be reflected in the philosophy of each commune and are bound to be discussed, debated, experimented with, and resolved in many different ways. The literature on communes is large, but to this date there does not seem to have been a systematic effort to study the topic of leisure and the formation of leisure attitudes within this context.

There are other subgroups in our culture that invite the study of their effect on the formation of leisure attitudes. One might want to study leisure attitudes in The Armed Forces, as an example of a highly controlled and organized environment. One might want to look at leisure attitudes in prisons and public institutions, like large hospitals with chronic wards. There are

171

groups such as families on welfare, the chronically unemployed, migrant farm workers, and many others.

Last, but not least, there are the leisure attitudes of the aged. This is, no doubt, the group for which these attitudes are of most relevance if for no other reason (and there are many others) than that the elderly tend to have the most free time. We shall discuss these issues further in our chapter on leisure and gerontology.

Leisure attitudes determine that proportion of variance in leisure behavior that is not a function of the immediate environment, the opportunities provided by society, but reflecting the personal, the subjective, the unique. If we wish to provide adequate leisure services, if we wish to improve such services and anticipate what people really want, it is an absolute necessity that we know what their attitudes on leisure are. An understanding of how these attitudes are formed will certainly help us comprehend better the dynamics involved in leisure behavior.

CHAPTER 7

EXPERIMENTAL LEISURE RESEARCH

ONE INDICATION OF THE development of a science is the degree to which experimentation is employed in its research efforts. The progression usually is one from unsystematic data collection and description, to loosely formulated ideas about possible relationships, to systematic data gathering and classification of these, to formal theory building, and, finally, to a testing of these through experimentation. Viewed from this perspective, the scientific investigation of leisure is still at a primitive stage. In the first edition of this book (1974a, p. 131) we stated that

> much information has been collected but few comprehensive theories have been proposed, and experimentation is practically nonexistent or, perhaps, just beginning.

The hope was expressed, however, that future editions would require a considerable enlargement of this chapter "to cover all the work that will have been done by that time" (p. 142).

There is little doubt that experimentation relevant to leisure has been on the increase, but how much of that relates specifically to the leisure experience, that is, leisure conceived of as a state of mind? Mannell (1980, p. 68), in an exploration of techniques for the experimental study of leisure as a subjective or mental state, indicates that relatively little progress has been made in that respect:

> With the exception of two experiments completed in our laboratory (Mannell, 1978, 1979; Backman and Mannell, 1978) and a field experiment reported by Csikszentmihalyi (1975), most leisure research examining the experience has been correlational. Experimental studies that manipulate situational or psychological variables in either laboratory or natural settings and then measure the resulting effects on dependent measures which operationalize leisure experiences

have not been reported.

Mannell (1980) quotes as a possible explanation for this lack of research our argument about the difficulty of operationalizing leisure and also adds that the humanistic orientation of many leisure theorists prevents them from accepting the possibility that leisure can occur or be studied in experimental settings.

Nevertheless, there has been and continues to be a considerable amount of experimental research on leisure related variables (as defined in our paradigm), particularly on *intrinsic motivation*, without, however, making this relevance to leisure explicit. Finally, there is work being done in what we have called "leisure related areas." Among these one could obviously include play, thus expanding the field vastly. We have chosen not to do so, for reasons given shortly.

THE NEED FOR EXPERIMENTATION

Why is experimentation important? Why is it considered critical in the development of scientific knowledge? One answer is to recognize that an operational definition implies an experimental approach and that no science can progress or even exist without operational definitions. The definition of an *operational definition* has itself undergone many changes over the years, and many social and experimental psychologists "no longer maintain that every construct must be denotable" (Berkowitz, 1963). The basic idea of the operational definition is still that the concept defined must at least be unambiguously inferable, if not observable, through some measurement procedure. To measure something unambiguously, however, means to be able to exclude concomitant or confounding variables, and thus, in the words of Underwood, "my particular way of viewing an operational definition is that it becomes an experimental design" (1957 p. 14).

One argument for the experimental approach, then, is that it is needed in testing the validity of the constructs used, certainly an important issue in leisure research. The other and even more cogent reason for advocating this approach has to do with discovering and demonstrating *causal* relationships. A well-

174

accepted dictum is that correlation does not prove causation and that just about the only way causation can be inferred is through an adequate experimental design. Some alternative methods have been investigated (e.g. Campbell and Stanley, 1963; Heise, 1970; Duncan, 1970; Kahle and Berman, 1979; Kenny, 1979), and it is likely that concurrent with the increasing emphasis on nonexperimental multivariate research designs their use will become more frequent. Nevertheless, experimental research will remain an essential tool for establishing the validity of leisure hypotheses and confirming causal relationships among variables in the leisure domain.

Advantages and Disadvantages of Experimentation

If experimentation is so critical to the advancement of knowledge, why has there been hardly any in the field of leisure research? The answer partly lies in the nature of the experiment. An experiment is usually very time-consuming and often expensive to carry out; it is difficult to set up; it requires considerable know-how for its performance and consequent data analyses. Most importantly, it presupposes that the concepts dealt with can be operationally defined, that the independent variable can be manipulated and that the dependent variable can be validly measured. While there are purely explorative experiments, as a rule, experiments test specific hypotheses. The level of theorizing in the leisure domain, however, is only now reaching the point of producing some testable hypotheses.

Another factor that helps delay progress in this area are certain biases against experimentation. Probably the most frequent criticism is that generalizations from an experimental situation to the real life situation are inappropriate. To give an example: a doctoral student (at a university other than The City College), who wanted to do an experiment on leisure for his thesis, was discouraged from doing so by his committee chairman because, so the argument went, the condition of leisure cannot possibly be created in the laboratory. This type of objection results from a misunderstanding of the purpose of an experiment and from a failure to make a distinction between *experimental realism* and *mundane realism* (Aronson and Carlsmith, 1968). Generalization to a real life situation is not the primary goal of experimentation. The purpose of an experiment is more likely to be the clarification and validation of some construct and its effects in some very limited but precisely defined situation. The experimenter must first be concerned that the subjects in the experiment validly experience the variables that the experimenter manipulates, that they are truly involved in what they are doing, and that the experimental situation is real to the subjects (*experimental realism*). A laboratory experiment is always an abstraction from reality with intentionally isolated variables, a situation that hardly ever exists in real life. To copy the real life situation in the experimental setup (*mundane realism*), while desirable, is only of secondary concern. The emphasis on field experimentation in recent research does make this type of realism more common.

The difficulties involved in creating the conditions that generate the leisure experience (e.g. perceived freedom and intrinsic motivation) are no greater than those of manipulating most psychological variables. As we shall see shortly, it is being done quite frequently in social psychological experiments, and it certainly is possible to create a leisure experience within the context of a field experiment.

The major advantage of the laboratory experiment is the degree of control maintained. The experimenter creates the situation; what will happen is known before it happens; the levels of change in the variables are manipulated, and the sequence of events is under control. Validity checks on the manipulations can be arranged to see whether the manipulations "took," and as many measures of the dependent variable can be introduced as are deemed necessary. One of the most important aspects of such an experiment is that it can be repeated an indefinite number of times by the experimenter or by somebody else, under identical conditions. This possibility of replication gives the experiment its greatest potential strength. Unfortunately, not too many experiments are ever replicated.

Types of Experimental Studies

One way to overcome limited generalizability in experimentation is to carry out experiments in real life situations. The trend of moving the laboratory into the field is becoming more prevalent in social psychological research. It may be useful to examine briefly the various methods employed, following a classification of research methods by Cartwright and Zander (1960).

FIELD STUDY. These are investigations which subject some existing group to study without in any way attempting to influence it. Data are collected without interfering in what goes on and without creating disruption. Since no manipulation occurs, this type of study does not qualify as an experiment. Survey studies may fit into this category as may participant observations.

NATURAL EXPERIMENT. This type of investigation takes advantage of some meaningful event that takes place "naturally," like a new policy introduced by a company, the opening of a new recreation facility, or some such event. Thus, the introduction of a shorter workweek in sections of a large company could be worked into a natural experiment. The manipulation here (i.e. the shortening of the workweek for some but not for others) is one that takes place whether the experiment is being carried out or not. It is a "natural" phenomenon. The advantages of this type of experiment are great, but unfortunately the opportunities for them are rare.

FIELD EXPERIMENT. Changes are introduced into the natural environment with the explicit purpose of testing some hypothesis. The manipulation is under the control of the experimenter who works in a real life situation. This method is probably optimal in terms of generalizability, but it is generally very difficult to gain access to situations that make this type of study possible.

NATURAL GROUPS IN THE LABORATORY. In this type of investigation an existing group is lifted out of its natural setting and brought into the laboratory. Thus, if one wants to investigate interactions among members of a bowling team, one might bring the whole team into the laboratory for certain experimental manipulations. One combines here a certain amount of reality (i.e. the group is real; their feelings about each other are real) with the artificiality of the laboratory that, however, provides better means of control.

ARTIFICIAL GROUPS OR INDIVIDUALS IN THE LABORATORY. This is the classical experiment carried out under completely controlled conditions. It deals either with individuals or with groups that are formed for a particular purpose in the laboratory. It provides the experimenter with the best means for abstracting variables, but it has the disadvantage of having limited generalizability to real life situations.

It is hard to say which of these methods is best for any given research problem, and the choice of method is frequently dictated by the situation rather than the experimenter.

EXPERIMENTAL LEISURE STUDIES

Our purpose, as stated previously, is not to provide a review of the literature but to refer the reader to certain studies as exemplars of what can and has been done. We shall restrict ourselves to experiments that deal specifically with psychological aspects of leisure. This reduces the potential field considerably. For example, we would not consider *Experiments in Recreation Research* (Burton, 1971b), as an appropriate example for this section. It is an excellent treatment of techniques of assessment, measurement, and projection in the supply and demand aspects of recreation, but it does not really deal with experiments. The author uses the term experiment "to mean investigations which utilize experimental methods, such as matching, even though these investigations cannot be undertaken in a situation which is totally controlled." Furthermore, the book deals with applied aspects of recreation rather than with theoretical issues derived from leisure hypotheses.

The first edition of *The Psychology of Leisure* described only two studies of experimental leisure research. The first was that of Bishop and Witt (1970), dealing with the general problem of sources of behavioral variability due to situation, personality, and type of response, and specifically with the hypothesis that behavior can best be understood as the interaction of these three factors. This hypothesis had previously been tested in respect to hostility and anxiety behavior (Endler, Hunt and Rosenstein, 1962; Endler and Hunt, 1968). Bishop and Witt chose to replicate these studies in the leisure domain, in part because two classical viewpoints of leisure behavior enabled them to test out hypotheses about the effects of either personality or the environment. The "personologist's" view of leisure behavior, as represented by Aristotle, sees it as free, unobligated, and relatively unaffected by environmental demands. According to this view each person would tend to develop certain characteristic modes of leisure responses, and leisure behavior could best be explained in terms of a *person by mode of response* interaction. The contrasting "situational" view of leisure, as represented by theories of leisure such as the relaxation theory, the surplus energy theory, and the compensation theory, assumes that situational events induce a need-state that can be satisfied by appropriate leisure responses. According to this second view, the situation tends to be more critical than the person in determining leisure behavior, and thus the *situation by mode of response* interaction should best explain leisure behavior.

While the subjects in this study were not actually manipulated in the manner of a classical experiment, they were asked to respond to ten imagined (and described) situations. This procedure may be considered a quasi-experimental manipulation and qualifies this study as an experiment. The method of analysis used was analysis of variance, which allows for the investigation of the relative proportions of variance associated with each of the independent variables, persons, situations, and responses, and their interactions.

The study is too complex to permit a brief summary. Following is the abstract as printed in the originial article, and the reader is strongly encouraged to consult the source for details and inspiration.

Two samples of subjects rated how much they would feel like participating in each of a set of leisure activities in each of ten hypothetical

179

situations. The resulting matrices of responses were analyzed into the estimated variance components associated with persons, situations, modes of response, and their various interactions. These sources of variance in leisure behavior were compared to those reported by Endler and Hunt for hostility and anxiety. The results showed major differences between the relative contributions of the sources of variance to leisure behavior and their contributions to hostility and anxiety. There were also some differences between the sexes in sources of variance, both within and across the three domains of behavior. In addition, the implications of two classical views of leisure behavior were tested by comparing the Persons X Modes of Response and Situations X Modes of Response interaction variances. The results showed some support for both views, although sex differences suggested that these classical views might be differentially applicable to males and females (Bishop and Witt, 1970).

A second study that also relied on a role playing technique was an unpublished honor's thesis by Margit Winckler (1972), who investigated changes in connotative leisure, job, and self-profiles as a function of two fantasy conditions. Condition *1* was the subjects' present (reality) life situation; Condition *2* required the subjects to hold a job (any job they chose) with $100,000 per year income guaranteed; Condition *3* guaranteed a $100,000 per year income without the need for holding a job. Changes in concept profiles were obtained through a semantic differential technique. In spite of a relatively small sample, fifty-six full-time, working adults, the author obtained significant differences between conditions and found mainly that all three concepts became more positive as the subjects went from reality to the two fantasy conditions. Given greater personal freedom, subjects perceived leisure, the job, and themselves as more interesting, active, sociable, meaningful, and honest. Of the three concepts investigated, the perception of the concept job changed the most over the three conditions, that of leisure the least.

Let us now turn to the previously mentioned studies by Mannell (1978) and Backman and Mannell (1978). In both of these studies, perceived freedom of choice was the independent variable and the leisure experience the dependent one. In addition, the first also involved level of competition and the second, the internal-external locus of control orientation of the subjects as additional independent variables. The unique aspect of these studies was that operationalized phenomenological aspects of the leisure experience were used as dependent variables, namely *time duration estimates, situational awareness,* and *mood change.* Mannell hypothesized that the leisure experience would be accompanied by the perception of the loss of time, decreased awareness of the incidental features of physical and social surroundings, and accompanied by positive affect. Mannell (1980) reports support for the first two of these hypotheses in the Mannell (1978) study but conflicting results in the Backman and Mannell (1978) experiment.

Mannell's major thrust, however, lies not in his experiments but rather in the theoretical discussions surrounding them (Mannell, 1979, 1980). Since many of these have direct reference to our work on leisure attitudes as well as to our leisure paradigm, some comments are in place.

Mannell (1979) deplores the lack of conceptual and operational definitions of the leisure state as a major barrier to a developing psychology of leisure, a position with which we fully agree. Mannell sets out to study specifically the leisure experience rather than, for example, leisure attitudes. He sees a confusion prevailing among professionals between leisure as an experience and leisure as an attitude. He then seems to ascribe to me the argument "that leisure attitudes encompass the totality of the mental state referred to as leisure" (p. 182). Not only do I agree with Mannell that leisure attitudes "should not be considered the total leisure state," but I have expressed myself quite explicitly on that point:

> Leisure is sometimes referred to as an attitude, when intending to refer to it as a state of mind. An attitude is indeed a state of mind, but as traditionally defined a very specific one. It is a disposition to respond in certain ways (i.e. cognitively, affectively, and connotatively) *toward an object or event.* Thus, one has an attitude or attitudes toward leisure or aspects of leisure. But having an attitude toward leisure is not the same as being in a state of leisure! (Neulinger, 1978, 1981, p. 199)

181

Mannell also raises an objection to my leisure paradigm that is based on a misunderstanding of its purpose. He states that Neulinger (1974) and others have argued that the primary dimensions of leisure are perceived freedom and intrinsic motivation (Mannell, 1979, p. 182). He then continues:

> It can be argued though, that these factors are not characteristics of the leisure experience. Rather they are characteristics which are attributed (correctly or incorrectly) to the situation or activity engaged in. Perceived freedom of choice and intrinsic/extrinsic motivation are more correctly conceived as causal influences on the leisure experience affecting its quality and duration.

The point, however, is that there is no argument. Mannell is right; these factors (perceived freedom and intrinsic motivation) are not characteristics of the leisure experience, but rather are the conditions necessary to bring that experience about. My leisure paradigm specifies the variables that need to be manipulated to bring about the state of leisure. This is in line with what Kerlinger (1973, p. 31) calls an *experimental* operational definition, as distinct from a *measured* operational definition. Kerlinger (1973, pp. 31-32) uses the following example:

> Barker, Dembo, and Lewin, apparently influenced by the definition of Dollard et al., operationally defined frustration by describing children put into a playroom with "a number of highly attractive, *but inaccessible*, toys."

Nobody would argue that the inaccessible toys, or even that the conceptual phrase "being prevented from reaching a goal" characterizes the phenomenological experience of frustration. These merely spell out the conditions that will bring about frustration!

Mannell's work is indeed valuable in that he provides *measured* operational definitions, ways of how a variable can be measured. In describing his experimental procedure, Mannell (1979, p. 185) makes the same distinction. He speaks of "the manipulation of several factors as independent variables that may influence the leisure experience" (the prime one turns out to be freedom of choice!) and providing "a setting in which to conveniently measure variations in the experience," . . . "means by which . . . properties of the leisure experience may be operationalized." These properties, as already stated, were *situational awareness, time duration estimates*, and *mood change*.

One more comment on Mannell's theoretical position. It seems quite clear that Mannell attempts to delineate the leisure experience, a psychological state. Yet, he restricts the term *leisure* "only to a subset of the total range of experiences that may accompany recreation, entertainment, or art engagements" (Mannell, 1980, p. 76). The rationale given is that

> leisure requires higher levels of psychological involvement — involvement characterized by a narrowing of attention, loss of awareness of the passage of time, and mood elevation (p, 76).

Why such levels of involvement could not apply to occupational or professional activities, for example, is not clear to us.

The third experimental study mentioned by Mannell (1980) is that of Csikszentmihalyi (1975). This author has become involved quite extensively in the study of autotelic activity, that is, activity that "required formal and extensive energy output on the part of the actor, yet provided few if any conventional rewards" (Csikszentmihalyi, 1975, p. 10). In analyzing what makes such activities enjoyable, Csikszentmihalyi developed the concept of *flow* that is closely related to that of *autotelic experience*, "a psychological state, based on concrete feedback, which acts as a reward in that it produces continuing behavior in the absence of other rewards" (p. 23). *Flow* differs from the autotelic experience in that it may be associated with activities that also carry external goals or external rewards. [1] *Flow* is seen to be a function of action opportunities and action capabilities and is experienced "when people perceive opportunities for action as being evenly matched by their capabilities" (p. 50). Csikszentmihalyi distinguishes between *macroflow* and *microflow* experiences, the former

---

[1] In terms of our leisure paradigm, the autotelic experience would be relevant to Cell 1 *pure leisure*, while *flow* would refer to Cells 1 through 3, *pure leisure, leisure-work,* and *leisure job.* This is not to imply, however, that the concept flow is identical with the concept *leisure,* as we use it.

referring to complex, structured activities that produce full-fledged flow experiences, and the latter to the simple unstructured activities that people perform throughout the day (p. 54). Examples of macroflow activities described are chess, rock climbing, rock dancing, and surgery. [2] Microflow activities reported included "social" ones, like talking and joking with other people, parties, browsing, shopping, and sexual activity; "kinesthetic" ones, like body movements and muscle movements; and others like daydreaming, spectatorship, and others. The experiment referred to examined what would happen if people were to stop doing these kind of unnecessary, simple behaviors that tend to produce microflow *experiences*.

> Twenty subjects, mostly students at the University of Chicago, (were asked) to keep a detailed record of all playful, noninstrumental but rewarding behavior that they did during a forty-eight — hour period. Before and after this forty-eight — hour observation/recording period, each subject took a battery of tests . . . A week later, each subject was to stop all enjoyable, noninstrumental behavior for a forty-eight — hour period. At the end of flow deprivation, the battery of tests was given a third time (Csikszentmihalyi, 1975, p. 143).

From the above and additional tests and interviews a preliminary picture of microflow patterns and their function was constructed. Csikszentmihalyi reports some truly fascinating results in respect to the physical feelings, cognitive functioning and self-perception, and behavioral aspects of the subjects. As the author, however, recognizes the study has severe limits in terms of the small number of subjects, the relatively short duration of deprivation, and the possibility of deception; we shall thus limit ourselves to a brief summary of results, given in the conclusion section:

When people stop noninstrumental behavior, they feel more tired

---

[2] Note that surgery is not recreation, entertainment, or an art engagement. It was picked as an activity that is "completely removed from the field of leisure and even artistic expression . . . We need to show that jobs can also have some of the structural elements of flow activities, and hence that they are able to provide intrinsically rewarding experiences" (Csikszentmihalyi, 1975, pp. 123, 124).

and sleepy and less healthy and relaxed. They report more headaches. They judge themselves in more negative terms, and they especially feel less creative and reasonable. Normal daily activities become more of a chore, and they are accompanied by irritability, loss of concentration, depression, and the feeling of having turned into a machine (Csikszentmihalyi, 1975, p. 176, 177).

Why are we including the above study in our section on experimental leisure research? First, because it is an *experiment,* there is a manipulation of flow activities and, thus, the flow experience. Second, flow activities are characterized by intrinsic motivation, and they may further be assumed to be carried out voluntarily under conditions of perceived freedom. In the deprivation conditions, subjects were asked *not* to engage in these noninstrumental activities; thus, their perceived freedom was limited. While I agree with Mannell (1980, p. 86) in terms of not wishing to supplant the term *leisure experience* with that of *flow* or *peak experience,* we are certainly dealing with very similar phenomena.

Testing Leisure Paradigms

Iso-Ahola (1980, p. 187) carried out "two quasi-experimental studies" to test empirically the validity of dimensions used in two leisure paradigms. One study, based upon Kelly's (1972) and Neulinger's (1974a) theoretical models, examined the relative contributions of *perceived freedom, intrinsic-extrinsic motivation,* and *work-relation* to one's perception of leisure (Iso-Ahola, 1979a). The other study, based on Neulinger's 1974a) model only, examined *perceived freedom, intrinsic-extrinsic motivation,* and *goal orientation,* as they affect one's perception of leisure (Iso-Ahola, 1979b).

In both studies, male and female undergraduates were presented with eight hypothetical situations and asked to rate on a scale from 1 (not leisure at all) to 10 (leisure at its best) what their participation in any given leisure activity would mean to them as leisure under each hypothetical condition. The situations were described in terms of the characteristics of three dimensions, with two levels in each (Iso-Ahola, 1980, p. 187).

Since descriptions of these studies are readily available in sev-

185

eral sources, we shall not go into the details of the studies. We must acknowledge that we are very happy about the outcomes. As summarized by Iso-Ahola (1980, p. 187):

> These findings were entirely consistent with Neulinger's and Kelly's theorizing, in that it was freedom rather than lack of it, intrinsic rather than extrinsic motivation, low work-relation rather than high work-relation, and final goals rather than instrumental goals, which increased the subjects' perceptions of leisure.

In addition, it was also evident that the effect of perceived freedom was far greater than that of the other variables. Moreover, while motivation and goal had some impact on the perception of leisure, that effect was mainly perceived under conditions of high perceived freedom. This is, indeed, entirely in line with the hierarchical nature (and not, as mistakenly stated by Iso-Ahola, 1979a, 1979b, linear assumptions) of our model, which posits *perceived freedom* as the overriding and determining dimension of leisure, suggesting other dimensions, however, as potential modifiers of either the leisure or the nonleisure state.

One more comment as regards the study that is presented as a test between "two rival theoretical models" (Iso-Ahola, 1979a). Kelly's and Neulinger's models are not rival models but are models at different levels of analyses, i.e. one sociological and the other psychological. This makes such a test not only inappropriate but conceptually quite impossible. Note the author's recognition that "the definition of free time for the subjects included the absence of work, which possibly biases the effect of work-relation in favor of Kelly and in disfavor of Neulinger." You cannot test a psychological model using sociological concepts, or *vice versa*. One might investigate which of two models accounts independently for more of certain variance in behavior, but that is different from throwing them together into one model that is designed to fit neither.

LEISURE RELATED VARIABLES

In a summary of the 1975 symposium of the American Psychological Association meetings, devoted to issues of leisure, we stated that

The variables that have been used to define leisure, i.e. *perceived freedom* and *intrinsic motivation,* have recently been studied intensively by social psychologists (e.g. Notz, 1975), within the context of work, although only one article so far has referred explicitly to leisure as a possible dependent variable (Calder and Staw, 1975) (Neulinger and Crandall, 1976).

Much theoretical and experimental work continues to be carried out in relation to these variables, yet the connection to leisure is still rarely spelled out. For example, the following books do not even mention leisure in their subject index: *Intrinsic Motivation* (Deci, 1975), *Locus of Control: Current Trends in Theory and Research* (Lefcourt, 1976), *The Determinants of Free Will* (Easterbrook, 1978), *Choice and Perceived Control* (Perlmutter and Monty, 1979). It is to be hoped and expected that the two recent works by Iso-Ahola (1980a,1980b) will contribute greatly to making the link between leisure and social psychology explicit.

Recognizing that "the study of the processes underlying intrinsic motivation has direct and far-reaching implications for the study of leisure behavior, . . .", Barnett (1980, p. 158) has presented a thorough review on research related to intrinsically motivated behavior. Much of this work has been carried out within an attributional or self-attributional framework.

> Self-perception theory suggests that to the extent the individual perceives external reinforcement contingencies to be controlling his behavior, he will come to attribute the motivation for his behavior to these controlling circumstances. If external contingencies are not perceived, or if they are ambiguous or psychologically insufficient to account for his behavior, the individual will attribute the cause of his behavior to his own disposition, interest, or desires (Barnett, 1980, p. 144).

We thus see a link from intrinsic motivation to internal causality, or to a feeling of self-determination. This trend was spelled out by deCharms (1968, p. 328) as follows:

> Whenever a person experiences himself to be the locus of causality for his own behavior . . . he will consider himself to be intrinsically motivated. Conversely, when a person perceives the locus of causality for his behavior to be external to himself . . . he will consider himself to be extrinsically motivated.

DeCharms used the term *pawn* for a person acting in a situation in which the perceived locus of causality was external, and the term *origin* when it was internal. "Roughly speaking, the pawn is perceived as pushed around, and the origin is perceived as originating his or her own behavior" (deCharms, 1979). DeCharms concedes that the concepts of personal causation and locus of control of reinforcement are often used as almost synonymous.

Our model of leisure treats *perceived freedom* and *intrinsic motivation* as separate variables, that are "logically distinct, even though statistically they may, unfortunately, not always be orthogonal" (Neulinger, 1974a, p. 17). Our conceptual definition of *perceived freedom* is intentionally naive and rather crude: a state in which the person feels that what he/she is doing, is done by choice and because one wants to do it (p. 15).

A large amount of recent theorizing and experimentation relates to the clarification of the concepts of causation and control, freedom and choice. For example, deCharms now feels that the concept of personal causation and that of locus of control are based on two distinct models. "The stress is on the total experience of personal causation rather than on just the perception of it, or just the attribution of it to others, or just the behavioral correlates of it" (deCharms, 1979, p. 33). Personal causation (the *origin* aspect) is now seen as the *experience* of causing something yourself, rather than merely the perception of it. Similarly, the *pawn* aspect refers to the *experience* of being pushed around, and not just the perception of it.

A distinction between perceived freedom and perceived control was also spelled out by Harvey et al. (1979, p. 276):

> Perceived freedom may be thought of as an experience associated with the *act* of deciding upon the alternatives that we will seek . . . (while) . . . perceived control does not seem to be so wedded to the act of deciding . . . We characterize perceived control as more of a continuing experience than perceived freedom.

Let us add one more distinction between the terms *control* and *choice*. In an article on "Three kinds of reported choice," Steiner (1979, p. 17) states the issue as follows:

> The individual presumably experiences control when feeling that he
> or she, rather than other people, luck, or unmanageable forces, de-
> termines whether desired outcomes will be received. He or she ex-
> periences choice when concluding that the self is the agent who de-
> cides which of two or more options will be accepted.

The author then elaborates further that choice refers to at least
three different kinds of experience, each of which may have different behavioral consequences.

We have two rather contradictory intentions in presenting the
prior examples of the kind of theorizing and research being
done in this area. One was to provide the reader interested in this
line of inquiry with some directions. These are very sophisticated, detailed and sensitive analyses that are necessary to ad-
vance knowledge and help us penetrate to the very elements of
behavioral and cognitive processes; however, we also feel a certain amount of unease with this type of research. It represents a
molecular if not atomistic approach. It brings to mind the kind of
research that has brought social psychology to where it is
today—in dead-end territory. This statement should not be mis-
understood as implying that I am not in favor of preciseness of
thought and expression or that I even would want to discourage
the prior type of research. I do want to express, however, a plea
for *also* encouraging research on a more molar level of analysis,
with variables that represent broad ranges of experiential states,
as long as these ranges of experiences can be clearly differen-
tiated from each other. Otherwise leisure research will become
as lacking of social relevance as is most of social psychological research of today.

LEISURE RELATED STUDIES

There are a number of areas that are at least tangentially related to leisure in which a considerable amount of experimental
research is being carried out. Perhaps the one most closely related is that of play. We admit that the prime reason for not including this topic in this section is that there is too much research
and theorizing related to play to be treated in a few pages and
that there are sources readily available for that information (e.g.

Ellis, 1973; Ellis and Scholtz, 1978; Erikson, 1977; Levy, 1978; Lieberman, 1977; Sutton-Smith, 1980). But, there are other reasons. For example, is play really a tangential topic related to leisure, or is it leisure? Intuitively, we may feel that leisure and play are not the same and that we denote different phenomena with these concepts. What exactly are these differences, and what is the overlap? Since there are no universally agreed upon definitions of either concept available, these are hard questions to answer, and we shall leave that task for some other day or for somebody else to attempt.

Let us then turn to some topics that clearly are not leisure but are intimately related to the leisure experience.

Time

The relevance of time to leisure is demonstrated by the inclusion of the concept of time in the most popular definition, i.e. the residual definition, of leisure. Time is used here as a frame, something that provides the temporal space for things to occur in. Time, or rather a specific type of time (free time), sets the outer limits for the duration of potential leisure activities. Time, or some type of time, is, however, essential in that sense for any activity, leisure or not.

Another sense in which time is relevant to leisure is as an experienced entity. When we speak of "time on one's hand," "killing time," or similar expressions, time represents something that can be felt and that can affect our behavior. This aspect of time ought to be of great interest to the person concerned with leisure behavior. Just when do we become aware of time in this sense? What are the conditions under which free time turns into "felt time?" Are these the conditions that are usually associated with boredom, or is waiting the basic condition for the awareness of time's passage, as suggested by Fraisse (1963). Do we find individual differences in the perception of time, and to what factors are these related?

Many of these questions have been investigated. A large number of these deal with methodological problems of time studies. For example, Hornstein and Rotter (1969) compared

190

three methods of estimating short visual time intervals: (1) verbal estimation, (2) production of a duration specified by the experimenter, and (3) reproduction by the subject of a duration produced by the experimenter. Verbal estimates were found to be too long, while production and reproduction judgments tended to be too short. The authors suggest that greater activity (during production and reproduction) leads to overestimation of time that agrees with the common sense observation that "time flies" when one is busy.

Among the factors that have been investigated are those of arousal states. Cahoon (1969), for example, found that a state of high arousal sped up subjective time rates, although the effect seemed limited to states of natural arousal (anxiety) and not to induced arousal (through electric shocks). Fraisse (1963) found that boredom tended to be generally accompanied by a feeling of slowness of the passage of time. A study that dealt with what we consider to be a critical dimension of leisure, i.e. extrinsic-intrinsic motivation, by Schiff and Thayer (1970) did not find significant effects for this factor on time judgments; they did confirm that verbal estimation tends to exceed reproduction estimation.

In a different and quite fascinating approach some studies are treating time (i.e. clock-speed) as an independent variable (e.g. Rotter, 1969; Aaronson, 1966; Craik and Sarbin, 1963; Lewis, Lobban and Shaw, 1956). For example, Rotter (1969) hypothesized that the slower the clock-speed, the slower would be the perceived time-rate. He further investigated whether the manipulated perceived time rate affected the judgment of the dullness of a task. He worked with four clock speeds: normal (100%), 50 percent, 25 percent, and 12½ pecent of normal. Rotter found that clock-speed indeed influenced subjects' experience of the speed of time. Interestingly enough, at normal and 50 percent of normal clock-speeds, the sensation of time-flow was experienced as being faster than normal. This might explain why subjects even in the 12½ percent condition accepted the clock readings as veridical. Task interest (rating of reading material), contrary to the hypothesis, did not differ significantly among the four conditions of clock-speed. Yet overall, higher reading interest was associated with an experienced faster flow of time (r = .35; p < .001). This somewhat inconsistent finding may represent a flaw in the procedures used and awaits further clarification.

Another line of research deals with individual differences in the subjective experience of time (e.g. Wessman, 1973; Brayley and Freed, 1971; Cottle, 1971; Calabresi and Cohen, 1969, Epley and Ricks, 1963). Wessman (1973), for example, identified four factors of time perception and their personality correlates, as follows:

> An *Immediate Time Pressure* factor (harassed lack of control vs. relaxed mastery and adaptive flexibility) was correlated with high emotionality and nervous tension, imaginative fantasy and self-absorption, and sensitivity. A *Long-Term Personal Direction* factor (continuity and steady purpose vs. discontinuity and lack of direction) correlated with happiness and elated mood levels, and self-esteem and identity. A *Time Utilization* factor (efficient scheduling vs. procrastination and inefficiency) correlated with precision and orderliness, and confidence and initiative. A *Personal Inconsistency* factor (inconsistency and changeability vs. consistency and dependability) correlated with affective lability and low repression, and with impulsiveness.

This study, in line with others, supports the view that characteristic ways of experiencing and utilizing time vary greatly among individuals. There is a strong logical argument that these differences will affect the person's attitudes toward and experience of leisure.

That no major field of sociological research exists that deals specifically with time has been pointed out by Bull (1978). He feels, however, that the sociology of leisure has made the concept of time more explicit. He distinguishes three main uses of the concept. One, *time as duration*, that is as applied to the measurement of the duration of an activity. Two, *time and synchronization*, that is, "a definition of temporal order when studying the scheduling or ordering of activities." Three, *temporal orientation*, referring to the anchorage point of a person's cognitions. This last usage relates closest to the psychological perspectives of time, and reference is made, for example, to people's varying orientation to time in different cultures and subcultures.

Let us conclude this section by referring the reader to a most comprehensive look at *The Personal Experience of Time* (Gorman and Wessman, 1977). This volume not only reports on a plethora of research, but it also offers stimulating theoretical discussions many of which are intimately related to the leisure experience.

Boredom

The state of boredom is frequently, but not exclusively, associated with free time. Boredom can occur during job time, particularly when the work carried out is of a monotonous nature. Explanations of boredom and behavior associated with it have ranged from the stipulation of a "boredom drive" (Fowler, 1965), reducible by sensory variation, freedom of action, etc., through "titillation" and "tedium" theories (Walker, 1959). "Titillation" theories seek explanations of exploratory and alternation behavior in terms of characteristics of the stimulus situations that are approached. "Tedium" theories are cast in terms either of some form of response inhibition or decrement or of adaptation to or satiation with the stimulus situation previously experienced (Appley, 1970).

Boredom has been studied in relationship to time perception, as noted earlier (e.g. Fraisse, 1963). Industrial psychologists have investigated it extensively as to its affect on work and the conditions by which it is brought about or can be avoided (e.g. Smith, 1953, 1955; N. Maier, 1965; Nelson and Bartley, 1968). The problem of boredom is also of great concern to those who must maintain people in relative isolation for long periods of time, in arctic weather stations or future space flights.

The relationship between job boredom and recreation participation has been investigated by Grubb (1975) in a study of auto assembly line workers. The principal index of job boredom was derived from Ornstein's (1970) cognitive theory of time experience suggesting that boredom is related to perception of time duration. Results indicated that

193

> Those who experienced relatively greater job boredom appeared to
> engage, and to want to engage more frequently in certain activities
> which were important because of the stimulation which they provided
> the participant (Grubb, 1975).

The previously mentioned work of Csikszentmihalyi (1975)
also relates to this section because it not only deals with the *flow*
experience, but this experience also is seen as bordering on the
one side worry and eventual anxiety and on the other boredom
and again anxiety. *Flow* is experienced when opportunities for
action are perceived as being evenly matched by one's
capabilities. When these opportunities become too demanding,
the resulting stress leads first to worry and then anxiety; when
skills are greater than demands, boredom results at first and
eventually becomes anxiety.

A clearer understanding of the conditions for boredom could
contribute much to a better understanding of leisure. Treating
boredom as a dependent variable, one might want to investigate
the conditions that bring about various intensities of boredom.
What are individual differences in this respect, and what aspects
of personality are they related to? Treating boredom as an independent variable (assuming that one has mastered its valid
manipulation), one might investigate its motivational force in
terms of letting people escape boredom via a range of increasingly unpleasant tasks. One might also study individual differences in tolerance levels of boredom.

The condition of boredom certainly differentiates a leisure
activity from a mere free-time activity. It is quite conceivable that
one feels bored with what one does during one's free time. It is
inconceivable to be bored while *leisuring*, that is, while one is
doing what one wants to do for its own sake. The moment boredom enters, leisure leaves.

Sensory Deprivation

The relationship of sensory deprivation to leisure may need
some elaboration. There are two ways in which this experience
may touch the leisure domain. One concerns one of the two directions that a person's leisure orientation may take: an intensive

194

involvement with the outside world coupled with an increased consumption of goods and services, or an inner involvement, withdrawal and quiet contemplation. The latter state in its extreme form may come to resemble sensory deprivation. The second way deals with the type of situation mentioned in the previous section on boredom, periods of relative isolation, such as in space flights or underwater explorations. While these conditions are not ones of total sensory deprivation, they do deprive the person of many sensory inputs to which he is normally accustomed.

Research on hallucinations experienced after sensory deprivation may be of interest to the person who attempts to achieve psychic changes through meditation or contemplation (e.g. Bexton, Heron, and Scott, 1954; Heron, 1957, 1961; Lilly and Shurley, 1958; Zuckerman and Cohen, 1964; Zubek, 1969). The person concerned with problems of prolonged partial deprivation would look for findings in regard to a person's ability to endure such conditions, including that of social deprivation (e.g. Casler, 1961; Yarrow, 1961, 1964; Zigler, 1966).

What other areas could one consider relevant as experimental research into the leisure experience? In a narrower sense, any area that can be shown to be affected by or affects perceived freedom and/or intrinsic motivation (e.g. daydreaming, making moral judgments, competing, maintaining or raising work satisfaction, and others) is relevant. In a broader sense, the whole domain of personality is relevant — the manipulation of any personality trait or syndrome for the sake of achieving changes in leisure states or the manipulation of leisure states for the sake of studying differential outcomes in various personality types. Such experimentation ought to be carried out, of course, within an environment-personality interaction model, thus widening the range of possibilities no end.

In closing this chapter, we may conclude that aside from continued experimental research in leisure related areas, some work into the theoretical foundations of the leisure experience is appearing, and much work is being carried out on leisure related variables. In most of the latter research, however, the link to leisure is not yet fully recognized or made explicit. I venture to predict that this will change and that the last two decades of the twentieth century will see a vast growth of leisure research, including leisure experimentation.

CHAPTER 8

TIME ON OUR HANDS:
THE CHALLENGE TO LEISURE
(Leisure and Gerontology)

ONE OF THE TRUISMS of life is that the prime task of living is survival. The major proportion of people's time and energy tends to be devoted to this task. In the past, only a small minority of most societies were able to escape that burden, usually at the expense of those who did not have the power to provide similar conditions for themselves. During the industrial age, a growing large middle class was created and given the chance to taste during their so-called leisure (i.e. free time) what a life without labor might be like. The illusion was promoted that during that brief period the worker could become a member of the leisure class and experience leisure just as they did.

The problem with this assumption is that the nature of a state of mind is not determined by time periods but by certain conditions that prevail. Green (1968, p. 71) illustrated this point in terms of the concept *love*. Love is a state of mind, and it certainly does not come about just as a function of time. You do not love your child from 12 to 1 during your lunch hour, and not before and after. You either love your child, or you do not. Time is merely the medium necessary for all experiences.

Leisure, as a state of mind, does not emerge as a function of free time but of certain conditions that must prevail. It is true that free time *may* provide some of these conditions, but as I have pointed out before, free time is neither the necessary nor the sufficient condition for leisure. Other states of mind (e.g. anxiety, awareness of pressing needs and obligations, pain) may severely inhibit the attainment of leisure during free time. The person whose primary task remains that of survival is always under the disadvantage of the limitations set by the awareness of this un-relenting demand.

There is good news! As we (and hopefully, soon the rest of the world) are about to enter the postindustrial era, an ever larger proportion of our population has available to them in one large block a growing amount of free time.[1] I am referring, of course, to the later years of life. Moreover, postindustrial society has the potential to make this free time most suitable for the experience of leisure.

Let us consider the life of the elderly in terms of the task of survival. They are facing two alternatives (with obvious grada-tions in between) and one fact. The alternatives are as follows. One, they have achieved a level of sustenance that allows them to live the rest of their lives without having to worry about survival needs, at least from an economic standpoint. Two, they have not been able to achieve such a level of sustenance. We shall refer to the first group as the *sustenance assured* and the second as the *sustenance seekers*.

The fact we mentioned before refers to death. Death is await-ing us at the end of our lives. There is no getting away from this fact, as much as we would like to try. Nor can we realistically deny that this day is coming closer the older we get. The task of survi-val includes the recognition and benign acceptance of that fact. How we might achieve the necessary sense of *integrity* rather than *despair* (Erikson, 1950) to cope with this issue goes beyond the confines of this book. We would expect, however, that not hav-ing achieved at least a degree of that integrity would severely interfere with the experience of leisure because it deprives the person of the necessary sense of perceived freedom.

---

[1]By the postindustrial era or a *postindustrial society* we mean one that is so technologically advanced that the majority of the labor force no longer needs to be involved in the man-ufacture of goods. Instead the majority is engaged in providing services, such as educa-tion, entertainment, government, health care and welfare, and research and develop-ment. Two other characteristics usually associated with such societies are the increasing importance of the professional, scientific, and technical occupations and the role of theoretical knowledge in the solution of societal and social problems.

The Sustenance Assured

The sustenance assured are the elderly whose economic survival needs are (relatively safely) assured. Time and energy, those precious commodities, are available to them to spend on nonsurvival relevant tasks. We are particularly interested in this group because they bear greater personal responsibility for either experiencing leisure or suffering leisure lack, the absence of leisure.[2] They are confronting a number of years that could truly be called "the years of *their* life." They could enjoy a sense of sovereign autonomy similar to that once commanded by the so-called leisure elite. These years could be the culmination of life's efforts, a period one would want to enter as early as possible in one's life cycle. Not that we wish to denigrate the potential benefits and pleasures of the younger years; but for most, the conditions of economic freedom cannot be a reality until the later years of life.[3]

Is there a sustenance assured section of the elderly population in the United States? According to Havighurst (1978, p. 21), about 75 percent of the elderly "have incomes adequate enough to maintain the material standard of living to which they have been accustomed." Inflation, however, could seriously undermine this often hard-earned security. Nevertheless, this number represents an impressive proportion of the population to be in such a condition. Should we aim to raise this proportion to 100 percent? Is it not strange that we should even ask such a question?

Let me quote and paraphrase a few statements from a report by Dr. Neil McCluskey (1979), director of the Center for

---

[2]For a discussion of the concept *leisure lack,* see chapter 9.

[3]Note in this context the concept *time-banking.* "Time-banking is a novel idea that enables a company to hire an individual five years before starting work. . . . The advanced money is paid back over a long period of time." So explains Dr. Nellie Arnold, in discussing leisure alternatives for the future, in preparation as chair of the Education Program on Future's Impact with Leisure at the 1980 National Congress for Recreation and Parks (*Dateline,* June/July, 1980, Vol. 3, No. 3, 6). Is this trend to be applauded, neutrally accepted, or vigorously opposed? Should we let the credit card gambit lead us into a life of indenture? Is this the road to leisure?

Gerontological Studies at The City University of New York, describing a study-visit to Sweden:

> Life for the average older person in Sweden seems paradise when compared to the life lived by the elderly almost any other place in the world.
> Basic economic independence is assured to every Swede at age 65 through the general retirement pension . . . Everyone receives the identical amount irregardless of previous income or contributions.

This amount seems adequate for nearly everyone, although additional welfare help is available, if needed. In addition, people also receive a supplementary pension based upon a person's previous income, amounting to 60 percent of the average earned income from one's best fifteen earning years!

> Basic economic security then enables the individual to choose among the different styles and kinds of housing available, as well as among the many options in social welfare and medical care that are liberally provided by the government, many free or available at low cost.

The emphasis throughout these efforts and programs is on the right to self-determination and the right to normalcy. Perceived freedom clearly is given top priority! The coverage for financial and health needs is complete, and *"everyone* is covered."

Does that mean that everything is going smoothly in Sweden or that they have discovered the answer to all the problems that arise from that system? Of course not. One of the main problems remains the financing of these services, and as Dr. McCluskey reports, "One high government leader told me that if present rates of inflation and taxation continue, by 1985 every dollar earned by a Swede will have to go for taxes." Nevertheless, all political parties in Sweden agree that there must be no substantial cutback in the care program for the elderly. Dr. McCluskey concludes, "We in America have something to learn from the Swedish experience. Hopefully, soon."

The Sustenance Seekers

Let us now turn to the second group, those perhaps 25 percent or more who have not achieved an assured sustenance. These people still struggle for economic survival in their late years and *ipso facto,* do not have the same chance for leisure. Their leisure lack is more likely to have its roots in the situational and societal conditions in which they find themselves, compared to that of the first group. For this group, the ethics of the industrial society (the *work ethic*) may still be appropriate and functional. Their primary task remains one of survival, and all their leisure experiences are likely to be tempered by that fact.

The dichotomy of the elderly into these two groups, the sustenance assured and the sustenance seekers may be an exaggeration. But any consideration of the experience of leisure for the elderly without this distinction would be missing what is essentially new in our era: the potential of postindustrial society to assure the necessary conditions for leisure not to just a few of the elderly but to all of them.

Before turning to some of the specific issues facing the elderly in regard to leisure, let us take a look at some facts that reflect the changes that are taking place in our society. The rising interest in gerontology is, after all, not a coincidence but a direct outcome of these developments.

GERONTOLOGY AND AGE-RELATED FACTS

Gerontology is the study of aging. Surprisingly, it has only recently developed as a separate discipline. Work related to aging still tends to be carried out primarily in related disciplines, like medicine, nursing, psychiatry, psychology, sociology, and others. The National Institute on Aging, created through the National Research on Aging Act passed by Congress in 1974, represents a major force toward the independent development of gerontology.

One of the striking facts that one is quick to discover in the study of aging and that contradicts prevailing stereotypes, is the great diversity of the aged.

> Gerontology is the study of these differences in aging: how some persons may age successfully, how others may experience increasing difficulties, how one person may continue learning and growing while another gets stuck, lost in the past (Zarit, 1977).

Zarit (1977) sees as one task of gerontology the separation of myths of aging from what actually occurs as we grow older. He lists myths such as the belief that aging is a constant downhill course, and that all the elderly experience is problems rather than gains, such as unique perspectives and an increased aesthetic sense or personal awareness. He also points to the erroneous belief that help for the elderly is primarily a matter of biological breakthroughs. Many if not most of the problems of the elderly stem from social and societal conditions and could be alleviated through appropriate economic and political actions.

The Horatio Alger myth that initiative and hard work is all it takes to succeed in this land of golden opportunities might be a useful motivating force for persons starting their career. For the elderly who worked hard all their lives and often showed great initiative but find themselves still or again in rags, such a myth can be quite disturbing. Even more disturbing is that this myth colors our attitude toward the less affluent elderly.

Attribution theory has shown that we tend to attribute personal rather than environmental causes to others (Jones and Nisbett, 1971). A belief such as this myth is bound to heighten that tendency.

Fortunately, this trend is changing. That factors over which people have hardly any control are more often than not the key in determining the very course of their lives is beginning to be recognized. See, for example, the remarks made by George Maddox (1974), in a keynote address "Successful Aging: A Perspective":

> *The Importance of Environment: Matching Persons and Situations.* One does not investigate differences in human performance very long, however, without realizing the importance of environmental factors, particularly the structure of opportunities, which affect human performance.

Let us look next at what the National Institute on Aging has called "the most startling demographic characteristic of the twentieth century," namely "the vast increase in the absolute number and relative proportion of older people" (Special Report on Aging, 1977). The average life expectancy at birth in the United States in 1900 had been about forty-seven years; by 1970 this figure had risen to about seventy-one, an increase of twenty-four years. This trend is reflected in the following figures. In 1900, only 4 percent of the population consisted of individuals over sixty-five; by 1972, this percentage had risen to nearly 10 percent, and it is projected to be about 17 to 20 percent by 2030.

HEALTH STATUS. What is the health status of this increasing number of elderly? One indicator is the number of people who require to be institutionalized for health reasons. In the United States, this figure is reported to be about 5 percent. *Social Indicators: 1976* (1977) lists persons age sixty-five and over in Nursing Homes in 1973-74 as 3 percent for males and 5.5 percent for females. Note, however, that these figures include the full lifespan over sixty-five years. When we look at the data for those sixty-five to seventy-four years only, the percentages drop to 1.1 and 1.3, respectively. If you consider those eighty-five years and over, they become 18 percent and 29 percent, respectively.

Another clue to the health status of the elderly is the proportion of "persons unable to carry on major activity due to chronic conditions" (*Social Indicators: 1976,* 1977). Chronic is defined as (1) the condition existed three months before the date of reference, and (2) it is one of the conditions always described as chronic regardless of time of onset. Major activity refers to ability to work, keep house, or engage in school or preschool activities.

In 1973, the percent of such "unable" persons was 3.1 for all ages, 0.6 percent for those under forty-five years, 5.2 percent for those forty-five to sixty-four, and 16.1 percent for those sixty-five years and over. Note that about 84 percent of the elderly are *not* prevented by chronic conditions to the day of their death from carrying on a major activity. There are, however, major sex differences in this respect. The figures are as follows (female figures in parentheses): total population — 4.7% (1.6%); under 45 — 0.9% (0.4%); 45-64 — 8.6% (2.2%); and 65 and over — 27.5% (8.0%).

One more statistic in regard to health, the "Assessment of Own Health Status: 1973" (*Social Indicators: 1976,* 1977). Four categories of health status are used, and the data for the total population are as follows: 48.7 percent excellent, 38.4 percent good, 9.4 percent fair, and 2.8 percent poor. The most positive assessment is reported by those under seventeen years of age, and there is a steady decline as we move up the age ladder. The data for those sixty-five years and over are as follows: 29.1 percent excellent, 38.9 percent good, 22.4 percent fair, and 9.1 percent poor. Sex differences for those sixty-five years and over, within the four categories reported, do not exceed 2.8 percent.

Health, more precisely the assessment of own health status, is very much a function of family income. Comparing *excellent* versus *poor* rating of health we see that for *all ages* the figures are as follow: under $5,000 income, 32.4 percent excellent and 7.7 percent poor; $15,000 or more income, 60.7 percent excellent and 0.8 percent poor. For ages sixty-five years and over, the figures are as follows: under $5,000 income, 24.5 percent excellent and 11.4 percent poor; $15,000 or more income, 39.0 percent excellent and 4.4 percent poor.

INCOME. How does the income of the elderly compare to that of younger adults? A frequently stated figure is that the average family income at age sixty-five of family head (i.e. at time of retirement) drops by about 50 percent. For example, *Social Indicators: 1976* (1977) lists "Median family income, by age of family head" for 1974, as follows: all families: $12,836 (1.00); age of family head: 14-24 — $8,618 (.67); 25-34 — $13,000 (1.01); 35-44 — $15,117 (1.18); 45-54 — $16,709 (1.30); 55-64 — $13,645 (1.06); and 65 and over $7,298 (.57). The numbers in parentheses represent ratios of median income of age group to *all families.*

The primary public income maintenance program in the United States is the social security system. About nine out of ten persons age sixty-five and over are receiving social security benefits. These payments are the essential backbone of retirement income for the majority of the retired, as indicated by "as recently as 1971, over half of the married couple beneficiaries and over two-thirds of the nonmarried beneficiaries received less than $1,000 per year of retirement income from sources other than social security" (*Social Indicators: 1976*, 1977).

WORK STATUS. What is the proportion of the elderly, sixty-five years and over, who are included in an accounting of the civilian labor force? In 1975, this figure was 13.1 percent (2,939,000) of the then 22,400,000 elderly. It is estimated that this proportion will decrease to 12.3 percent by 1980, 11.3 percent by 1985, and 10.8 percent by 1990, while the expected number of people sixty-five years and over by 1990 is 28,833,000. Note that the respective figures for 1960 were 19.2 percent and for 1950, 24.5 percent.

These data reflect that an increasing number of people retire before they reach the age of sixty-five. In 1974, for example, sixty-two was the most common age at which workers would start receiving Social Security payments (Select Committee on Aging, 1977),[4] and the proportion of early retirees has been growing at a rate of two to three percent per year. Fritz (1978) reports that at least 89 percent of General Motors and Ford Motor Company employees retired before age sixty-five. Figures for other large companies indicate that only about 20 percent of the employees hold out to the mandatory retirement age of sixty-five.

What does this trend of early retirement imply about the assumption that people see mandatory retirement at sixty-five as a curtailment of their freedom to work or that workers see the lifting of mandatory retirement to seventy as allowing them to do what they really most want to do: work? It must be clear to the reader by now, that a discussion of this issue is meaningless unless we make the distinction between *a job* and *a work,* and ultimately, *a work* carried out by one's own choice (cells 6, 4, and ultimately 2, in our leisure paradigm). Unfortunately, but not surprisingly, there seems to be an inverse relationship between grasping this distinction and one's economic position in life. Fritz

---

[4]Note the title of the report of this Committee: *Mandatory Retirement: the Social and Human Cost of Enforced Idleness.* Retirement and idleness are equated! as a matter of fact!

(1978) points to the prevailing misunderstanding among "decisionmakers"[5] about the perceived reasons for retirement of most employees. They tend to see these as "company policy," i.e. mandatory retirement, a view that is at variance with many studies that have investigated motivations for retirement.

The relationship between the nature of one's job and one's motivation for retirement is made picturesquely clear in a quote from a *Time* article, reprinted in Fritz (1978):

> A blue-collar worker who has labored for 30 years at a grimy, bone-wearing task on an assembly line may welcome retirement with the enthusiasm of a sweepstakes winner. Says Nelson Cruikshank, chairman of the Federal Council on Aging: "If you talk to the black laundry worker about the 'privilege' of continuing to work after 65, she'll spit in your eye. The auto workers' slogan epitomizes this: '30 and out'." But people in more sedentary or fulfilling occupations, including most levels of management, may be inclined to linger ("Now, Revolt of the Old," 1977, p. 19).

The widespread belief that the elderly desire to hold on to their jobs is also questioned by Rapoport and Rapoport (1975, p. 272):

> The conception that older people wish to continue working needs revision except in a minority of cases. They wish to be 'occupied' and to have the companionship as well as the extra income a job provides. But the more general wish is to be able to enjoy a satisfying personal life — a wish that is more difficult for them to realize than many may have envisioned.

The recognition that the elderly may prefer early retirement to a continuing labor role carries significant political implications. The previously described retirement policies in Sweden are a reflection of the impact of such an orientation, but Sweden is not alone in this respect. Kaplan (1979, p. 50) points out that "Contrary to the U.S. moves for removal of mandatory retirement, in Italy, France, West Germany, Spain, and elsewhere the move is toward earlier retirement." He cites as an illustrative

---

[5]"Decision-makers" here refers to people in the private and public sector "who had responsibility for legislating and administering a broad range of policies and programs for older residents of Los Angeles County" (Fritz, 1978, p. 9).

example legislation in France that permits people to retire at sixty and receive 70 percent of their last salary for five years, at which point they go on normal pensions.

Keeping some of the facts in mind that we have just presented, let us now take another look at the elderly in the light of the advancing postindustrial society.

"What is new, Mr. and Mrs. Senior Citizen?"

The answer to this question is, nearly everything! It is not that the elderly did not experience challenges and problems in previous decades and centuries, since many of the most common ones are inherent in the human life cycle. It is the context of these happenings that has changed and is rapidly changing. In addition, there are some personal factors that are new, such as greater health and life expectancies for the average person.

It needs to be repeated that it is not a coincidence that suddenly we find an increased concern with the psychological aspects of leisure, that the concept of free time is no longer adequate to account for issues related to leisure, that the work/leisure dichotomy creates more problems than it solves, or that the work ethic, for so long a guiding principle of our lives, is becoming irrelevant in areas where it used to serve quite well. These developments are the direct outcome of our society moving from an industrial into a postindustrial era. Since this change is still in progress, however, it is affecting us in different ways and to different degrees as a function of our socioeconomic status, the nature of occupational activity, geographical location, and many other factors, but particularly our age. A child growing up during this period may not even be aware of anything changing because change itself has become a fact of life. The elderly, used to and remembering a period of stability in habits, life-styles, physical setting, and most of all, in values, may be overwhelmed by and unable to cope with all of these changes.

Leisure, as it refers to time periods and activities, is very much part of this changing life pattern. Not only do the elderly now find themselves with years of free time for which they have to take "personal responsibility," but this task of deciding what to

207

do has become so much more difficult because so much more is now considered quite appropriate for the elderly.

Our elderly were raised to expect meaning in life from two main sources: love and work. In both of these areas they are likely to experience major deprivations, but with more certainty and, one might say, hopefully earlier in the second one. It is ironic that what is so often described as the elderly's biggest problem, the yearning for a job, contriubtes much to reshaping our values and paving the way for a leisure ethic that eventually must replace the outdated work ethic.

The number one task in respect to leisure and the elderly is, then, a reshaping of values, in respect to the elderly themselves as well as to society as a whole. I have outlined elsewhere four types of professional involvement in the leisure domain: leisure resources consulting, leisure education, leisure counseling, and leisure therapy (Neulinger, 1981). Let us use this framework to consider issues related to the elderly, and let us also briefly review some basic assumptions.

Leisure is viewed as a state of mind that is desired by all but attained only by some, sometimes with great difficulty and always only for certain time periods. Difficulties may be of a personal nature or a function of the immediate environment or societal setting. Leisure lack is the term used to describe the absence of leisure.

Major problems of the elderly may be viewed as acts of separation: the "empty nest phenomenon" (separation from one's children), retirement (separation from the job), widowhood (separation from one's spouse), physical dislocation (separation from one's used-to environment), ailments (separation from one's health and habits depending on it), and finally death (separation from life). In each of these separations one is cut off from an important part of one's life, and feelings of loneliness and a loss of identity are the most frequent consequences. Both of these syndromes relate intimately to the quest for meaning, and it is this that makes leisure so important for the elderly. The leisure experience is based on intrinsically motivated activities, which is another way of saying that it is based on activities that provide meaning.

The degree to which personal rather than environmental factors will be involved in the attainment of leisure is different for the sustenance assured and the sustenance seekers. For the latter, much needs to be done "from the outside." Society must accept the obligation to provide at least minimal sustenance conditions for anyone who has been a member of that society for the greater part of their lives. The family used to carry that burden; in postindustrial society it must and can be shifted to society at large, with much less burden to any one individual. As regards the sustenance assured, the primary task of the leisure professional is to make them aware of the challenges and opportunities open to them and their right to experience them fully: the right to be a member of the leisure elite.

LEISURE RESOURCES CONSULTING. We are viewing this type of activity as primarily one of information giving, of "connecting" consumer and supplier interests. The relevance of this type of service for the elderly is quite obvious. Given the increased amount of time available, at least to the sustenance assured, and the now more urgent need to find meaningful activities, providing information about resources and opportunities becomes very important. Such efforts should not be restricted to a passive offering of information but should include outreach programs involving intensive mailings, visitations, and perhaps "gentle" encouragements.

LEISURE EDUCATION. This is the area in which most needs to be done. Two kinds of efforts are required, those directed toward the elderly themselves and those directed to the public at large. Leisure education for the elderly will relate primarily to issues of values and attitudes — that a changing society requires changing values; and that some previously useful and necessary values have become useless, unnecessary, and even destructive. Such leisure education will also deal with habits and life patterns that need revision in the light of the changing society.

Leisure education to the public at large will address itself to the perception of the elderly, to the previously referred to myths and stereotypes associated with the elderly, and to ageism as it is often called. It will consider society's role and obligation of providing for the elderly, not as a case of charity but out of a sense of self-interest and generativity. It will address itself to the implications of these demands and ways of realizing them. Leisure education must come to grips with political issues. It must arouse the public to insist on discussing these issues openly and widely and on striving to find solutions for them. Mostly, leisure education must dare to question basic beliefs that are prevailing in our society but of which many have become outdated. Leisure education is not telling people what to think or do, but it is telling them to question what they think and do and to reexamine it in the light of our changing society.

Leisure education must confront that our society includes many elderly sustenance seekers. Is this desirable, necessary, and unavoidable, or is it undesirable, unnecessary, and avoidable? Even if all our elderly were sustenance assured, leisure education remains a must. The quest for meaning is inversely related to one's concern with subsistence and existence needs. Therein lies the challenge of the future. The sustenance assured elderly have the time and energy to turn from vocational training to liberal arts, the chance to strive for perfection in whatever they do without worry about the bottom line — will it sell?

LEISURE COUNSELING. Leisure counseling addresses itself to individuals (although there may, of course, be group counseling), and it emphasizes motivational rather than informational aspects. Leisure counseling is a service designed for those who seek help in overcoming leisure lack. The elderly are particularly prone to this problem, since they are likely to experience sooner or later most of the previously mentioned acts of separation.

Leisure lack is also more likely to occur for the elderly than the young, since their values tend to be in conflict with present norms and behavior patterns. The freedom that the younger generation has to engage in these now acceptable behaviors may be absent for the elderly. Without perceived freedom there can be no leisure. Approaches used in leisure counseling the elderly will have to be tailored to the needs of the particular individual or individuals, but the goal will always be an increase in the person's experience of leisure.

Let us briefly at least mention here the concepts of *retirement* and *preretirement counseling.* Both of these services are becoming more common, in response to a very real need. From our viewpoint, these techniques should include aspects of both leisure education and leisure counseling, but this is particularly true of preretirement counseling. Many of the issues related to these services are quite distinct from leisure and obviously require a thorough coverage, but leisure, as a unique phenomenon and experience, must be an essential and major part of such programs.

LEISURE THERAPY. This type of service addresses itself to those who are severely handicapped or made disfunctional by leisure lack. Many of our elderly may require such therapy. Adjusting or changing values to which one has clung all one's life is not an easy process and requires intensive work. In many instances it may be advisable not to attempt changing values but rather adjusting to conditions as best as one can. Those are individual considerations that need to be explored with qualified professionals who themselves have become aware of the changing values of our society and are capable of incorporating this awareness into their therapeutic techniques. A dilemma may be posed by older therapists who, feeling akin to the problems of the elderly, may themselves be victims of leisure lack, and younger therapists, more attuned to changing values, may be insensitive to the plight of the elderly. Leisure therapy, as a subdivision of clinical therapy, really has hardly even begun to be developed.

Our treatment of leisure and the elderly must, by necessity, be a brief one. We have only enumerated the issues, each of which requires intensive elaboration. Both leisure and old age concern each of us most directly, one throughout our life cycle and the other at the final stage of our lives. It is generally assumed that a sense of integrity is an important aspect of a satisfying old age.

211

Integrity implies a sense of wholeness, of undividedness, and of being what one has become. If we had the opportunity and if we have learned to experience leisure in our youth and throughout our early adult years, it is likely that we shall carry that capacity into our final years. If we did not have the conditions that encouraged learning to leisure or if we did not take advantage of such conditions, much work may indeed be required during our later years to attain the state of leisure. A major contribution to this effort, however, remains the responsibility of society that may have contributed in the first place to our incapacity to experience leisure.

CHAPTER 9

LEISURE, LEISURE LACK, AND THE PROBLEM OF FREE TIME

AT NO TIME is it more critical to distinguish between leisure and free time than when we use the unfortunate phrase, *the problem of leisure*. Leisure, conceived of as a state of mind, is by definition a positive value given generally accepted beliefs of what is good. Free time, per se, is neutral but may take on positive as well as negative connotations, depending on what it is used for or how it affects the individual. It seems for many people that the more free time they have, the less valuable and the more disturbing it becomes. The so-called problem of leisure refers to this aspect of free time. The term *the problem of leisure* is also used to refer to what I have called *leisure lack* (Neulinger, 1978a, 1981), the relative absence of leisure, here understood as a state of mind.

This chapter is devoted to clarifying these two quite distinct types of problems and to showing how each of them relates in its own way to the social-psychological and societal-political context.

THE EXTENT OF THE PROBLEM: FROM THREAT TO CHALLENGE

Although it seems hardly necessary to document that leisure is viewed as a problem in our society, it may be worthwhile to look at a few concerned voices since they may reflect their conviction with more eloquence than can be offered here. Let us first look at the question whether we are gaining an increase in free time and whether, in that sense, there even is a problem of leisure?

There are some who argue, perhaps with validity, that people today do not have any more free time than their medieval ancestors had (e.g. de Grazia, 1962) or than they had a few decades ago (e.g. a private communication from the management of one of the ten largest corporations in the United States). While this may be true in some respects and for some people, there is no question that not so long ago we had a fifty, sixty, or even seventy-hour workweek, while today the average tends to be below forty hours. In addition, the number of people with increased free time in their later years has been significantly growing. More importantly, these time arguments are relevant only if we identify the problem of leisure with the problem of free time. Once we recognize that the problem of leisure, in modern times, stems from an alienation from work, a separateness of job and work, we come to understand that the problem of leisure is not a question of hours of free time or hours spent at work but is a question of the person being either an experiencing and autonomous self or an empty, goal-less person engaged in an endless struggle for survival.

Let us now look at some of the ways in which the problem of leisure has been phrased. As stated before, the most common view is to see it as the problem of free time. For example, Pregel (1959) sees it as follows:

> We shall have a large segment of the population that will have "too much time" on its hands, and not be at all prepared to use this leisure in a suitable and dignified manner. It looks as if a very common expression in our time, which is applicable to a certain part of our population, whom we designate as "poverty-stricken," will be replaced by a new and much larger one, which we could call "LEISURE-STRICKEN."

Leisure, thus, is a problem not only for individuals or families but also for governments. De Grazia (1962) puts it this way:

> We the people of plenty (at the moment) would admit that in a setting of brilliance our lives can be mean and brutish. Success discloses faults that failure conceals. Peace and prosperity are dangerous if a country doesn't know what to do with leisure (p, 4).

What is being done to prepare the country for the coming of the leisure age? The answer is, "Very little, if anything." The main agent of education in our society, namely the school system, is certainly not geared in the right direction. As Green

214

(1968) points out:

> ... unless some current trends in the structure and culture of American schools are reversed or strongly modified, we may find ourselves approaching a leisure society with a system of education that has been increasingly directed toward preparation for a job-oriented society. If that were to happen, it would mean that schooling would have become dysfunctional for the purpose of education. That would be, at the least, paradoxical; at its worst, it would be tragic (pp. 147-148).

The need for "education for leisure" is similarly stressed by Brightbill (1960), "The future will belong not only to the educated man but to the man who is educated to use his leisure wisely."

Leisure has also been viewed as a potential problem for the individual's mental health. For example, in a report on the psychiatrist's interest in leisure-time activities by The Group For The Advancement Of Psychiatry (1958), it was pointed out that "for many Americans leisure is dangerous," and reference was made to the clinical entity called "Sunday neurosis" (Ferenczi, 1918). This concept is used to describe the fact that some individuals experience an increase of symptomatology on their day off. Leisure seems to intensify their anxiety.

It is frequently said that our technological advances outrun our ability to cope with them. Charlesworth (1964), in a conference sponsored by The American Academy of Political and Social Science, entitled "Leisure in America: Blessing or Curse?" expressed this view as follows: "The salient fact about leisure is that it is growing much faster than is our capacity to use it wisely."

While leisure, then, is recognized as a growing problem, this recognition is paralleled by the realization of its tremendous potential positive aspects, the most important of which is to give fulfillment to an otherwise empty life. While we may wish to argue with "the first time" part of the following quote, we certainly agree that "For the first time in man's history leisure may become more important than work in giving meaning to life. This shift in emphasis gives no evidence of being temporary" (Miller and Robinson, 1963, p. 4).

A similar point is made by Douglas (1960):

> Leisure rather than work has become the dominant time factor which integrates life . . . To accept our leisure as seriously as we once did our work shifts a whole emphasis. The change necessitates new value systems as leisure makes life richer and more exciting.

The urgency of an adequate response to the challenge of leisure was depicted by Miller and Robinson (1963) as follows:

> The leisure age is just unfolding, and the prospect of a nation of two hundred million people working twenty hours a week and flooding any and all recreation facilities in their leisure hours is frightening and yet challenging. The nation, the recreation movement, and the recreation profession, all must respond to the demand for a completely different and profound leisure concept based upon a vastly increased leisure opportunity(p. 481).

Finally, as an ardent proponent of a state of mind conception of leisure, I want to take the freedom of quoting a few lines (somewhat out of context) from *Beyond Freedom and Dignity* (Skinner, 1971, pp. 169-172):

> A sensitive test of the extent to which a culture promotes its own future is its treatment of leisure.
> Leisure is the epitome of freedom.
> Leisure is a condition for which the human species has been badly prepared, . . .
> Leisure is one of the great challenges to those who are concerned with the survival of a culture because any attempt to control what a person does when he does not need to do anything is particularly likely to be attacked as unwarranted meddling.

What is needed is a new set of values that not only will permit us but also will encourage us to develop fully opportunities for leisure. It is up to the leisure profession to take an active voice in promoting these values. "The profession (professional leisure philosophers) must be ardent, not diffident, in advancing leisure values. The integrity of the profession depends precisely upon fulfilling this function" (Robinson, 1972).

It would not be difficult to find additional quotes that reflect concern about the various aspects of leisure in all circles of our society. The sampling given, however, should suffice to convey the scope, relevance, and urgency of the so-called problem of leisure.

THE NATURE OF THE PROBLEM

Traditionally, three major forces are held responsible for pushing the problems associated with leisure into the foreground: the shortened workweek, automation, and the combination of earlier retirement and a longer life span. Within the context of these issues, the problems are perceived primarily as ones of free time, and of the concept of leisure being placed in opposition to that of work. Thus, the person is thought of as being *either* at work *or* at leisure.

Leisure Lack: The Absence of Leisure is the Problem

What is it about free time, however, that makes it a problem? Free time itself is not a problem; it is how we experience it that makes it a problem. Automation is not a problem: it is how we feel about it and what it implies that makes it a problem. Problems associated with leisure relate to ways of coping (or not being able to cope at all) with conditions brought about by a technology that has developed everything but our capacity to deal with it. We see at least three distinct, but interrelated, aspects of these problems.

THE THREAT AND FRUSTRATION OF FREE TIME. Never before have so many people been given so much choice. The increased need to make decisions is brought about not only by the greater amount of free time, but also by the erosion of tradition and prescribed rules of behavior. The leisure class of old was brought up to believe that the world belonged to them, and indeed, it did. They were trained in the art of nonproductive behavior, and they could afford it. The leisure class of today, that is the masses, are brought up to believe that the world belongs to them, but indeed, it does not. They are trained in the art of productive behavior and, by encouraging continuous consumption of goods and services, are forced to maintain a highly productive lifestyle, but they are asked to engage in nonproductive behavior in their

217

free time and are expected to know how to enjoy it.

Thus, not only are people threatened by the prospect of free time because of a lack of inner resources and the capacity to handle choice, but the situation is made worse by dangling in front of them a set of demanding options created by a society whose only interest is to make them spend their last dollar, or better still, a dollar they have not even earned yet. They are not told that happiness can be a garbage strewn backyard turned into an oasis of nature, with blooming flowers and perhaps a little tree. No, they are told to jump on the next jet plane and depart for some mystical island where bliss is guaranteed, — and so may be twenty-four monthly payments. The freedom of free time is once more taken away from them by prescribing socially approved ways of spending their time that force them into a frenzy of galloping consumption.

THE FEAR OF HELL. People's incapacity to deal with free time is, however, related not only to their lack of inner resources and factors such as those mentioned previously, but it is also brought about by their feelings about free time and nonproductive activity. There is ample evidence that our society, from poor to rich, is permeated by the so-called Work or Protestant Ethic (Goodwin, 1972). This view made work an ultimate value and fostered an attitude of shame and guilt toward nonproductive activity. We have discussed these issues already in previous chapters and, at this point, simply want to restate our belief that a new Leisure Ethic is needed that will give us the assurance that *to leisure* is by far the greatest virtue, namely to be oneself and freely to actualize one's fullest potential.

THE LOSS OF SELF. There is, however, another force that contributes to the perception of leisure as a problem, a force that is stronger and more basic than any that may be related to the issues discussed before. This force results from changes that are taking place in our society in respect to the value and function of work. We tend to accept as a truism the premise that work plays the major part in the way people identify themselves. Work has been called one of the major components of self-esteem as well as the esteem given one by others (Neff, 1968). It has long been realized that one of the major problems of the retiring person is a loss of identity that, prior to this point in life, was provided by the work role. Could it be, however, that work is losing its capacity to serve as the basis for self-esteem and identity formation, even while the person is still at work?

What if indeed "work is dead!" What is to take its place? The answer may well be leisure. We may be approaching a point where

> the major moral satisfactions in life are to be sought through leisure, not work. Disengagement of self from occupational role not only is more common that it once was but it is increasingly regarded as *proper*. Alienation would seem almost complete when one can say with honesty and moral conviction, "I am not what I do; do not judge me by what I do for a living," and when one turns to nonworking life for values and identity (Berger, 1963).

One may wonder whether alienation, in this sense, is a bad thing. Green (1968) argues that it is not. Alienation from the job is only bad on the assumption that one's job should somehow have the character of providing one's life work. Green feels that alienation from work can be seen simply as the prelude to a leisure society that is already in our midst.

But Green's main point is that it is a fallacy to think that "a man's work and a man's job are in any respect one." A radical distinction ought to be drawn between the concept of work and the concept of job. A job is simply a way of making a living, having purely extrinsic utility. There is no need to infuse it with a sense of religious duty, the psychological burden of providing self-identity, justification, and a sense of personal worth. People need not find their central life-interest in their job. *A work, on the other hand, is* a way of finding meaning in one's life. It is an activity to which one devotes oneself and of which one can make a career. It has intrinsic value, because it is satisfying to the person engaged in it. Once this distinction between job and work is made, leisure and work are no longer at opposite sides. "Work and leisure remain opposing conceptions only so long as we persist in confusing the idea of having a work with the idea of having a job and insist that everyone has to find his work in his job" (Green, 1968, p. 92).

It is this aspect of leisure, its compatibility with *a work,* that is of tremendous relevance for modern life. It is most important to realize that it is neither leisure nor free time, but the lack of leisure, that is the problem here. Providing the potential for leisure becomes the challenge. With technology progressing at an accelerating rate, it can only be a matter of time before people will have to find a new basis for self-definition. They will probably always define themselves through *a work,* that is, through whatever activity is important and meaningful to them, but this activity need not necessarily be carried out during employment time. It may be, and hopefully will be, an activity engaged in freely and without constraints during free time.

> Paradoxical as it may seem, the problem of leisure in the modern sense will be resolved only in a leisure society in which the opportunities are multiplied and the possibilities maximized for every man to find a work (Green, 1968, p. 141).

The so-called problem of leisure has turned into the challenge of leisure. Leisure understood in the sense of self-fulfillment has only positive connotations. It implies an active person who has found *a work* (not necessarily, but possibly, one's employment) that gives meaning to one's life, that fills one with enthusiasm, and that enables one to find one's lost self again. The real culprit is *leisure lack,* a syndrome we shall turn to briefly next.

Leisure Lack. The problems discussed in this chapter were the impetus for the development of both leisure education and leisure counseling procedures during the 1970s. We shall turn to these in the next chapter. It was within the context of exploring the theoretical foundations of both of these activities, but particularly of leisure counseling, that the term *leisure lack* originated (Neulinger, 1978a, 1981).

Counseling tends to be problem oriented, frequently dealing with developmental tasks specific to certain ages, growth aiding, and concerned with the immediate situation rather than the client's past (Stefflre and Matheny, 1968, p. 8). It deals with

220

clients rather than *patients,* that is, with the so-called normal population, not the psychotic or the severe neurotic. The question that needed to be answered was what is the problem that brings the client to the leisure counselor and for which the leisure counselor is more appropriate than some other counselor or psychotherapist. *Leisure lack* was the term used to label that problem or, to put it differently, to identify a syndrome that one would associate with a person needing leisure counseling.

What is meant by leisure lack? At this point, it is a vague concept designed to capture the characteristics of a person and the conditions of his/her environment that interfere with the person's capacity to experience leisure. We would expect that leisure lack manifests itself in many different ways: a general feeling of dissatisfaction with one's life; or a feeling of lack of meaning, alienation, boredom, and at times, anxiety. These conditions may lead to states of frenzied activity or total apathy. We see the prime cause of leisure lack as consisting of a discord between the person's norm structure (superego) and that of his/her immediate as well as larger social environment. This discord, in contrast to one that might exist in what we might otherwise consider a psychopathological case, is brought about by persons suddenly finding themselves in a postindustrial society, yet carrying with them the norms of the industrial society. The syndrome, thus, is similar to *culture shock,* that is finding oneself suddenly in a strange culture for which one has not been prepared. It is not, however, that one has moved to a new culture but rather that the new culture, that is, the future has superimposed itself on one's accustomed surrounding. Yet, it is different from *future shock,* which refers to

> the distress, both physical and psychological, that arises from an overload of the human organism's physical adaptive systems and its decision-making processes. Put more simply, future shock is the human response to overstimulation (Toffler, 1970, p. 326).

Leisure lack may be caused, in part, by this unaccustomed overstimulation and its implications for pragmatic as well as moral decision making. Overstimulation, however, is only one of the many differences between industrial and postindustrial society. The crucial issues for leisure lack are the different values that are appropriate and adaptive for each of these societies.

A direct consequence of seeing leisure lack as rooted in a conflict between the person and his/her environment is that any attempt to deal with this phenomenon will have to address itself to both the person and the environment. Leisure education and leisure counseling thus require an interactionist approach, a point we shall pursue further in the next chapter.

Unfortunately, this shift in values appropriate for a postindustrial society and making leisure a highly positive concept, has not as yet permeated our society. For most, the advocacy of a leisure society is still associated with a feeling of uneasiness; to many leisure is still something negative, times left over after work, a wiling away of time, idleness. This is one of the reasons why it is so important to be clear to what we refer when using the term *leisure*. In this way a lot of unnecessary resistance can be avoided and positive support gained for making a leisure society come true.

AVENUES OF RESEARCH

In what ways can the social scientist, *qua* scientist, contribute to the solution of problems related to leisure. For the sake of discussion, we shall make a distinction between general and specific leisure related problem areas. In reality, of course, the problems and the concerns of these areas tend to overlap.

General Problem Areas of Leisure

The first task of the scientist is to gather facts. What is must be described as accurately as possible, before we can get involved in attempts to explain, predict, manipulate, or modify. To the degree that free time is an essential component of the problem, a prime task is to obtain valid information about its distribution in our society. While this is an area of the leisure domain in which research is quite abundant (i.e. via time-budget studies), the need for continued research is larger than ever, due to the increasing rate of change in the availability of free time and to the greater demand for information of this kind for planning purposes. A great deal of experimentation in changing work patterns is taking place (e.g. the four-day workweek, the "gliding working hours," *gleitende Arbeitszeit,*[1] sabbatical leaves in industry) that is bound to result in major life-style changes. Not only do we need to know about changes in the distribution of free time, but the psychologist in particular may wish to address concomitant changes that are of a more subjective nature. We need to know how people feel about these changes, what their leisure attitudes are, and what they relate to. A change in work policy, instituted by a governmental or industrial organization, may either be welcomed by the person involved or be perceived as threatening and undesirable, depending on the person's attitudes toward free time. Resistance to social change may result from motivation of which the person is quite unaware.

A fear of free time may not even imply a fear of free time. If this sounds like a contradiction, it is; but it means that people who expect additional free time (e.g. through a decrease in work hours or an additional day off per week) may see themselves not spending the gained hours as a free agent, but doing things they would rather not do. Thus, the husband with more time on his hands may suddenly find himself burdened with household chores that he previously managed to avoid. Or, the wife who gains free time may be back at the task she had been able to drop when taking a job in the first place. Thus, it seems imperative to gain information about expectations people have as regards what they might be doing with potential extra free time.

Much research is needed on the meaning of leisure and free time to special groups who are not part of a typical work routine, such as the unemployed, students, housewives, and the retired. What are the attitudes of the rich who choose to work or of those who do not? For each of these groups, free time may present different kinds of problems, and it is the task of the researcher to identify them.

---

[1] A work schedule introduced by *Lufthansa* in their new central office in Cologne, Germany, which allows employees to arrive at work more or less at their discretion, as long as they stay a given number of hours *(The New York Times,* July 12, 1971).

Let us now turn away from free time as the problem of leisure and discuss potential avenues of research related to what we have called "the loss of self." We have postulated as a major reason for this loss of identity the decreasing role of the job in modern day life. This decrease is reflected even in the very proportion of time spent either on the job or on free-time activities. Hartlage (1973) reports that Americans spend about 15.6 percent of their time at work as against 34.8 percent in their free-time activities. What issues, then, are of concern to persons who find themselves in such a position, that is, with a job that does not give them the opportunity for fulfillment and with much time to spend in free-time activities?

The first task, again, is to ascertain the relevant facts, particularly the person's feelings and expectations about the functions of the job and leisure. That the role of the researcher may overlap at this point with that of the promoter of leisure values will be discussed in the next chapter. To obtain valid findings about people's feelings as regards the issues involved, it is necessary first to clarify what is meant by *leisuring*, what is meant by *job*, and what is meant by *work*, as used by Green (1968). Although one cannot dictate how words are to be used, an effort should be made not to use the verb *to leisure* as an antonym of *to work*, but as an antonym of *to be engaged on a job* (that is, for pay). To ascertain meaningful attitudes about leisure, work and the job, the distinction between these concepts must be made clear to the respondents, a formidable task but one that may put leisure into a more positive framework, since it is no longer divorced from work.

The issues involved are closely linked to a topic of current concern: the guaranteed minimum income (e.g. Macarov, 1970). The fear that such an income would result in widespread idleness may be related to a failure to distinguish between job and work. The disbelief in the doctrine that people innately *want* to work may simply reflect the frequent experience that people do not want their jobs. Is this wrapping the Protestant Ethic in a new garment? Perhaps, but the goal is no longer the beautification of

God, but the beautification of the human being.

Another way of approaching the problem of "loss of self" is to deal with the question of self-definition directly. What does determine a person's self-image? What is important and why is it important? Surprisingly, the issue of the job in the person's self-concept has been neglected in traditional psychological literature. For example, a book entitled *The Self Concept* (Wylie, 1961), which claimed to be a critical survey of pertinent research literature, mentioned neither the word *work* nor the word *job* (nor the word *leisure)* in either its rather detailed, four-page table of contents or its subject index. This omission may relate to the psychologists' tendency to view the person's self-concept as being determined in early childhood. Whatever the reason, some work in this area is badly needed.

Another way of approaching this issue may be to ascertain the meaning that specific free-time activities have in the sphere of self-definition. Are certain activities associated with a particular self-image? Can a person count on being endowed with certain characteristics once it becomes known that he/she engages in specific free-time activities? Can the man who takes up skiing count on being considered masculine, daring, and adventurous? Can the woman who plays tennis be sure that she is seen chic, modern, independent, and intellectual? Are there stereotypes of free-time activities?

The study of stereotypes has shown them to be ubiquitous, relatively stable, and quite specific (e.g. Katz and Braley, 1933; Gilbert, 1951; Karlins, Coffman and Walters, 1969). Most of these studies, however, have concerned themselves with ethnic or national stereotypes. A study by Paluba and Neulinger (1976) confirmed that stereotypes based on free-time activities exist. Three profiles were delineated, the *golfer,* the *tennis player,* and the *bowler.* The knowledge of stereotypes may be useful for avocational guidance; it may help to explain why people are dissatisfied with what they do in their free time; it may also be useful for planners of recreation services.

That competence in free-time activities leads to a positive change in self-concept has been given empirical support by a study by Koocher (1971). The author, deploring the lack of experimental research in this area, showed that competence in swimming led to a more positive self-image among sixty-five boys, seven to fifteen, at a YMCA summer camp. While this study did not support a long-range effect, it demonstrated the potential function of free-time activities for self-definition.

As a final general research area we suggest the investigation into the leisure lack syndrome. This concept requires much further theoretical elaboration, but such endeavors should be accompanied, or at least followed, by relevant research to establish firmly the link between the construct and objective reality. Much will be gained by having leisure counselors explore the utility of this concept in their everyday work. There is also the need for fact-finding research and hypothesis testing.

Specific Problem Areas of Leisure

The problems discussed in the previous section, are the concern of everyone, although to different degrees. There are, however, problems that are restricted to certain groups of people, where leisure may be part of both the cause and the resolution of the problem. In this section we want to list some of these areas, fully realizing that each one would deserve an extensive discussion.

ALCOHOLISM. The scope of this problem may be indicated by the fact that alcoholism or problem drinking afflicts about nine million Americans and directly or indirectly affects some thirty-six million persons in the United States (National Institute on Alcohol Abuse and Alcoholism, 1971). While there are common-sense and theoretical reasons for linking alcoholism with leisure, there is little empirical research tying the two areas together (e.g. Sessoms and Oakley, 1969; Berg, 1974; Berg and Neulinger, 1976). There is some evidence that avocational guidance, recommendation of appropriate free-time activities during impatient treatment periods, may lead to a reduced relapse rate (Hartage, 1973).

DRUG ADDICTION. As with alcoholism, the problem lies not in

226

the drug but in the abuse of it. The scope of the problem may not be as extended as that of alcoholism, but the implications are equally serious. The relationship of drug use to leisure is of interest for several reasons. One is the issue of drug abuse and the possible role of leisure in the conditions that bring it about. Another is leisure as a potential preventive or theraputic factor. Finally, there is the issue of moderate drug use during free-time activities for the sake of pleasure (as one eats or drinks for pleasure) or for the achievement of heightened states of awarenwss, if not self-actualization, which is very much the business of leisure. There is little doubt that a great deal of research is needed in this area before appropriate policies could even be suggested.

OLD AGE. The role of leisure in old age is obviously a very special one and we have discussed relevant issues in the previous chapter.

THE DISADVANTAGED. The term refers to inner-city people, likely to be ethnic minority group members, and all those who, primarily for economic reasons, are unable to share in the many conveniences and luxuries that the majority of us take for granted. Their plight has been documented by Nesbitt, Brown, and Murphy (1970), and valuable guidelines have been offered by these authors for improvements in these areas.

This concludes our listing of some of the areas that deserve special attention. Surely the reader could think of others to add to the list.Much work needs to be done in these areas and as regards the general problems discussed in the previous section. Research however, can do only so much; it can bare the facts; it can reveal relationships, and it can stimulate and arouse feelings. But, eventually these findings must be translated into social, economic, and political action, if they are to bring about social changes. The next and final chapter of this book will be devoted to social action implications and the attempt to bring our society one step closer to the ideal: a leisure society.

CHAPTER 10

LEISURE AND THE QUALITY OF LIFE

This FINAL CHAPTER addresses itself to humanity's ultimate goal: leading a life of leisure. Humanity's ultimate goal: a life of leisure! The issue is intentionally phrased in its most extreme form to provoke disagreement, to arouse the emotions. How can one help but *feel* in response to this statement. Whether one agrees or disagrees, one is bound to experience at least a feeling of uneasiness. Who can claim to agree without some feeling of guilt, or shame, or doubt about one's right to such a goal. Who can disagree without ever having at least fantasized about such a life, even if only for a short while.

Most people disagree with the statement that leisure is humanity's ultimate goal, and unfortunately we have data to show this (Neulinger and Breit, 1971). We are convinced, however, that this disagreement is not a real one, that it is based on a conception of the term *leisure* that is misleading and that stems from an era that our century has outgrown. If we can convey a new meaning to the term *leisure* and, concurrently, to the term *work*, we shall have taken the first step in providing the conditions under which a new Leisure Ethic can flourish.

The New Leisure Ethic

It may be necessary, at this point, to repeat some of the things we have said earlier. We have expressed the conviction that people have a natural desire to develop themselves to their greatest potential, to fulfill themselves. In making this belief our basic premise we are not lifting people out of their natural realm. We feel that a flower, too, wants to bloom and develop into the

229

most perfect form of which it is capable. Is this a regression to a teleological explanation of behavior? No, we are not implying that the plant consciously or unconsciously acts to achieve such a goal; we are simply saying that we have in the perfected and completed form of the flower a criterion by which to judge the development of this type of flower. Similarly with people, we can take the perfected, fully-developed form as the criterion for which to strive. There are, however, two major differences between the flower and a person. One, it is relatively easy to discover what the perfected form of a flower is; it is far more difficult, if not impossible, to agree on what a person's perfect nature is. The second distinction is that the flower is not and cannot become aware of imperfections, and even if it could, it would have little means to do anything about it. People are aware or, at least, have the potential of being aware; they can form conceptions of the nature of the person, and they can be aware of their imperfections. Most importantly, however, they have the potential to do something about these imperfections and develop themselves to their ultimate potential.

For hundreds of years, people (and particularly men) in our society have been told that the context within which they have to develop themselves and the terms in which they have to define themselves are their work. After the Reformation, with the spreading of the Protestant Ethic and the development of an industrial society, this work became *the job*. People were taught to identify themselves through their job. They became their job.

As long as work demanded an involvement of skills, a task to be conquered, a challenge to overcome, it had the potential to contribute to one's development and thus, self-fulfillment. But "a new technology has spilled us into another era..." (Fackre, 1972). The belief that the job can provide the basis for self-definition is simply no longer appropriate for millions and millions of people. A radical change in the belief of what the function of the job is has to take place and is probably already taking place in many quarters. People have to abandon the idea that they have to find meaning in their job. "...'Alienation from work,' drudgery and repetition in jobs, is not something to be feared, but rather something to be celebrated" (Green, 1968). This does not imply that people have to give up the idea of work, that is, meaningful activity. It means that they must look for such activities in areas other than the job. Ironically enough, people may have to find this work in their free time. As Green puts it, "It is simply *finding a work independently of job* that is the problem of leisure."

As we approach the twenty-first century we must develop a new conception of the job, work, and leisure. As long as we hold the belief that our job *has* to give meaning to our life and that we *have* to define ourselves in terms of what we do on the job, we will be in trouble to the degree that the nature of our job does not permit us to do so. We must realize that what is truly important is to find an activity that is fulfilling and in which we can work with enthusiasm while developing ourselves. If our job does fulfill these conditions, then we will be one of the few lucky ones, because we shall be paid for our leisure. If the job does not meet these criteria, we must be free to recognize that the function of the job is to provide us with the conditions that will enable us to have *a work,* that is *to leisure,* in our free time. We should be able to do so without guilt.

Dumazedier (1975) expresses this sentiment in discussing free time in industrially developed countries:

> Part of what yesterday was considered as egoism, selfishness, a certain expression of the dreams of the individual, is today part of human dignity....the first Marxist who sensed this expression of individual connected with industrialization, was not Karl Marx, but his son-in-law, Paul Lafargue, who wrote in 1883 that man has the right to be lazy.

It is easy to see that the new Leisure Ethic requires a major promotional job. No less than the change of basic cultural norms is intended, not a small task, indeed! To think that any one person, any one book, or any one organization could achieve such a goal, would be to suffer from delusions of grandeur. Hope, however, exists because the advocated changes in beliefs and values are part of the *Zeitgeist;* the ideas are "blowing in the wind." They merely need fertile soil and patient pampering to burst into full bloom.

There are several spheres in which an explicit promotion of the new Leisure Ethic ought to be carried out. One is the area of education, guidance, and counseling. Another is mass communication, particularly the mass media. Finally, the government, local, state, and federal, must actively participate in that process. Glasser (1975) advocates such a position in the strongest and, we feel, totally justified manner:

> We face...not just the question of leisure, but whether humane society can survive.
>
> There are only two options. One is to continue on the present road,...a policy that permits business to exercise ethical power without responsibility. The other is to take this persuasion power away from business and for the State to use it, with democratic safeguards,...

Yes, as leisure professionals, we shall find ourselves unavoidably emersed in political issues. It is the link between leisure and the quality of life that makes such an involvement a necessity.

EDUCATIONAL AND COUNSELING PROCEDURES

Let us take a brief look at two modes of direct impact that the leisure profession is developing to optimize opportunities for a leisure experience: leisure education and leisure counseling. There is general agreement that there is, at this point, no agreed upon definition of either of these terms, nor are there commonly used techniques or clearly relevant theories. Reviews of *Leisure Counseling: An Aspect of Leisure Education* (Epperson, et al., 1977), a book that reviews much of the work going on in that area, conclude that the "state of the art" has not progressed enough to provide theories of leisure counseling (Tinsley, 1980) and "that it is difficult to draw from this book a universally accepted theory and approach to leisure counseling" (Caverly, 1980).

The lack of agreement is not too surprising for at least two reasons. *One,* there is as yet no agreed upon definition of leisure, and the term continues to be used (by professionals!) as sometimes denoting a time period, sometimes an activity, and sometimes a state of mind.[1] Thus, we cannot even agree on what it is we are educating or counseling about. *Two,* professionals getting involved in this area stem from different sources: health, physical education and recreation; therapeutic recreation; leisure studies; counseling; education; psychology; and others. To these must be added the many nonprofessionals who attempt to become involved in this burgeoning field and are either looking for training or feel that "life" has prepared them adequately for this role. Thus, each different background tends to bring with it a different orientation.

This is not the place to discuss either of the two areas in detail.[2] We shall merely exemplify each, briefly state our orientation, and leave a more extensive consideration for another day.

Leisure Education

A quite prevalent orientation in leisure education is represented by the following definition:

> Leisure education...can best be described in terms of process rather than content. It is viewed as a total developmental process through which individuals develop an understanding of self, leisure, and the relationship of leisure to their own life-styles and the fabric of society. People go through a process of determining the place and significance of leisure in their own lives (Mundy and Odum, 1979, p. 2).

This description is followed by a long list of statements telling what leisure education is, and what it is not.[3]

A similar orientation is expressed in a resource package designed for leisure education and published by The Leisure Edu-

---

[1] In chapter 7 we already referred to the fact that *leisure* lately has also been used as referring to an attitude!

[2] See Neulinger (1981), for a more extended discussion of leisure education and leisure counseling.

cation Program of the Ministry of Culture and Recreation in Toronto, Ontario. [4] The goals of leisure education are stated as

To have people:

- Experience and enjoy leisure
- Develop ongoing habits of creative leisure involvement
- Explore new ideas and leisure directions
- Take responsibility for their own leisure lifestyle

The four main objectives of leisure education are given as follows:

- To develop personal knowledge and understanding about leisure
- To develop the skills and personal resources for involvement in a wide range of leisure pursuits
- To identify and assess personal leisure needs, interests and barriers and make appropriate leisure choices
- To develop and express positive attitudes and clarify personal values relating to leisure

Our orientation to leisure education is quite different from the one exemplified here. It would be difficult not to agree with the above goals of leisure education, or even with the objectives. We feel, however, that these programs do not go far enough and do not really address themselves to what is new about *leisure* in the last two decades of the twentieth century and certainly what will be new in the century to come. They are programs related to healthy living, healthy life-styles and could have been just as appropriate in the nineteenth century. There is no head-on confrontation with the relevant issues: the impact of postindustrial society on our values, our life-styles, our resources; the changing

---

[3] For a critical review of this orientation, see *Leisure Education; a Serious Task, Not Self-delusion Nor Child's Play* (Neulinger, 1979c). Available in microfiche and paper copy through ERIC, *Resources in Education,* Clearinghouse on Teacher Education, One Dupont Circle, N.W., Suite 616, Washington, D.C., 20036, document number SP 015 351, ED 184 991.

[4] The three-volume leisure education resource package is published by The Leisure Education Program, Ministry of Culture and Recreation, 77 Bloor St. W., 5th Floor, Toronto, Ontario M7A 2R9, and can be ordered from the Ontario Government Bookstore, 880 Bay Street, Toronto, Ontario, Canada, M7A 1N8.

meaning and function of the concepts *job, work,* and *leisure;* the changing population structure; necessary changes in political and economic systems; and so on.

Perhaps, it is best to state first explicitly that leisure education does not mean teaching people certain skills, hobbies, sports, or amusements in which they can engage during their free time; nor does it mean adult education programs or similar efforts. Such programs are of great value in their own right, and the intention is not to undermine or discredit them in any way.

Leisure education has two prime tasks. One is providing the individual with information about societal developments relevant to the leisure experience, and another is engaging in a conscious and systematic effort to bring about an attitude favorable toward leisuring as defined previously. It is, thus, an attempt at attitude change, a change in the person's beliefs and feelings about and actions as regards leisure. Let us look at this process in terms of two developmental stages.

LEISURE EDUCATION IN CHILDHOOD. In discussing the formation of leisure attitudes it was suggested that the person's value system is rooted in early childhood experiences. It follows that there is no better time than childhood for establishing basic attitude patterns or bringing about their change. If for the moment we set aside the family as the major socialization agent, the educational system seems to remain as the best potential promoter of desired changes. In what ways, then can the school system, including preschool nursery training, be helpful in developing the kind of attitudes that allow individuals to maximize their leisure experiences? To arrive at an answer, let us consider once more three additional questions: what is meant by leisureing, what does leisuring imply, and what might consequences of leisuring be?

What is meant by leisuring? Leisuring means to engage in an activity freely, without compulsion either from outside forces or inner neurotic drives. It involves an awareness of the spontaneity of the action, the freedom of being one's own master, accompanied by an aura of pleasantness, unhurriedness, and relaxation. It means engaging in an activity because one finds the activity itself satisfying and doing it for its own sake or for the perfection of that which is the final goal.

What does leisuring imply? It presupposes a large degree of freedom. This includes freedom from the needs usually referred to as subsistence and existence needs. It includes freedom from social pressure, from norms, from the forces of conformity. It must also include freedom from the compulsion of inner psychic forces that can destroy the person's autonomous strivings. It implies nothing less than the ability to be oneself. No wonder that some doubt that most of us are capable of leisuring. De Grazia (1962) is a spokesman for such a pessimistic view:

> Anybody can have free time. Not everybody can have leisure. Free time is a realizable idea of democracy. Leisure is not fully realizable, and hence an ideal not alone an idea. ...Leisure refers to a state of being, a condition of man, which few desire and fewer achieve (p. 5).

More recently he wrote:

> . . . "not everyone has the temperament for leisure. For most people, leisure lacks sufficient guidance and sense of purpose. The leisure life is too hard. Those who have the toughness, or psychological security for it are not many" (de Grazia, 1972).

De Grazia has been criticized as being antidemocratic and propounding a type of intellectual-elitist-aristocratic snobbery. Perhaps he is merely opening our eyes to see that most of us are not properly prepared, either psychologically or intellectually, an ideal, it is removed from anybody's total grasp. One only strives for an ideal, one never reaches it. It is important, however, that leisuring becomes a goal for which our society should strive.

What might be the consequences of leisuring? Leisuring might affect the person in many ways, but we feel that the critical outcome will be personal growth. It would bring about a feeling of inner satisfaction that comes from having done that which you really wanted to do, from having been able to do that which you wanted to do, and from doing it well. Somehow, leisuring implies doing things well, since the criterion is the satisfaction obtained in being active.

Does this sound selfish? Does it imply that everyone would be concerned only with their happiness, with doing their thing, and never mind anybody else? Certainly not. Leisuring can be altruistic through identification with others and with society at large, and it can be altruistic through a sharing of one's goals. Furthermore, it is only people with feelings of inner worth who can give themselves or of themselves to others. Besides, nobody will be leisuring at all times; perhaps nobody would want to leisure at all times. There are the realities of life, existence and subsistence needs. There are chores to be done that nobody will ever want to do. Thus, the job will always remain an important aspect of life. But it must be stripped of its excess meaning and of the functions it cannot and need not fulfill.

It must be clear by now that leisure education is a difficult task. In the broadest sense, it implies teaching children to be themselves, to be autonomous, self-reliant, and aware. These are goals that have repeatedly been proclaimed in education and are equivalent to striving for a state of optimal mental health. It may be hard to promote such values because they are, to some degree, contrary to the needs of society, or at least to the "upholders" of society, the so-called establishment. To maintain the *status quo*, citizens ought to be easily controlled, influenced, and governed. They ought to conform and be dependent. They ought to have the very characteristics that disqualify them for leisuring. We have no solution for this dilemma. The importance to children of autonomy and independent thinking and acting is well recognized in educational circles. The trend in modern education is clearly in this direction and there is little we could suggest that has not already been proposed. We can merely restate the goals, reemphasize their importance, and give the goal a new and enlarged meaning.

One aspect that deserves special emphasis is a switching from the use of extrinsic to the use of intrinsic rewards as reinforcement in teaching. This is probably the purest form of education for leisure: learning to want to do things, not for some external reward, like a pat on the shoulder, verbal praise, a good grade, a piece of candy, or a large salary, but wanting to do things for the satisfaction that is inherent in the very activity. Again, this is not a new idea; learning through play is probably the best known form of this approach. The emphasis here, however, is different. This method should be used not only to teach the child whatever needs to be taught but also to instill in him a preference for the kind of activity that is intrinsically rewarding as opposed to the one that is not.

How can we achieve this? It can be done perhaps by providing the child with more opportunities to engage in such activities, perhaps by modelling more such activities for him, perhaps by actively discouraging and disparaging games that are extrinsically rewarding. We do not have the answer. Clearly, a lot of research needs to be done in this area.

LEISURE EDUCATION IN ADOLESCENCE. The same general recommendations that apply to primary education are relevant to secondary education, the high school and college level. An emphasis on intrinsic rewards should supplement and supplant the prevailing habit of using extrinsic rewards in teaching. The common outcry against the present grading system indicates a trend in the desired direction. Unfortunately, the reasons given for abolishing the grading system are often the wrong ones: grading is unfair; it is invalid; or it is not needed. If grades are unfair and invalid, then one ought to make them fair and valid, not abolish the system. Some method of evaluation is necessary as a barometer of knowledge gained, but somehow, and that is where the real difficulty lies, the grading system ought not to be used as a method of reward and punishment. The unresolved question is how to disentangle evaluation from reinforcement. By permitting grades to serve this latter function, we encourage students to learn to do things for extrinsic rewards; we remove the incentive and learning stops.

The main problem, of course, is that most subjects taught in school are not of intrinsic interest to students. Green (1968) provides a critical, but unfortunately valid observation:

238

> Whether we like it or not, the evidence is convincing that the function of schooling in American society is not what it once was—to develop an informed electorate and a common culture. Instead, it is increasingly to shape the human resources of the nation so as to "fit" the economic and military requirements of the United States (p. 164).

What is worse, we no longer even feel that this is an indictment of the American or any other school system but have come to accept it as desirable. Perhaps it can be otherwise; perhaps the day is near when people will refuse to be shaped into preexisting forms to fill slots in some gigantic economic mold. Perhaps this is what the student unrest of the sixties was all about; students recognized that "the schools now serve certain functions that are dysfunctional for the purpose of education" (Green, 1968). "The war cry of youth has become relevance,..." and "To grapple with this issue of relevance in the curriculum is to go to the heart of the problem of leisure" (Obermeyer, 1971).

What can be done? One, a major revision of the curriculum must take place. A greater emphasis on liberal education rather than specialized, applied technological skills is indicated (see Hawkins, 1972; Kraus, 1964). New forms of expression in art, in music, in communications should be explored. Science, as the path to truth and thus the most exciting and ennobling experience, should be promoted, rather than science as the path to an improved Ford Model T, a better color TV, or a better way of killing more people with less effort.

A new curriculum is not enough; a new spirit of teaching, as well as learning, is necessary; a new set of goals and values is required. We need a renaissance that will awaken apathetic students who are bored by their courses and hate what they do but know that they must do it to survive in this society. Can it be done? The time seems ripe, but the forces working against change are tremendous. A society that has grown fat and complacent stands like an immovable block in the way of innovation. The greatest threat to America's survival is its success. It has produced an affluent society that holds on to what it considers important in life, material goods and a standard of living that for its maintenance keeps everybody on the run.

Let us conclude our discussion of leisure education by stressing that the prime task is one of making the individual aware of the nature of the leisure experience and the conditions that bring it about. This implies becoming involved not only in the individual's characteristics but also in his/her societal setting and societal issues in general. It means exploring and educating about the conditions that will lead to an improvement of the quality of life.

Leisure Counseling

The field of leisure counseling is, no doubt, even more diversified than that of leisure education. McDowell (1977, p. 139) sees at least three leisure counseling orientations pervading the field: "(1) an information retrieval-dissemination service, and/or (2) a developmental-education service, and/or (3) a remedial-therapeutic service." These labels are fairly self-explanatory. The first category deals primarily with matching individuals to available resources. The second involves traditional counseling procedures designed to develop self-awareness and assertiveness traits, all in reference to leisure. The final category deals primarily with people who are unable to function in some leisure-related area, on the basis of a physical or mental inadequacy.

McDowell (1977, p. 138) defines leisure counseling

> as that helping process which facilitates interpretive, affective, and/or behavioral changes in others toward the attainment of their total leisure well-being. More specifically, I believe that as both therapeutic recreators and counselors we are attempting to solicit a type of leisure life-style development in our clients.

Our view of present-day leisure counseling is in agreement with the conclusions of the previously cited reviewers that the field lacks a theoretical underpinning rooted in the concept of leisure (Tinsley, 1980; Caverly, 1980). We suggest that we begin the formulation of leisure counseling by identifying a set of conditions or problems that are unique to this service. In this spirit we define leisure counseling as a guidance and enabling process

240

specifically designed to help individuals overcome the syndrome *leisure lack,* the chronic absence or relative infrequency of a leisure experience (Neulinger, 1981). Leisure lack may be the consequence of a number of intrapersonal inadequacies, but I would use this term primarily for the case when it is the result of a discord between the person's norm structure and that of the relevant environment. Attention to *content* as well as *process* will thus be an important part of leisure counseling. That is to say the task includes making the person aware of the nature of this discord, its reasons, and potential advantages or disadvantages resulting from it. These explorations of the person's and the environment's value system will be undertaken, however, not by a value free counselor, not *in vacuo,* but with the conviction that leisure is *a good* and that it is the task of the leisure counselor to help clients optimize their potential for leisure experiences. Given our model of leisure, this translates into optimizing conditions for perceived freedom and intrinsic motivation.

How do leisure education and leisure counseling relate to each other? We have suggested elsewhere that a four-way categorization of professional involvement in this domain may be useful: *leisure resources consulting, leisure education, leisure counseling,* and *leisure therapy* (Neulinger, 1981, p. 198). The primary distinguishing characteristic of these services is their ratio of informational to motivational components, with *leisure resources consulting* being highest in informational and *leisure therapy* in motivational content. Implications of this categorization relate to minimal education requirements of the professionals involved, appropriateness of target populations, and approaches or techniques used.

In concluding this section, we want to emphasize once more that the very reason for the development of all of these services is because our society is moving into an era (i.e. the postindustrial one) that is both qualitatively and quantitatively different from anything that ever existed on this planet.

Leisure and Society at Large: Spreading the Gospel

The leisure age is about to be upon us. Or is it? The

technological development of this country is certainly advanced enough to make such an age a real possibilty. The national output in goods and services is sufficient to provide every citizen with subsistence and existence needs in return for a relatively small number of hours of labor. Why then does it seem unlikely that we shall have anything like a leisure society in the near future?

There are at least two compelling reasons why the life of leisure is still a far-off dream. One is that, while the United States and perhaps a few other countries could switch to a leisure economy if they really wanted to, for most countries in the world such a move is as yet unfeasible. The satisfaction of existence and subsistence needs is still a full-time job in most parts of the world. The Garden of Eden, however, will have to cover all of earth, not just part of it, if for no other reason (and there are many others) than that the justification for such a state could never be maintained unless it were shared by all.

The second and more serious obstacle is that such a leisure society is based on values contrary to the basic assumptions and practices of our economic system. Our society is based on the belief that consumption is good, desirable, necessary, and to be encouraged.

> It is essential for the economy, at this present stage of growth, that the average family buy the equivalent of four trash cans full of new goods twice a week, convert them to real trash, clear them from the house and return to the marketplace next week prepared to buy again (Russell Baker, 1967).

Day in and day out we are bombarded with messages telling us to buy, to spend, to use up. Everything we buy is made to last for the shortest possible time so that we have to buy again, and again, and again. To add insult to injury, we are evaluated by what we possess; we become our possessions. All this is presented under the guise of providing higher living standards and achieving the American dream.

Does leisure have a chance? Perhaps it does if we stop keeping up the race with the Joneses and if we "unseat the goddess of

242

getting ahead" (Fackre, 1972). We need a revolution for leisure, but the motivation for revolutions comes from hunger, not from satiation. The youth of the sixties — the flower children, the hippies, the demonstrating students — presented a strong force in our culture for leisure and against the consuming society. Unfortunately, their motivation sprang from satiation rather than hunger. This might explain why their revolt was mainly negative, their actions often destructive, and their demise predictable. A hunger for leisure is needed, a real desire for the good life. The first step in creating such a desire is to explain and let it be known what leisure really is. "Leisure cannot exist where people don't know what it is" (de Grazia, 1962).

Once the true nature of leisure has been understood, it is unlikely that there would be many with a negative view toward it. A life of leisure is bound to be more satisfying than a life of conspicuous consumption. Leisure is a virtue and must once again become the goal toward which each individual and society at large will strive.

A LEISURE SOCIETY

It must be clear to the reader, by now, that we have long passed the point at which our position could be called a detached one; we have obviously adopted an advocacy role. We are claiming for leisure a high position on the scale of values. We have declared it to be "the criterion of the quality of life" (Neulinger, 1978b). Let us play the game a bit further. Let us fantasize that we had succeeded in convincing the majority of our people and our government that *to leisure* is, indeed, the ultimate goal for which to strive. What might then be some of the conditions necessary for a leisure society to exist, and what are some of the issues that would have to be worked through?

Clearly, a major economic and political change would be required to bring about such a society. I have elaborated on these issues elsewhere (Neulinger, 1981) and shall merely list some essential points here. A leisure society would have to guarantee to its citizens at least the following: a minimum subsistence income, the provision of health services, and education relevant to non-

243

free and free time. In return for these services, citizens would be obligated to carry out necessary jobs for a certain number of hours per week, during a relatively small number of years per life. Obviously, there would have to be a tax structure to support state expenses. How will all this be possible? An advanced technology will provide the means and a political system will have been instituted to arrange the just and equitable distribution of goods and obligations. A dream, yes; but I do not believe that the main obstacles to its realization are economic issues. I am convinced that the critical problems are our present-day attitudes and values and unfortunately, I suspect, some quite deeply rooted human characteristics.

Perhaps, the strongest justification for a psychology of leisure is because the realization of a leisure state (both in the sense of an intrapersonal phenomenon as well as in that of a political system) is dependent on subjective conditions: attitudes, values, and our very personality. If any real change is to take place in our society, a major upheaval in these systems will have to take place.

We may pose, then, the following questions: Will a major personality change be the result of value changes made necessary by changing societal conditions; or will a changed personality be the necessary condition to bring about value changes needed to cope with changed societal conditions? In either case, psychologists will have important tasks to accomplish. If the former, psychologists will be engaged primarily in observing and reporting the phenomena. If the latter, however, their task will be more critical. Psychologists, as leisure educators, will need to encourage actively such necessary personality changes and do everything in their power to bring them about.

At this late stage of the book, I hardly need to justify such a position, except to restate once more that all educators, counselors, therapists, and scientists hold to fundamental values. Every one of them, though to varying degrees, is engaged in promoting values. Some of these values are more adaptive than others to the survival of the individual as well as that of society. It is the unique task of the leisure profession to be involved in the evaluation of these values as well as their promotion.[5]

Let me conclude, however, by stressing once again that leisure is not the exclusive domain of any one discipline. Nearly all areas of human endeavor are intimately involved with it and contribute to its realization. In the final analysis, we are dealing with one of the external mysteries of human existence: how can necessity and freedom, determinism and free will coexist? How can we attain and maintain a state in which we perceive as willed what is necessary in terms of our nature and that of the universe? Perhaps leisure is play after all!

---

[5]Note in this context that during the founding meeting of *The Academy of Leisure Sciences* (October 18, 1980), one of the first topics suggested for in-depth exploration was that of leisure values.

APPENDIX A

A STUDY OF LEISURE

A PROGRAM OF LEISURE RESEARCH
JOHN NEULINGER AND MIRANDA BREIT

THE CITY COLLEGE OF THE CITY UNIVERSITY OF NEW YORK

138th Street and Convent Avenue
New York, NY - 10031

A STUDY OF LEISURE
Form 0769

Within the framework of a program of leisure research, conducted at The City College of The City University of New York, we are making a survey related to issues of leisure and work. We are asking for your cooperation in this study.

Many prominent scholars and economists feel that leisure may become a serious problem in the near future. An excess of free time may have great psychological and social implications. With this questionnaire we are trying to obtain information that will help to evaluate leisure in all its aspects.

This questionnaire is a long one; there are many questions and some of these may seem personal and inquisitive. However, you are guaranteed complete confidentiality and anonymity.* Your questionnaire will be identified by a number only and nobody, not even the staff of the project, will know who the person is who completed a questionnaire.

Thus, we ask you to answer the questions as openly and sincerely as possible. Think about the questions; take your time in answering them. We are not trying to trick you into any answers or play games with you. The kind of questions asked are not questions of fact: there are no true or false answers. This is *not* an intelligence test.

We are interested in opinions, specifically *your* opinions, beliefs and attitudes about leisure.

In completing the questionnaire, please disregard the numbers in parentheses that are next to the items. These are for purposes of IBM coding only.

Your cooperation and patience in completing this questionnaire are very much appreciated.

---

*If you would like to cooperate in further studies, put your name and address on this form so that we can contact you at a later date. Of course, all information will still be kept confidential and your data will be identified by a number only.

(1) Below are listed a number of free time activities. Using the scale values given, indicate what in your opinion society's position regarding these activities should be.

This activity should be:	SCALE VALUES
very strongly encouraged	7
strongly encouraged	6
encouraged	5
neither encouraged nor discouraged	4
discouraged	3
strongly discouraged	2
very strongly discouraged	1

FREE TIME ACTIVITIES:
                                                              Your
                                                            Position

a—activities emphasizing mental endeavors such as studying, taking adult education courses, etc... _____ (1)

b—activities involving the taking of habit forming drugs .... _____ (2)

c—activities that consist basically of doing nothing, being idle, "hanging around," etc. .... _____ (3)

d—activities involving active participation in social affairs, such as volunteer work, club activities, etc. .... _____ (4)

e—activities involving creative and/or artistic efforts, such as writing, painting, or playing an instrument. .... _____ (5)

f —activities involving the consumption of alcohol _____ (6)

g—activities involving productive efforts, such as certain hobbies like woodworking, leather tooling, sewing, etc. .... _____ (7)

h—activities involving physical exercise, such as sports and calisthenics, hunting and fishing, or just walking. .... _____ (8)

(2) Given the most ideal conditions of any society you can think of, how many weeks of vacation should a

person get who has been employed Number
by a company for 10 years? of weeks _____ (9,10)
(3) How many weeks of vacation per Number
year would you like to have? of weeks _____ (11,12)
(4) How many days per week would
you want to spend working for a Number
living? of days _____ (13)
(5) Given the present state of our society, what should be the *workweek,*
that is, how many days per week Number
should be spent working for a of
living? days _____ (14)
(6) Given a five-day workweek, how Number
many hours per day would you want of
to work for a living? of hours _____ (15,16)

~~~~~~

(7) Below are listed a number of statements. Indicate your own
position on each of these by using the number of the label
which comes closest to your opinion.

L A B E L S
7 ...... I agree very strongly
6 ...... I agree strongly
5 ...... I agree moderately
4 ...... I am undecided, uncertain or don't know
3 ...... I disagree moderately
2 ...... I disagree strongly   Assign
1 .....: I disagree very strongly   numbers
                                       here:

a—My personal ambitions can be more fully realized
on the job than in my free time. .... _____ (17)
b—Very little of my free time is actually leisure ..... _____ (18)
c—I would prefer to be famous for something I had
done on my job (like an invention) rather than for
something I had done in my free time (like cross-
ing the ocean in a rowboat) .... _____ (19)

d—I always seem to have more things to do than I
have time for .... _____ (20)

e—It is more important for me to be good at my free
time activities than at my work activities .... _____ (21)

f—I have enough leisure .... _____ (22)

g—My leisure activities are more satisfying to me than
my work. .... _____ (23)

h—I would like to have more free time than I have
now. .... _____ (24)

i—My leisure activities express my talents and capabilities better than does my job. .... _____ (25)

(8) In our society nearly everybody works. Now, assume that you
were given the chance to live a life of complete leisure, never
again having to work for a living.

Indicate on the scales below how you think you might feel
about certain aspects of such a life.

a—How much would you like to lead such a "life of leisure"?(26,27)

.... / .... / .... / .... / .... / .... /

| Not at all | probably dislike it | uncertain | would like it | like it very much | extremely so | would be the fulfillment of my greatest dreams |

b—How long could you "stand" such a life? (28,29)

/ .... / .... / .... / .... / .... / .... /

| For a month or less | half a year | one year | two years | five years | ten years | for-ever |

c—Would you feel "guilty" about living such a life of leisure?

(30,31)

/ .... / .... / .... / .... / .... / .... /

| Not at all | probably not | uncertain | somewhat | quite a bit | very much | extremely so |

d—If you had (or have) children, would you like them to
live such a life of leisure?

(32,33)

/ .... / .... / .... / .... / .... / .... /

| Certainly not | probably not | uncertain | somewhat | quite a bit | very much | extremely so |

252

(9) How much of your free time activities could be called "killing time"? (34-36)

Indicate your estimate on the scale below:

/......./....../....../....../....../....../....../....../....../....../....../

None   10   20   30   40   50   60   70   80   90   All

PERCENT

(10) Place a check next to the statement below that *best* describes the society in which you would want your children to live in. (37)

_____ a society where everyone has a life of leisure

_____ a society where the emphasis is on leisure

_____ a society where the life of work and leisure are balanced

_____ a society where the emphasis is on work

_____ a society where everyone has a life of work

(11) If you were to divide your time into two parts: one work time and the other free time—how much time would you want for each?

Let the bar below represent your time. Draw a line dividing the bar according to the way you would divide your time between work time and free time. Label the work part "W" and the free time part "F." (38,39)

(12) Below are seven statements which describe different positions society could take regarding a person's free time. First, read all statements and then indicate by a check mark *the one statement* with which you agree most. (40)

_____ society should prohibit certain free time activities and prescribe certain others

_____ society should prohibit certain free time activities

_____ society should encourage certain free time activities and discourage certain others

253

_____ society should discourage certain free time activities

_____ society should encourage certain free time activities

_____ society should make available information about free time activities but not actively encourage or discourage what a person does in his free time

_____ what a person does in his free time is none of society's concern

✕✕

(13) Check the statement below which *best* describes you: (41)

_____ my leisure time is always filled with thousands of things I want to do

_____ I usually have no trouble finding things to do during my leisure time

_____ I sometimes do not know what to do in my leisure time

_____ I usually do not know what to do in my leisure time

_____ I sometimes feel quite bored during my leisure time

_____ I usually feel quite bored during my leisure time

_____ I always feel quite bored during my leisure time.

(14) Below are nine paragraphs each describing a particular kind of free time activity.

First, read all nine paragraphs.

Then, rank them in order of your preference, from *1* to *9*. Start by placing a *1* next to the activity you like most; then place a *9* next to the one you like least. Continue in this manner until you have ranked all paragraphs, that is, assign a *2* to the activity you like second best, and an *8* to the activity you like second least, and so on.

DO NOT USE THE SAME NUMBER FOR MORE THAN ONE PARAGRAPH!

FREE TIME ACTIVITIES

a—This activity gives you a chance to organize and arrange things. It demands precision and neatness. It requires a sense of planning, order and forethought. _____ (42)

b—This activity allows you to do as you please regardless of rules or conventions. It provides for adventure,

254

change and independence, involving a minimum of rules. ＿＿ (43)

c—This activity provides for the enjoyment of aesthetic feelings and of sensuous impressions. It may involve the enjoyment of one or more of the arts, and indulging in sensory pleasures and feelings. ＿＿ (44)

d—This activity involves reflection, thinking, analyzing and asking questions. It involves seeking scientific and philosophic truth and an understanding of life. ＿＿ (45)

e—This activity enables you to tackle a difficult task and to achieve high standards. It offers recognition for your accomplishments. It involves determination and the will to succeed. ＿＿ (46)

f—This activity involves forming and furthering sexual relationships. It involves the enjoyment of feelings of love. It provides the opportunity for attracting others and flirting. ＿＿ (47)

g—This activity gives you a chance to be with others and meet new people. It provides the opportunity for cooperation with others and engaging with them in common activities. ＿＿ (48)

h—This activity gives you an opportunity to help others who are in need and to protect and support them. It may involve being with children or taking care of animals. ＿＿ (49)

i—This activity gives you a chance to be "on the go." It relieves the feeling of listlessness and provides for action. It keeps your mind off things because it requires your full attention. ＿＿ (50)

(15) Below are sixteen 7-point scales each referring to a word pair. Use these scales to describe what *leisure* means to you.

The scale points indicate the following:

1 = extremely
2 = quite
3 = slightly
4 = neutral or unrelated

5 = slightly
6 = quite
7 = extremely

Put a check mark at that point on the scale which best describes what leisure means to you.

For example, if the word pair is
beautiful   1   2   3   4   5   6   7   ugly

and you feel that leisure is *quite* beautiful, you would check 2 on the scale; on the other hand, if you feel that leisure is *extremely* ugly, you would have checked 7 on the scale.

WORD PAIRS

LEISURE is:

boring	1	2	3	4	5	6	7	interesting	(51)
solitary	1	2	3	4	5	6	7	sociable	(52)
honest	1	2	3	4	5	6	7	dishonest	(53)
empty	1	2	3	4	5	6	7	full	(54)
desirable	1	2	3	4	5	6	7	undesirable	(55)
necessary	1	2	3	4	5	6	7	unnecessary	(56)
powerful	1	2	3	4	5	6	7	powerless	(57)
mature	1	2	3	4	5	6	7	developing	(58)
valuable	1	2	3	4	5	6	7	worthless	(59)
meaningful	1	2	3	4	5	6	7	meaningless	(60)
passive	1	2	3	4	5	6	7	active	(61)
satisfying	1	2	3	4	5	6	7	unsatisfying	(62)
thin	1	2	3	4	5	6	7	thick	(63)
good	1	2	3	4	5	6	7	bad	(64)
refreshing	1	2	3	4	5	6	7	tiring	(65)
pleasant	1	2	3	4	5	6	7	unpleasant	(66)

(16) Now, repeat what you did on the previous page, but this time use the scales to describe what *work* means to you.

The scale points, as before, indicate the following:

1 = extremely
2 = quite
3 = slightly
4 = neutral or unrelated
5 = slightly
6 = quite
7 = extremely

WORK *is:*

	1	2	3	4	5	6	7		
boring	1	2	3	4	5	6	7	interesting	(1)
solitary	1	2	3	4	5	6	7	sociable	(2)
honest	1	2	3	4	5	6	7	dishonest	(3)
empty	1	2	3	4	5	6	7	full	(4)
desirable	1	2	3	4	5	6	7	undesirable	(5)
necessary	1	2	3	4	5	6	7	unnecessary	(6)
powerful	1	2	3	4	5	6	7	powerless	(7)
mature	1	2	3	4	5	6	7	developing	(8)
valuable	1	2	3	4	5	6	7	worthless	(9)
meaningful	1	2	3	4	5	6	7	meaningless	(10)
passive	1	2	3	4	5	6	7	active	(11)
satisfying	1	2	3	4	5	6	7	unsatisfying	(12)
thin	1	2	3	4	5	6	7	thick	(13)
good	1	2	3	4	5	6	7	bad	(14)
refreshing	1	2	3	4	5	6	7	tiring	(15)
pleasant	1	2	3	4	5	6	7	unpleasant	(16)

(17) If you were to describe yourself to someone in terms of (17,18) what is most important to you about yourself, how

much would you talk about your work and how much would you talk about your free-time activities?

Indicate your position by a check mark on the scale below:

′ .... ′ .... ′ .... ′ .... ′ .... ′ .... ′

talk only about work	talk mostly about work	talk a little more about work than free time	talk equally about work and free time	talk a little more about free time than work	talk mostly about free time	talk only about free time

Below are sets of statements relating to beliefs and attitudes about sex. For each set of statements indicate the *one* with which you agree more by placing a check mark in front of that statement.

(18) ____ I feel that the main reason for having sexual relations should be to have children.

____ I feel that having sexual relations for pleasure only is fine.

____ I prefer not to answer this question. (19)

∞∞∞∞∞∞∞∞∞∞∞∞∞∞∞∞∞∞∞∞∞∞∞∞∞∞∞∞∞∞∞∞∞∞∞∞

(19) ____ I feel that a person should engage in sexual relations only after he or she is married.

____ I approve of premarital sex.

____ I prefer not to answer this question. (20)

∞∞∞∞∞∞∞∞∞∞∞∞∞∞∞∞∞∞∞∞∞∞∞∞∞∞∞∞∞∞∞∞∞∞∞∞

(20) ____ I feel that children should not be aware of the fact that their parents engage in sexual relations until the parents feel it is necessary to introduce the subject.

____ I feel that it is all right for children of any age to be aware of the fact that their parents engage in sexual relations.

____ I prefer not to answer this question. (21)

∞∞∞∞∞∞∞∞∞∞∞∞∞∞∞∞∞∞∞∞∞∞∞∞∞∞∞∞∞∞∞∞∞∞∞∞

(21) ____ I feel that society should permit only heterosexual (male-female) relationships.

____ I feel that society should be permissive of all types of sexual relationships.

____ I prefer not to answer this question. (22)

258

(22) _____ I feel that the institution of marriage, as we know it today, should be here to stay.

_____ I feel that the institution of marriage, as we know it today, should be abolished.

_____ I prefer not to answer this question. (23)

≫≫≫≫≫≫≫≫≫≫≫≫≫≫≫≫≫≫≫≫≫≫≫≫≫≫≫≫≫≫≫≫≫≫≫≫≫≫≫

(23) Do you make a distinction between *free time* and *leisure*?

_____ Yes; _____ No. (24)

(24) If "Yes," indicate on the scale below how much of your *free time* you consider *leisure*. (25,26)

None	10%	20%	30%	40%	50%	60%	70%	80%	90%	All

BACKGROUND INFORMATION

Sex: male _____ (1)   Age: _____   Religious preference: (30)
(27) female _____ (2)   (28,29)   Protestant _____ (1)
                                    Catholic _____ (2)
What is your occupation or   Jewish _____ (3)
profession: Other _____ (4)
(31,32) _____   None _____ (5)

Race: (33)   Marital status: (34)
  White _____ (1)   single, never married _____ (1)
  Black _____ (2)   married _____ (2)
  Oriental _____ (3)   separated, divorced _____ (3)
  Other _____ (4)   widowed _____ (4)

What was the last grade you completed in school? (35)
to 6 years _____ (1) 12 years (high school graduate) _____ (4)
7-9 years _____ (2) 13-15 years (some college) _____ (5)
10-11 years _____ (3) 16 year (college graduate) _____ (6)
                       17 years or more (graduate work) _____ (7)

Adding up the income from all sources, what was your total family income last year? (Under family include only those people you actually lived with) (36)

  under $5,000 _____ (1) $11,001-13,000 _____ (5)
  $5,001-7,000 _____ (2) $13,001-15,000 _____ (6)
  $7,001-9,000 _____ (3) $15,001-20,000 _____ (7)
  $9,001-11,000 _____ (4) $20,000 or over _____ (8)

What is your present work status?   (37)

work full-time	____ (1)	laid off, or on stike	____ (5)
work part-time	____ (2)	retired	____ (6)
unemployed	____ (3)	housewife	____ (7)
student	____ (4)	other: _____	____ (8)

Country of birth: (38)   Physical fitness: (39)

U.S.	____ (1)	poor ____ (1) good	____ (3)
other	____ (2)	fair ____ (2) excellent	____ (4)

Your sleep: (40)

poor ____ (1); fair ____ (2); good ____ (3); excellent ____ (4)

Indicate your family size: (41)

I come from a family of . . .

____ one child (that is, I am an only child)
____ two children
____ three children
____ four children
____ five children
____ six children or more

What is your position in the family?   (42)

First-born and/or only	____ (1)	Fourth-born	____ (4)
Second-born	____ (2)	Fifth-born	____ (5)
Third-born	____ (3)	Sixth or later-born	____ (6)

Indicate sex of siblings: (include yourself in this list)   (43)

	male (1)	female (2)	
Oldest (and/ or only)	____	____	(43)
Second-born	____	____	(44)
Third-born	____	____	(45)
Fourth-born	____	____	(46)
Fifth-born	____	____	(47)
Sixth-born	____	____	(48)

CODING INSTRUCTIONS FOR LEISURE ATTITUDE DIMENSIONS A STUDY OF LEISURE

Appendix

CODING INSTRUCTIONS FOR LEISURE ATTITUDE DIMENSIONS A STUDY OF LEISURE

Form 0769

General information: A factor analysis was carried out on 32 variables and 335 subjects, using a principle component method and a Varimax rotation to five factors.

Items assigned to each factor are listed below. Three items were excluded as factor definers because they had loadings of less than .40, and one item because it was tied on two factors by a difference of less than .10.

For each item are listed item numbers, card number and column location, factor loadings, standard deviations and means based on the *Norm* group.

FACTOR 1 (N = the number of items = 5)

Item Number	Card	Cols.	Factor Loading	Standard Deviat'n	Mean
8b How long could you "stand" such a life	81	28,29	.806	21.81	26.21
8a How much would you like to lead a "life of of leisure"	81	26,27	.753	16.67	22.52
8d Would you like your children to live such a life	81	32,33	.681	16.86	17.64
11 Free time vs work time allotment	81	38,39	.575	5.44	16.94
8c Would you feel "guilty" about living such a life	81	30,31	−.571	16.64	19.64

FACTOR 2* (N = 5)

	Card	Cols.	Factor Loading	Standard Deviat'n	Mean
1g Productive efforts	81	7	.704	.98	5.37
1e Creative and/or artistic efforts	81	5	.628	.98	5.56

*To obtain a nondirectional factor score, first convert all 3's into 5's, all 2's into 6's, and 1's into 7's. Discouraging implies as much of an active role as encouraging!

263

1d Participation in social affairs	81	4	.572	.93	5.29
1h Physical exercise	81	8	.545	.98	5.76
1a Mental endeavors	81	1	.467	.96	5.80

FACTOR 3 (N = 6)

7i Leisure activities express talents and capabilities	81	25	.692	1.86	3.64
7g Leisure activities are more satisfying	81	23	.667	1.74	4.03
17 Self-description through free-time activities ..	82	17,18	.655	11.90	33.13
7e More important to be good in free-time than work activities	81	21	.499	1.52	2.89
7c Prefer fame for job rather than something done in free time	81	19	-.403	1.77	4.21
7a Ambitions more realized on job than free time	81	17	-.640	1.80	4.09

FACTOR 4 (N = 6)

7f I have enough leisure	81	22	.607	1.72	2.99
13 Leisure time felt to be boring	81	41	.412	.98	2.18
9 How much free time is "killing time"	81	34-36	.396	18.74	19.94
7b Little of my free time is actually leisure	81	18	-.411	1.78	4.58
7h I would like more free time than I have	81	24	-.553	1.49	5.51
7d I always have more things to do than I have time for	81	20	-.611	1.74	5.22

FACTOR 5 (N = 4)

3 How many weeks of vacation would you like to have	81	11,12	-.783	8.62	7.73
2 Given the most ideal conditions how many weeks of vacation should a person have	81	9,10	-.728	8.05	7.43
5 Given the present state what should be the *work week*	81	14	.463	.61	4.41
4 How many days per week you want to work ..	81	13	.666	.91	4.01

Coding information:

Items 8a through d, 17, code from 0 to 60 (one for each dot).

Items 1a through h, 7a through i, code as indicated (1-7).

Item 11: divide bar into 32 parts, and score "F" part; possible range = 0 to 32.

Item 9, code from 0 to 100 (i.e., 0,3,4,5,6,7,10,13,14,15,16,17,20,23, 24, 25,26,27,30,33, etc.)

Item 13, code from 1 (my leisure time is . . .) to 7 (I always feel quite bored . . .)

Items 2,3,4,5: code as given.

Factor scores: F

a—turn raw scores into z-scores (z) , using s and $\overline{X}$ as given.

$$z = (X - \overline{X})/s$$

b—multiply z-scores by respective factor loadings (1), sum these cross-products for each factor, and divide by N.

$$F = \frac{\Sigma \, z \, l}{N}$$

BIBLIOGRAPHY

Aaronsen, B.S.: Hypnosis, time-rate perception, and psychopathology. Paper read at the Eastern Psychological Association, Atlantic City, April, 1966.

Allport, Gordon W.: The historical background of modern social psychology. In Lindzey, Gardner, and Aronson, Elliot (Eds.): *The Handbook of Social Psychology,* 2nd ed. Reading, Addison-Wesley, 1968, Vol. I, pp. 1-80.

American Academy of Arts and Sciences: Toward the year 2000: work in progress. *Daedalus, J Am Acad Arts and Sciences, 96, 3:* Summer 1967.

American Academy of Political and Social Science: Social goals and indicators for American society. *The Annals, J Am Acad Pol Soc Sci, No. 1 and 2:* September, 1967.

Anderson, Harold H.: Creativity as personality development. In Anderson, H.H. (Ed.): *Creativity and Its Cultivation.* New York, Har-Row, 1959.

Appley, M.H.: Derived motives. In Mussen, Paul H., and Rosenzweig, Mark R. (Eds.): *Ann Rev Psychol.* Palo Alto, Annual Reviews, 1970, Vol. 21.

Armstrong, J.S., and Soelberg, P.: On the interpretation of factor analysis. *Psychological Bulletin, 70:*361-365, 1968.

Aronson, E., and Carlsmith, J.M.: Experimentation in social psychology. In Lindzey, Gardner, and Aronson, Elliot (Eds.): *The Handbook of Social Psychology,* 2nd ed. Reading, Addison-Wesley, 1968, Vol. II, pp. 1-79.

Ausubel, D.P.: Causes and types of narcotic addiction: a psychosocial view. *Psychiatr Q, 35:*523-531, 1961.

locus of control on transient "leisure" experiences. Paper presented at the Second Canadian Congress on Leisure Research, Toronto, 1978.

Baker, Russell: Observer: The west wind policy won't do. *The New York Times:* August 20, 1967.

Barnett, L.A.: Theorizing about play: Critique and direction. *Leisure Sciences,* 1978, *1, 2:* 113-129.

Barnett, L.A.: The social psychology of children's play: effects of extrinsic rewards on free play and intrinsic motivation. In Iso-Ahola, S.E. (Ed.), *Social Psychological Perspectives on Leisure and Recreation.* Springfield, Charles C Thomas, Publisher, 1980.

Barret, W.: *The Illusion of Technique.* Garden City, NY, Anchor Press/Doubleday, 1978.

Bauer, R.A. (Ed.): *Social Indicators.* Cambridge, MA: MIT Pr, 1966.

Beaman, J.: Comments on the paper "the substitutability concept: implications for recreation research and management," by Hendee and Burdge. *Journal of Leisure Research, 7:* 146-151, 1975.

Bennett, M.K.: On measurement of relative national standards of living. *QJ Economics*, 317-335, February, 1937.

Berelson, Bernard, and Steiner, Gary A.: *Human Behavior, an Inventory of Scientific Findings.* New York, Harcourt, Brace & World, 1964.

Berg, C., and Neulinger, J.: The alcoholic's perception of leisure. *JS Alcohol, 37*, 11: 1625-1632, 1976.

Berger, B.M.: The sociology of leisure: some suggestions. In Smigel, E.O. (Ed.): *Work and Leisure.* New Haven, Coll & U Pr, 1963, pp. 21-40.

Bergler, R.: *Psychologie Sterotyper Systeme.* Bern, Huber, 1966.

Berkowitz, L.: Social psychological theorizing. In Marx, Melvin H. (Ed.): *Theories in Contemporary Psychology.* New York, Macmillan, 1963, pp. 369-388.

Berlyne, D.E.: Arousal and reinforcement. In Levine, David (Ed.): *Nebraska Symposium on Motivation.* Lincoln, U of Nebr Pr, 1967.

Berlyne, D.E.: Laughter, humor, and play. In Lindzey, Gardner, and Aronson, Elliot (Eds.): *The Handbook of Social Psychology,* 2nd ed. Reading, Addison-Wesley, 1969, Vol III, pp. 795-852.

Bexton, W.H.; Heron, W., and Scott, T.H.: Effects of decreased variation in the sensory environment. *Can J Psch, 8*:70-76, 1954.

Biderman, A.D.: Social indicators and goals. In Bauer, R.A. (Ed.): *Social Indicators.* Cambridge, MA, MIT Pr, 1966.

Bird, J.W., and Bird, L.P.: *The Freedom of Sexual Love.* Garden City, NY, Doubleday, 1967.

Bishop, D.W.: Stability of the factor structure of leisure behavior: analyses of four communities. *Journal of Leisure Research, 2:* 160-170, 1970.

Bishop, D.W.: A comment. *Journal of Leisure Research, 3:* 194-197, 1971.

Bishop, D., Jeanrenaud, C., and Lawson, K.: Comparison of a time diary and recall questionnaire for surveying leisure activities. *Journal of Leisure Research, 7:* 73-80, 1975.

Bishop, D.W., and Witt, P.A.: Sources of behavioral variance during leisure time. *J Pers Soc Psychol, 16*:352-360, 1970.

Bogardus, E.S.: Avocations and personality. *Sociological and Social Research, 18*:275-281, 1934.

Borow, H.: Development of occupational motives and rules. In Hoffman, M.L., and Hoffman, L.W. (Eds.): *Review of Child Development Research.* New York, Russell Sage, 1966, Vol. II.

Bradburn, N.M., and Caplovitz, D.: *Report on Happiness.* Chicago, Aldine, 1965.

Brayley, L.S., and Freed, N.H.: Modes of temporal orientation and psychopathology. *J Consult Clin Psychol, 36:* 33-39, 1971.

Breit, M. Explorations in leisure types. Unpublished honors thesis, Psychology Department, The City College of the City University of New York, New York, 1969.

Bibliography

Brightbill, Charles K.: *The Challenge of Leisure*. Englewood Cliffs, P-H, 1960.

Brightbill, Charles K.: A remark in the precis of the conference. In Charlesworth, James C. (Ed.): *Leisure in America: Blessing or Curse?* Philadelphia, Am Acad Pol Soc Sci, April 1964, Monograph 4, p. 88.

Brim, Orville G., Jr.: Socialization through the life cycle. In Brim, Orville G., Jr., and Wheeler, S.: *Socialization After Childhood: Two Essays*. New York, Wiley, 1966.

Brim, Orville G., Jr., Glass, D.C., Neulinger, John and Firestone, I.J.: *American Beliefs and Attitudes about Intelligence*. New York, Russell Sage, 1969.

Bronfenbrenner, U.: Socialization and social class through time and space. In Maccoby, E.E., Newcomb, T.M., and Hartley, E.L. (Eds.): *Readings in Social Psychology*. New York, Henry Holt, 1958.

Brownwell, Baker: *Art is Action*. New York, Har-Row, 1939.

Bryan, H., and Alsikafe, M. The case of university professors (Sociological Studies No. 3). University of Alabama, Bureau of Public Administration, 1975.

Buchholz, R.A. : The work ethic reconsidered. *Industrial and Labor Relations Review, 31:* 450-459, 1978.

Bull, N.C.: One measure for defining a leisure activity. *Journal of Leisure Research, 3:* 120-126, 1971.

Bull, N.C.: Chronology: the field of social time. *Journal of Leisure Research, 10:* 288-297, 1978.

Burch, W.R., Jr.: The social circles of leisure: competing explanations. *Journal of Leisure Research, 1:* 125-148, 1969.

Burdge, R.J.: The development of a leisure orientation scale. Unpublished master's thesis, Columbus, Ohio State University, 1961(a).

Burdge, R.J.: The Protestant Ethic and leisure-orientation. Paper presented at Ohio Valley Sociological Society, Cleveland, 1961(b).

Burdge, R.J.: Levels of occupational prestige and leisure activity. *Journal of Leisure Research, 3:* 262-274, 1969.

Burton, T.L.: Identification of recreation types through cluster analysis. *Society and Leisure, 1:* 47-64, 1971(a).

Burton, T.L.: *Experiments in Recreation Research*. Totowa, NJ, Rowman & Littlefield, 1971(b).

Cahoon, R.L.: Physiological arousal and time estimation. *Percept Mot Skills, 28:* 259-268, 1969.

Calabresi, R., and Cohen, J.: Personality and time attitudes. *J Abnorm Psych, 73:* 431-439, 1969.

Calder, B.J., and Staw, B.M.: The self-perception of intrinsic and extrinsic motivation. *J Pers Soc Psychol, 31:* 599-605, 1975.

Campbell, Angus: Aspiration, satisfaction, and fulfillment. In Campbell, Angus, and Converse, Philip E. (Eds.): *The Human Meaning of Social Change*. New York, Russell Sage, 1972, pp. 441-466.

269

Campbell, D.T., and Fiske, D.W.: Convergent and discriminant validation by the multitrait multimethod matrix. *Psychol Bull, 56:* 81-105, 1959.

Campbell, D.T., and Stanley, J.C.: *Experimental and Quasi-Experimental Designs for Research.* Chicago, Rand, 1963.

Cantril, H.: *The patterns of human concern.* New Brunswick, NJ, Rutgers University, 1965.

Cartwright, D., and Zander, A. (Eds.): *Group Dynamics,* 2nd ed. Evanston, Row, Peterson, 1960.

Casler, L.: Maternal deprivation: a critical review of the literature. *Monographs of Social Research and Child Development,* 26: No. 2 (whole No. 80), 1961.

Caverly, M.: Book review of *Leisure Counseling: an Aspect of Leisure Education.* In *Leisure Sciences, 3:* 305-306, 1980.

Census of Population, *Alphabetical Index of Occupations and Industries, rev.* Washington, D.C., U.S. Government Printing Office, 1960.

Charlesworth, J.C.: A comprehensive plan for the wise use of leisure. In Charlesworth, J.C. (Ed.): *Leisure in America: Blessing or Curse?* Philadelphia, Am Acad Pol Soc Sci, 1964.

Cheek, N.H., Jr., and Burch, W.R., Jr.: *The Social Organization of Leisure in Human Society.* New York, Harper & Row, 1976.

Cicchetti, Charles J.: A review of the empirical analyses that have been based upon the National Recreation Surveys. *Journal of Leisure Research, 4:* 90-107, 1972.

Clarke, Alfred C.: The use of leisure and its relation to levels of occupational prestige. *Sociol Rev, 21:*301-307, 1956. Also in Larrabee, Eric, and Meyersohn, Rolf (Eds.): *Mass Leisure.* Glencoe, Free Pr, 1958, pp. 205-214.

Clausen, John A.: Family structure, socialization, and personality. In Hoffman, Lois W., and Hoffman, Martin L. (Eds.): *Review of Child Development Research.* New York, Russell Sage, 1966, Vol, 2, pp. 1-53.

Clawson, Marion: How much leisure, now and in the future? In Charlesworth, James C. (Ed.): *Leisure in America: Blessing or Curse?* Philadelphia, Am Acad Pol Soc Sci, 1964.

Conner, K.A., and Bultena, G.L.: The four-day workweek: an assessment of its effects on leisure participation. *Leisure Sciences, 2:* 55-69, 1979.

Converse, P.E. and Robinson, J.P.: 1965/66 Survey Research Center study. University of Michigan, 1966.

Cottle, Thomas J.: The politics of pronouncement, In *Science, Heritability, and IQ.* Harvard Educational Review, 1969, pp. 50-62.

Cottle, Thomas J.: Temporal correlates of dogmatism. *J Consult Clin Psychol, 36:70-81,* 1971.

Craik, K.H., and Sarbin, T.R.: The effect of covert alterations of clock rate upon time estimates and personal tempo. *Percept Mot Skills, 1:*597-610, 1963.

Bibliography

Crain, W.C.: *Theories of Development.* Englewood Cliffs, NJ, Prentice-Hall, 1980.

Crandall, R., and Slivken, K.: The importance of measuring leisure attitudes. Presented at the *NRPA Research Symposium,* National Recreation and Park Association, Miami Beach, October, 1978.

Crandall, R., and Slivken, K.: Leisure attitudes and their measurement. In Iso-Ahola, S.E. (Ed.), *Social Psychological Perspectives on Leisure and Recreation.* Springfield, Thomas, 1980.

Csikszentmihalyi, M.: *Beyond Boredom and Anxiety.* San Francisco, Jossey-Bass, 1975.

Cunningham, David A., Montoye, Henry J., Metzner, Helen L., and Keller, Jacob B.: Active leisure activities as related to occupation. *Journal of Leisure Research,* 2:104-111, 1970.

Dale, Edwin L., Jr.: A guaranteed income. *The New York Times:* May, 1968.

deCharms, R.: *Personal Causation, the Internal Affective Determinants of Behavior.* New York, Academic Press, 1968.

deCharms, R.: Personal causation and perceived control. In Perlmutter, L.C., and Monty, R.A. (Eds.), *Choice and Perceived Control.* New York, Wiley, 1979.

Deci, E.L: Effects of externally mediated rewards on intrinsic motivation. *J Pers Soc Psychol,18:*105-115, 1971.

Deci, E.L.: *Intrinsic Motivation.* New York, Plenum, 1975.

de Grazia, Sebastian: *Of Time, Work and Leisure.* New York, The Twentieth Century Fund, 1962.

de Grazia, Sebastian: American Institute of Planners' statement. Quoted in Staley, Edwin J., and Miller, Norman P. (Eds.): *Leisure and the Quality of Life.* Washington, D.C., AAHPER, 1972, p. 161.

Deutsch, Martin: Happenings on the way back to the forum. In *Science, Heritability, and IQ.* Harvard Educational Review, 1969, pp. 63-97.

Dewey, John: *A Cyclopedia of Education,* Monroe, Paul (Ed.). New York, Macmillan, 1925, Vol. 14.

Diagnostic and Statistical Manual of Mental Disorders (DSM-III), Task Force on Nomenclature and Statistics, *American Psychiatric Association,* Washington, D.C., 1978 (draft version).

Ditton, R.B., Goodale, T.L., and Johnsen, P.K.: A cluster analysis of activity, frequency, and environment variables to identify water-based recreation types. *Journal of Leisure Research,* 7:282-295, 1975.

Dohrenwend, B.P., and Dohrenwend, B.S.: *Social Status and Psychological Disorder.* New York, Wiley, 1969.

Dollard, J., Doob, L., Millern, N., Mowrer, O., and Sears, R.: *Frustration and Aggression.* New Haven, CT, Yale, 1939.

Donald, Marjorie N., and Havighurst, Robert J.: The meanings of leisure. *Social Forces,* 37:355-360, 1959.

Douglas, Paul: The administration of leisure for living. *Bulletin of the American Recreation Society, 12:* No. 3, 1960.

Dowell, L.J.: Recreational pursuits of selected occupational groups. *Research Quarterly, 38:* 719-722, 1967.

Dubin, R.: Industrial worker's worlds: a study of the "central life interests" of industrial workers. In Smigel, Erwin O. (Ed.): *Work and Leisure.* New Haven, Col & U Pr, 1963, pp. 53-72. Also in *Social Problems:* January, 1956.

Dubin, R., and Goldman, D.R.: Central life interests of American middle managers and specialists. *Journal of Vocational Behavior, 2:* 133-141, 1972.

Dumazedier, Joffre: *Toward a Society of Leisure.* London, Collier Macmillan, 1967.

Dumazedier, J.: *Sociology of Leisure.* Amsterdam, Elsevier, 1974.

Dumazedier, J.: The conception of changes in leisure and education. *Society and Leisure, 7:* 57-62, 1975.

Duncan, D.J.: Leisure types: factor analyses of leisure profiles. *Journal of Leisure Research, 10:* 113-125, 1978.

Duncan, O.D.: Partials, partitions, and paths. In Borgatta, Edgar F., and Bohrnstedt, George W. (Eds.): *Sociological Methodology 1970.* San Francisco, Jossey-Bass, 1970, pp. 38-48.

Dunn, D.R.: Book review, Szalai: *The Use of Time. Journal of Leisure Research, 6:* 84-86, 1974.

Easterbrook, J.A.: *The Determinants of Free Will.* New York, Academic Press, 1978.

Edwards, P.B.: Sex is not leisure. *Leisure Information Newsletter, 6, 2:* 8-9, 1979.

Ellis H.: *Studies in the Psychology of Sex.* New York, Random, 1936, Vol. II.

Ellis, M.J.: Play and its theories re-examined. *Park and Recreation,* Special Issue: Leisure — a new dawn in America: 51-55, August, 1971.

Ellis, M.J.: *Why People Play.* Englewood Cliffs, NJ, Prentice-Hall, 1973.

Ellis, M.J., and Scholtz, G.J.L.: *Activity and Play of Children.* Englewood Cliffs, NJ, Prentice-Hall, 1978.

Endler, N.S., Hunt, J. McV., and Rosenstein, A.J.: An S-R inventory of anxiousness. *Psychological Monographs, 76:* No. 17 (whole No. 536), 1962.

Endler, N.S., and Hunt, J. McV.: S-R inventories of hostility and comparisons of the proportions of variance from persons, responses, and situations for hostility and anxiousness. *J Pers Soc Psychol, 9:* 309-315, 1968.

Ennis, Philip H.: The definition and measurement of leisure. In Sheldon, Eleanor B., and Moore, Wilbert, E. (Eds.): *Indicators of Social Change.* New York, Russell Sage, 1968.

Epley, D., and Ricks, D.F.: Foresight and hindsight in the TAT. *Journal of Projective Techniques, 27:* 51-59, 1963.

Bibliography

Epperson, A., Witt, P.A., and Hitzhusen, G.: *Leisure Counseling: an Aspect of Leisure Education.* Springfield, Thomas, 1977.

Erikson, E.H.: *Childhood and Society.* New York, Norton, 1950.

Erikson, E.H.: *Identity, Youth and Crisis.* New York, Norton, 1968.

Erikson, E.H.: *Toys and Reasons.* New York, Norton, 1977.

Fackre, Gabriel: The new leisure: planner and citizen in partnership. In Staley, Edwin J., and Miller, Norman P. (Eds.): *Leisure and the Quality of Life.* Washington, D.C., AAHPER, 1972, pp. 71-92.

Faris, R.E.L., and Dunham, H.W.: *Mental Disorders in Urban Areas: An Ecological Study of Schizophrenia and Other Psychoses.* Chicago, University of Chicago, 1939.

Fechner, G.T.: *Elemente der Psychophysik* (2 vols). Leipzig, Breitkopf and Hartel, 1860.

Fehr, F.S.: Critique of hereditarian accounts. In *Science, Heritability, and IQ.* Harvard Educational Review, 1969, pp. 40-49.

Ferenczi, S.: Sunday neuroses (1918). In Ferenczi, S.: *Further Contributions to the Theory and Technique of Psycho-Analysis,* 2nd ed. New York, Basic, 1950.

Ferguson, G.A.: *Statistical Analysis in Psychology and Education.* New York, McGraw, 1966.

Festinger, L: *A Theory of Cognitive Dissonance.* Stanford, Stanford U Pr, 1957.

Fishbein, M. (Ed.): *Readings in Attitude Theory and Measurement.* New York, Wiley, 1967.

Fishbein, M., and Ajzen, I.: *Belief, Attitude, Intention and Behavior: An Introduction to Theory and Research.* Reading: Addison-Wesley, 1975.

Fiss, B.L.: Flexitime. In *Alternative Work Patterns: Changing Approaches to Work Scheduling.* Scarsdale, N.Y., Work in America Institute, 1976.

Flanagan, J.C.: A research approach to improving our quality of life. *Am Psychol, 33:*138-147, 1978.

Foote, N.: Methods for study of meaning in use of time. In Kleemeier, Robert W. (Ed.): *Aging and Leisure.* New York, Oxford Pr, 1961.

Fort, Joel: Why people use drugs and what should be done about it. In Blachly, Paul H. (Ed.): *Progress in Drug Abuse.* Springfield, Thomas, 1972.

Fowler, H.: *Curiosity and Exploratory Behavior.* New York, Macmillan, 1965.

Fraisse, P.: *The Psychology of Time.* New York, Har-Row, 1963.

Frank, Lawrence K.: *Society as the Patient.* New Brunswick, Rutgers U Pr, 1948.

Freud, Sigmund: Three essays on sexuality. In Strachey, J. (Ed.): *The Standard Edition of The Complete Psychological Works.* London, Hogarth Pr, 1953. (First German edition: 1905.)

Friedlander, F.: Importance of work versus nonwork among socially and occupationally stratified groups. *J Appl Psychol:* December, 1966.

Friedman, G.: *The Anatomy of Work.* Glencoe, Free Pr, 1961.

Fritz, D.: *The Changing Retirement Scene: A Challenge for Decision Makers.* Los Angeles, The Ethel Percey Andrus Gerontology Center, 1978.

Fromm, E.: *The Sane Society.* New York, Rinehart, 1955.

Fromm, E.: *To Have or To Be?* New York, Harper and Row, 1976.

Gentry, J.W., and Doering, M.: Sex role orientation and leisure. *Journal of Leisure Research, 11:*102-111, 1979.

Gilbert, G.M.: Stereotype persistence and change among college students. *J Abnorm Soc Psychol, 46:*245-254, 1951.

Ginzberg, E., et al.: *Occupational Choice.* New York, Columbia U Pr, 1951.

Glasser, R.: Life or tranquiliser? *Society and Leisure, 7:*17-26, 1975.

Godbey, G.: Leisure: nearing the receding horizon. *Parks and Recreation: 33,* August, 1971.

Goldhammer, H., and Marshall, A.W.: *Psychosis and Civilization: Studies in the Frequency of Mental Disease.* Glencoe, IL, Free Pr, 1953.

Goodwin, L.: *Do the Poor Want to Work?* Washington, D.C., Brookings Institution, 1972.

Gorman, B.S., and Wessman, A.W. (Eds.): *The Personal Experience of Time.* New York, Plenum, 1977.

Gratton, L.C.: Analysis of Maslow's need hierarchy with three social class groups. *Social Indicators Research, 7:*463-476, 1980.

Green, T.F.: *Work, Leisure, and The American Schools.* New York, Random, 1968.

Groos, Karl: *The Play of Man.* New York, D. Appleton, 1901.

Group for the Advancement of Psychiatry: The psychiatrist's interest in leisure-time activities. New York, August, 1958, Report No. 39.

Grubb, E.A.: Assembly line boredom and individual differences in recreation participation. *Journal of Leisure Research, 7:*256-269, 1975.

Guilford, J.P.: *Fundamental Statistics in Psychology and Education.* New York, McGraw, 1965.

Gulick, Luther Halsey: *A Philosophy of Play.* New York, C Scribner, 1920.

Gurin, G., Veroff, J., and Feld, S.: *Americans View Their Mental Health.* New York, *Basic Books,* 1960.

Hall, G. Stanley: *Adolescence: Its Psychology and its Relations to Physiology, Anthropology, Sociology, Sex, Crime, Religion, and Education.* New York, Appleton, 1904, Vol. 1.

Hanhart, D.: *Arbeiter in der Freizeit.* Bern, Hans Huber, 1964.

Harshbarger, T.R.: *Introductory Statistics.* New York, Macmillan, 1971.

Hartlage, Lawrence C.: A computerized approach to the problem of leisure. Paper presented at the American Psychological Association meeting, Montreal, 1973.

Harvey, J.H., Harris, B., and Lightner, J.M.: Perceived freedom as a central concept in psychological theory and research. In Perlmutter, L.C., and Monty, R.A. (Eds.): *Choice and Perceived Control.* New York, Wiley, 1979.

Hautaluoma, J., and Brown, P.J.: Attributes of the deer hunting experience: a cluster-analytic study. *Journal of Leisure Research, 10:*271-287, 1978.

Havighurst, Robert J.: *Human Development and Education.* New York, Longmans, Green, 1953.

Havighurst, Robert J.: The leisure activities of the middle-aged. *Am J Sociol, 63:*152-162, 1957(a).

Havighurst, Robert J.: The social competence of middle-aged people. *Genet Psychol Monogr, 56:*297-395,1957(b).

Havighurst, Robert J.: and Feigenbaum, K.: The principal values of leisure for adults. Unpublished manuscript, 1960.

Havighurst, Robert J.: The nature and values of meaningul free-time activity. In Kleemeir, Robert W. (Ed.): *Aging and Leisure.* New York, Oxford Pr, 1961, pp. 309-344.

Havighurst, Robert J.: Youth in exploration and man emergent. In Borow, H. (Ed.): *Man In a World at Work.* Boston, H M, 1964, pp. 215-236.

Havighurst, Robert J.: Social change: the status, needs, and wants of the future elderly. In Herzog, B.R. (Ed.): *Aging and Income.* New York, Human Sci Pr, 1978.

Hawkins, Donald: Leisure Education. In Staley, Edwin J., and Miller, Norman P. (Eds.): *Leisure and the Quality of Life.* Washington, D.C., AAHPER, 1972, pp.107-126.

Heider, F.: *The Psychology of Interpersonal Relations.* New York, Wiley, 1958.

Heise, D.R.: Causal inference from panel data. In Borgatta, Edgar F., and Bohrnstedt, George W. (Eds.): *Sociological Methodology 1970.* San Francisco, Jossey-Bass, 1970, pp. 3-27.

Hendee, J.C., and Burdge, R.J.: The substitutability concept: implications for recreation research and management. *Journal of Leisure Research, 6:*155-162, 1974.

Hendrick, Clyde, and Jones, Russell A.: *The Nature of Theory and Research in Social Psychology.* New York, Acad Pr, 1972.

Henle, Peter: Recent growth of paid leisure for U.S. workers. In Smigel, Erwin O. (Ed.): *Work and Leisure.* New Haven, Coll & U Pr, 1963, pp. 182-203.

Heron, W.: The pathology of boredom. *Sci Am, 196:*52-56, 1957.

Heron, W.: Cognitive and physiological effects of perceptual isolation. In Solomon, P., Kubzansky, P.E., Leiderman, P.H., Mendelson, J.H., Trumbull, R., and Wexler, D. (Eds.): *Sensory Deprivation: A Symposium Held at Harvard Medical School.* Cambridge, Harvard U Pr, 1961.

Hinckley, E.D.: The influence of individual opinion on construction of an attitude scale. *J Soc Psychol, 3:*283-296, 1932.

Hoffman, M.L., and Hoffman, L.W. (Eds.): *Review of Child Development Research.* New York, Russell Sage, 1964, Vol. 1.

Hollingshead, A.B., and Redlich, F.C.: *Social Class and Mental Illness: A Community Study.* New York, Wiley, 1958.

Hornstein, A.D., and Rotter, G.S.: Research methodology in temporal perception. *J Exp Psychol, 79:*561-564, 1969.

Hovland, C., Janis, I., and Kelley, H.: *Communication and Persuasion.* New Haven, CT, Yale U Pr, 1953.

Hovland, C., Lumsdaine, A., and Sheffield, F.: *Experiments on Mass Communication.* Princeton, NJ, Princeton U Pr, 1949.

Hovland, C., and Sherif, M.: Judgemental phenomena and scales of attitude measurement: item displacement in Thurstone scales. *J Abnor Soc Psychol, 47:*822-832, 1952.

Huizinga, Johan: *Homo Ludens: A Study of the Play Element in Culture.* London, Routledge & Kegan Paul, 1955.

Hunt, J. McV.: Traditional personality theory in the light of recent evidence. *Am Sci, 53:*80-96, 1965.

Insko, C.A.: *Theories of Attitude Change.* New York, Appleton, 1967.

Iso-Ahola, S.E.: Basic dimensions of definitions of leisure. *Journal of Leisure Research, 11:*28-39, 1979(a).

Iso-Ahola, S.E.: Some psychological determinants of perceptions of leisure: preliminary evidence. *Leisure Sciences, 2:*305-314, 1979(b).

Iso-Ahola, S.E.: *The Social Psychology of Leisure and Recreation.* Dubuque, Iowa, Wm. D. Brown, 1980.

Jackson, R.G.: A bicultural study of value orientations, leisure attitudes and activity preferences. Unpublished doctoral dissertation, The University of New Mexico, 1971.

Jackson, R.G.: A preliminary bicultural study of value orientations and leisure attitudes. *Journal of Leisure Research, 5, 4:*10-22. 1973.

Jensen, Arthur R.: How much can we boost IQ and scholastic achievement? In *Environment, Heredity, and Intelligence.* Harvard Educational Review, 1969, pp. 1-123.

Johnston, D.F..: Foreword. In Rossi, R.J., and Gilmartin, K.J., *The Handbook of Social Indicators: Sources, Characteristics, and Analysis.* New York, Garland STPM Press, 1980.

Jones, E.D.: The rocky road from acts to dispositions. *Am Psychol, 34:* 107-117, 1979.

Jones, E.E., and Gerard, H.B.: *Foundations of Social Psychology.* New York, Wiley, 1967.

Jones, E.E., and Nisbett, R.E.: *The Actor and the Observer: Divergent Perceptions of the Causes of Behavior.* Morristown, NJ, General Learning Press, 1971.

Kahle, L.R., and Berman, J.J.: Cross-lagged panel correlation and personality. *New Directions for Methodology of Behavioral Science, 2:*17-32, 1979.

Kahn, Herman, and Wiener, Anthony J.: Black population in major cities, Appendix G. In Nesbitt, John A., Brown, Paul D., and Murphy, James F. (Eds.): *Recreation and Leisure Service for the Disadvantaged.* Philadelphia, Lea & Febiger, 1970, p. 593.

276

Bibliography

Kahn, Robert L.: The meaning of work: interpretation and proposals for measurement. In Campbell, Angus, and Converse, Philip E. (Eds.): *The Human meaning of Social Change.* New York, Russell Sage, 1972, pp. 159-204.

Kaplan, M.: *Leisure in America: A Social Inquiry.* New York, Wiley, 1960(a).

Kaplan, M.: The use of leisure. In Tibbitts, C. (Eds.): *Handbook of Social Gerontology.* Chicago, U of Chicago Pr, 1960(b), pp. 407-443.

Kaplan, M.: *Leisure: Theory and Policy.* New York, Wiley, 1975.

Kaplan, M.: *Leisure: Lifestyle and Lifespan.* Philadelphia, Saunders, 1979.

Karlins, M., Coffman, T.L., and Walters, G.: On the fading of social stereotypes: studies in three generations of college students. *J Pers Soc Psychol, 13:*1-16, 1969.

Kass, R.A., and Tinsley, H.E.A.: Factor analysis. *Journal of Leisure Research, 11:*120-138, 1979.

Katz, D., and Braly, K.W.: Racial stereotypes of one-hundred college students. *J Abnor Soc Psychol, 28:*282-290, 1933.

Katz, Daniel, and Stotland, Ezra: A preliminary statement to a theory of attitude structure and change. In Koch, Sigmund (Ed.): *Psychology: A Study of a Science.* New York, McGraw, 1959, Vol. 3.

Kelly, J.R.: Work and leisure: a simplified paradigm. *Journal of Leisure Research, 4:*50-62, 1972.

Kelly, J.R: Two orientations of leisure: processual theory-building. Paper at the American Sociological Association meeting, New York, August 1976.

Kelly, J.R.: A revised paradigm of leisure choices. *Leisure Sciences, 1:*345-363, 1978.

Kenny, D.A.: *Correlation and Causality.* New York, Wiley, 1979.

Kenyon, G.S.: The significance of adult physical activity as a function of age, sex, education, and socio-economic status. Paper presented at the Midwest District Convention of The American Association for Health, Physical Education, and Recreation, Detroit, 1964.

Kenyon, G.S.: A conceptual model for characterizing physical activity. *Research Quarterly, 39:*96-105, 1968.

Kenyon, G.S.: Six scales for assessing attitude toward physical activity. In Morgan, William P. (Ed.): *Contemporary Readings in Sports Psychology.* Springfield, Charles C Thomas, 1970, Chapter 8, pp. 82-94.

Kerlinger, F.N.: *Foundations of Behavioral Research.* New York, Holt, Rinehart and Winston, 1973.

Kiesler, C.A.; Collins, B.E., and Miller, N.: *Attitude Change.* New York, Wiley, 1969.

Kleiber, D.A.: Fate control and leisure attitudes. Leisure Sciences, *2:*239-248, 1979.

Kleiber, D.A., and Kelly, J.R.: Leisure socialization, and the life cycle. In Iso-Ahola, S.E.(Ed.): *Social Psychological Perspectives on Leisure and Recreation.* Springfield, Thomas, 1980.

Kluckhohn, C., and Murray, H.: *Personality in Nature, Society and Culture,* 2nd ed. New York, Knopf, 1962.

Koocher, G.P.: Swimming, competence, and personality change. *J Pers Soc Psychol, 18:*275-278, 1971.

Kornhauser, A.: *Mental Health of the Industrial Worker.* New York, Wiley, 1965.

Kraus, Richard: *Recreation and the Schools.* New York, Macmillan, 1964.

Kraus, Richard: Negro patterns of participation in recreation activities. In Nesbitt, John A.; Brown, Paul D., and Murphy, James F. (Eds.):*Recreation and Leisure Service for the Disadvantaged.* Philadelphia, Lea & Febiger, 1970, pp. 324-343.

Kraus, Richard: *Recreation and Leisure in Modern Society.* Santa Monica, CA, Goodyear Publishing, 1978.

Krech, D., Crutchfield, R.S., and Ballachey, E.L.: *Individual in Society.* New York, McGraw, 1962.

Lafitte, P.: *Social Structure and Personality in the Factory.* London, Routledge, 1958.

Lange, Konrad: Arts as play. From Schertel, Max, and Rader, Melvin (Translators):*Das Wesen der Kunst,* 1901; In Rader, Melvin (Ed.): *A Modern Book of Esthetics.* New York, Henry Holt, 1935.

Lange, N.: Beitrage zur Theorie der Sinnlichen Aufmerksamkeit und der aktiven Apperception. *Philosophische Studien, 4:*390-422, 1888.

Larrabee, Eric, and Meyersohn, Rolf (Eds.): *Mass Leisure.* Glencoe, Free Pr, 1958.

Lazarsfeld, Paul F.: Sociological reflections on business: consumers and managers. In Dahl, Robert A., et al.: *Social Science Research on Business: Product and Potential.* New York, Columbia U Pr, 1959.

Lee, Joseph: *Play in Education.* New York, Macmillan, 1929.

Lefcourt, Herbert M.: The function of the illusions of control and freedom.*Am Psychol, 28:*417-425, 1973.

Lefcourt, Herbert M.: *Locus of Control: Current Trends in Theory and Research.* New York, Wiley, 1976.

Levy, J.: Risk taking as a determinant of competitive play behavior: an extension of Atkinson's theory of achievement motivation (Part I). *Canadian Association of Health, Physical Education, and Recreation Journal:* 31-37, March-April, 1972.

Levy, J.: Leisure module: an objective-subjective model for leisure-time planning. Unpublished doctoral dissertation, University of Waterloo, Faculty of Environmental Studies, 1975.

Levy, J.: *Play Behavior.* New York, Wiley, 1978.

Lewin, K.: *Field Theory in Social Science.* New York, Harper, 1951.

Lewis, P.R., Lobban, M.C., and Shaw, T.I.: Patterns of urine flow in human subjects during a prolonged period of life on a 22-hour day. *J Physiol, 133:*659-669, 1956.

Lieberman, J.N.: *Playfulness.* New York, Academic Press 1977.

Light, Richard J., and Smith, Paul V.: Social allocation models of intelligence. In *Science, Heritability, and IQ.* Harvard Educational Review, 1969, pp. 1-27.

Lilly, J.C., and Shurley, J.T.: Experiments in solitude in maximum achievable physical isolation with water suspension on intact, healthy persons. *Symposium,* Boston, Harvard Medical School, June, 1958.

Liu, Ben-Chieh: *Quality of Life Indicators in U.S. Metropolitan Areas, 1970.* Washington, D.C.: U.S. Environmental Protection Agency, Washington Environmental Research Center, 1975.

Lundberg, G., Komarowski, M., and McInerny, M.: *Leisure: A Suburban Study.* New York, Columbia U P, 1934.

Lynd, Robert S., and Lynd, Helen M.: *Middletown.* New York, Harcourt, Brace, 1929.

Lynd, Robert S., and Lynd, Helen M.: *Middletown in Transition.* New York, Harcourt, Brace, 1937.

Macarov, David: *Incentives to Work.* San Francisco, Jossey-Bass, 1970.

MacDonald, A.P., Jr.: Relation of birth order to morality types and attitudes toward the poor. *Psychol Rep, 29:*732, 1971.

MacDonald, A.P., Jr.: More on the Protestant Ethic. *J Consult Clin Psychol, 30:*116-122, 1972.

Maddi, S.R.: The search for meaning. *Nebraska Symposium on Motivation, 18:*137-186, 1970.

Maddox, G.: Keynote address, successful aging: a perspective. In Pfeiffer, E. (Ed.): *Successful Aging.* Durham, NC, Duke University, Center for the Study of Aging and Human Development, 1974.

Maier, H.W.: *Three Theories of Child Development.* New York, Har-Row, 1965.

Maier, Norman R.F.: *Psychology in Industry,* 3rd ed. Boston HM, 1965.

Mancini, J.A., and Orthner, D.K.: Recreational sexuality preferences among middle-class husbands and wives. *The Journal of Sex Research, 14:*96-106, 1978.

Mannell, R.C.: Leisure research in the psychological lab: leisure a permanent and/or transient cognitive disposition? Paper presented at the Second Canadian Congress on Leisure Research, Toronto, 1978.

Mannell, R.C.: A conceptual and experimental basis for research in the psychology of leisure. *Society and Leisure, 11:*179-196, 1979.

Mannell, R.C.: Social psychological techniques and strategies for studying leisure experiences. In Iso-Ahola, S.E. (Ed.): *Social Psychological Perspectives on Leisure and Recreation*. Springfield, Thomas, 1980.

Martin, John B.: Preface to *Toward a National Policy on Aging*. Proceeding of the 1971 White House Conference on Aging. Washington, D.C., U.S. Government Printing Office, 1971.

Maslow, Abraham H.: *Motivation and Personality*. New York, Harper and Brothers, 1954.

Maslow, Abraham H.: Creativity in self-actualizing people. In Anderson, H.H. (Ed.): *Creativity and Its Cultivation*. New York, Har-Row, 1959.

Maslow, Abraham H.: *Toward a Psychology of Being*. Princeton, D. Van Nostrand, 1962.

McClelland, David C.: *The Achieving Society*. Princeton, D. Van Nostrand, 1961.

McClelland, David C., Davis, William N., Kalin, Rudolf, and Wanner, Eric: *The Drinking Man*. New York, Free Pr, 1972.

McCluskey, N.G.: Sweden: a preview of where America's elderly might be? *On Aging*, Newsletter of the CASE Center for Gerontological Studies, The City University of New York, 4, 2:12-13, 1979.

McDowell, C.F., Jr.: Leisure counseling; a review of emerging concepts and orientations. In Epperson, A., Witt, P., and Hitzhusen, G. (Eds.): *Leisure Counseling: An Aspect of Leisure Education*. Springfield, Thomas, 1977.

McGuire, W.J.: Toward social psychology's second century. Paper presented at the American Psychological Association meeting, New York, September, 1979.

McKechnie, G.E.: The psychological structure of leisure: past behavior. *Journal of Leisure Research, 6,* 27-45, 1974.

Meyer, Harold D., Brightbill, Charles K. and Sessoms, Douglas H.: *Community Recreation: A Guide to Its Organization*. Englewood Cliffs, P-H, 1956.

Meyersohn, Rolf: The sociology of leisure in the United States: Introduction and bibliography, 1945-1965. *Journal of Leisure Research, 1:*53-68, 1969.

Meyersohn, Rolf: Leisure. In Campbell, Angus, and Converse, Philip E. (Eds.): *The Human Meaning of Social Change*. New York, Russell Sage F, 1972.

Miller, Norman P., and Robinson, Duane M.: *The Leisure Age*. Belmont, Wadsworth, 1963.

Mirels, H.L., and Garrett, J.B.: The Protestant Ethic as a personality variable. *J Consult Clin Psychol, 36:*40-44, 1971.

Mischel, W.: *Personality and Assessment*. New York, Wiley, 1968.

Mischel, W.: Continuity and change in personality. *Am Psychol, 24:*1012-1018, 1969.

Moore, Wilbert E.: *Man, Time, and Society*. New York, Wiley, 1963.

Moore, Wilbert E.: Foreword. In Cheek, N.H., Jr., and Burch, W.R., Jr., *The Social Organization of Leisure in Human Society*. New York, Harper and Row, 1976.

Bibliography

Mundy, J., and Odum, L.: *Leisure Education, Theory and Practice.* New York, Wiley, 1979.

Murphy, J.: *Recreation and leisure services.* Dubuque, W.C. Brown, 1975.

Murray, Henry A., et al.: *Explorations in Personality.* New York, Oxford Pr, 1938.

Nahrstedt, W.: *Die Entstehung der Freizeit.* Gottingen, Vandenhoech & Ruprecht, 1972.

National Commission on Technology: Automation, and economic progress, improving public decision making. In *Technology and the American Economy,* Vol. 1. Washington, D.C.: U.S. Government Printing Office. 1966.

National Institute on Aging: Special Report on Aging: 1977. U.S. Department of Health, Education, and Welfare, DHEW Publication No. (NIH) 77-1121.

National Institute on Alcohol Abuse and Alcoholism: Publication No. (HSM) 72-9019. Rockville, U.S. Department of Health, Education, and Welfare, 1971.

Neff, W.E.: *Work and Human Behavior.* New York, Atherton, 1968.

Nelson, T.M., and Bartley, S.H.: The pattern of personal response arising during the office work day. *Occupational Psychology, 42:*77-83, 1968.

Nesbitt, J.A., Brown, P.D., and Murphy, J.F.: *Recreation and Leisure Service for the Disadvantaged.* Philadelphia, Lea & Febiger, 1970.

Neulinger, John: Person types and environment types and resultant forces. Unpublished doctoral thesis, New York University, 1965.

Neulinger, John: A preliminary survey on leisure. Unpublished manuscript, The City College of the City University of New York, 1967(a).

Neulinger, John: The psychology of individual similarities: the use of the self as an independent variable. Paper presented at the New York State Psychological Association, Buffalo, May, 1967(b).

Neulinger, John: Progress Report #1, An Investigation of Leisure. Unpublished manuscript, The City College of The City University of New York, 1968.

Neulinger, John: Leisure and mental health: a study in a program of leisure research. *Pacific Sociological Review, 14:*288-300, 1971.

Neulinger, John: Into leisure with dignity. Symposium at the American Psychological Association meeting, Montreal, August, 1973.

Neulinger, John: *The Psychology of Leisure.* Springfield, Thomas, 1974(a).

Neulinger, John: Comments on the 1973 American Psychological Association symposium on leisure. *Society and Leisure, 6,* 3:119-120, 1974(b).

Neulinger, John: The need for and the implications of a psychological conception of leisure. *The Ontario Psychologist, 8,* 2:13-20, 1976(a).

Neulinger, John: Education for leisure: An issue of attitude change. *Leisure Today: Journal of Physical Education and Recreation, 47,* 3:5-6, March 1976(b).

Neulinger, John: *What Am I Doing? A Self-exploration (WAID).* New York, The Leisure Institute, 1977.

Neulinger, John: Leisure counseling: process or content? Paper presented at the Dane County Recreation Coordinating Council Conference on Leisure Counseling, Madison, Wisconsin, September 27, 1978(a).

Neulinger, John: Leisure: the criterion of the quality of life; a psychological perspective. Presented as the Harold K. Jack lecture at Temple University, Philadelphia, April, 1978(b).

Neulinger, John: Sex and leisure, or sex as leisure. *Leisure Information Newsletter, 6*, 2:5-6, 1979(a).

Neulinger, John: Leisure: a state of mind that all desire but few achieve. Paper presented at the International Seminar on Molding Leisure Policies for Educational, Communal and Labor Frameworks. The Hebrew University of Jerusalem, Jerusalem, June 1979/b/.

Neulinger, John: Leisure education: A serious task, not self-delusion nor child's play. Paper prepared for the Fourth Annual Leisure Education Conference, The Pennsylvania State University, University Park, Pennsylvania, April 1979(c).

Neulinger, John: Empirical bases of value judgements: measuring the good life. Paper presented at the Morris R. Cohen Centenary Conference, The City College of New York, October, 1980.

Neulinger, John: *To leisure: An Introduction.* Boston, Allyn and Bacon, 1981.

Neulinger, John, Berg, Carl, and Weiss, H.: Leisure attitudes and alcoholism: an exploration. Unpublished manuscript, 1972.

Neulinger, John, and Breit, Miranda: Attitude dimensions of leisure. *Journal of Leisure Research, 1:*255-261, 1969.

Neulinger, John, and Breit, Miranda: Attitude dimensions of leisure: a replication study. *Journal of Leisure Research, 3:*108-115, 1971.

Neulinger, John and Crandall, Rick: The psychology of leisure: 1975. *Journal of Leisure Research, 8:* 181-184, 1976.

Neulinger, John, Light, Steven, and Mobley, Tony: Attitude dimensions of leisure in a student population. *Journal of Leisure Research, 8:*175-176, 1976.

Neulinger, John, and Raps, Charles S.: Leisure attitudes of an intellectual elite. *Journal of Leisure Research, 4:*196-207, 1972.

Neumeyer, Martin H., and Neumeyer, Esther S.: *Leisure and Recreation: A Study of Leisure and Recreation in Their Sociological Aspects,* 3rd ed. New York, Ronald, 1958.

Nisbett, Richard E.: Birth order and participation in dangerous sports. *J Pers Soc Psychol, 8:*351-353, 1968.

Nixon, Eugene W., and Cozens, Frederick W.: *An Introduction to Physical Education.* Philadelphia, Saunders, 1941.

Bibliography

Notz, W.W.: Work motivation and the negative effects of extrinsic rewards: a review with implications for theory and practice. *American Psychologist, 30:*884-891, 1975.

Now, revolt of the old. *Time,* October 10, 1977, 18-20; 25-26; 28; 33.

Nunnaly, J.C.: *Psychometric Theory.* New York, Pantheon, 1967.

Obermeyer, Charles: Challenges and contradictions. In Kaplan, Max, and Bosserman, Phillip (Eds.): *Technology, Human Values, and Leisure.* Nashville, Abingdon, 1971, pp. 221-237.

Odaka, K.: Work and leisure: as viewed by Japanese industrial workers. Paper presented to Sixth World Congress of Sociology, Evian, 1966.

Opinion Research Corporation: 1957 survey. As described in de Grazia, Sebastian: *Of Time, Work, and Leisure.* New York, Twentieth Century Fund, 1962.

Ornstein, R.E.: *On the experience of time.* Baltimore, Penguin Books, 1970.

Orthner, D.K.: Excerpts from letter by Dennis K. Orthner to Patsy Edwards (May 22, 1979). *Leisure Information Newsletter, 6,* 2:8, 1979.

Orzack, L.H.: Work as a "central life interest" of professionals. In Smigel, Erwin O. (Ed.): *Work and Leisure.* New Haven, Coll & U Pr, 1963, pp. 73-84.

Osgood, C.E., Suci, G.J., and Tannenbaum, P.H.: *The Measurement of Meaning.* Urbana, U of ILL pr, 1957.

Osgood, C., and Tannenbaum, P.: The principle of congruity in the prediction of attitude change. *Psychol Rev, 62:*42-55, 1955.

Paluba, G., and Neulinger, J.: Stereotypes based on free-time activities. *Society and Leisure, 3:,* 89-95, 1976.

Parker, Stanley: *The Future of Work and Leisure.* New York, Praeger, 1971.

Parsons, T.: Age, sex, and social structure of the United States. In *Essays in Sociological Theory.* Glencoe, 1949.

Patrick, G.T.W.: *The Psychology of Relaxation.* Boston, HM, 1916.

Perlmutter, L.C., and Monty, R.A. (Eds.): *Choice and Perceived Control.* New York, Wiley, 1979.

Pieper, Josef: *Leisure, The Basis of Culture.* New York, The New American Library, 1963.

Poor, Riva (Ed.): *4 Days, 40 Hours.* Cambridge, Bursk and Poor, 1970.

Pregel, B.: Energy, economy and society in transition. *Transactions of the New York Academy of Sciences, 21:* No. 3, Ser. II, 206-219, 1959.

President's Research Committee on Social Trends: *Recent Social Trends in the United States.* New York, McGraw-Hill, 1933.

Ramsoy, N.R.: Social indicators in the United States and Europe: Comments on five country reports. In Van Dusen, R.A. (Ed.): *Social Indicators, 1973: A Review Symposium.* New York, Social Science Research Council, 1974.

Rapoport, R., and Rapoport, R.N.: *Leisure and The Family Cycle.* London, Routledge and Kegan Paul, 1975.

Recreation and Park Education Curriculum Catalog. Arlington, National Recreation and Park Association, 1972.

Reissman, L.: Class, leisure and social participation. *Am Sociol Rev, 19:*76-84, 1954.

Report of the President's Commission on National Goals for Americans: *Programs for Action in the Sixties.* New Jersey, Prentice-Hall, 1960.

Riesman, David: Foreword. In Dumazedier, Joffre: *Toward a Society of Leisure.* New York, Free Pr, 1967.

Riesman, David, Glazer, Nathan, and Denney, Reuel: *The Lonely Crowd.* New Haven, Yale U Pr, 1950.

Riley, J.W., Marden, C.F., and Lifshitz, M.: The motivational pattern of drinking. In Larrabee, Eric, and Meyersohn, Rolf (Eds.): *Mass Leisure.* Glencoe, Free Pr, 1958, pp. 327-334.

Ritchie, J.R.Brent.: On the derivation of leisure activity types — a perceptual mapping approach. *Journal of Leisure Research, 7:* 128-140, 1975.

Robinson, John P.: Social change as measured by time budgets. *Journal of Leisure Research, 1:*75-77, 1969.

Robinson, John P.: *How Americans Use Time.* New York, Praeger Publishers, 1977.

Robinson, John P., and Converse, Philip E.: 66 Basic Tables of Time-Budget Data for the United States. Survey Research Center, Institute for Social Research, University of Michigan, Ann Arbor, June, 1966.

Robinson, John P., and Converse, Philip E.: Social change reflected in the use of time. In Campbell, Augus, and Converse, Philip E. (Eds.): *The Human Meaning of Social Change.* New York, Russell Sage, 1972, pp. 17-86.

Robinson, Duane: Comment—The new leisure: Planner and citizen in partnership. In Staley, Edwin J., and Miller, Norman P. (Eds.): *Leisure and the Quality of Life.* Washington, D.C., AAHPER, 1972, pp. 103-106.

Roe, A.: *The Psychology of Occupations.* New York, Wiley, 1956.

Roebuck, Julian B., and Kessler, Raymond G.: *The Etiology of Alcoholism.* Springfield, Thomas, 1972.

Rokeach, Milton: *The Nature of Human Values.* New York, Free Pr, 1973.

Romesburg, C.H.: Use of cluster analysis in leisure research. *Journal of Leisure Research, 11:*144-153, 1979.

Rosenberg, M.J., Hovland, C.I., McGuire, W.J., Abelson, R.P., and Brehm, J.W.: *Attitude Organization and Change.* New Haven, Yale U Pr, 1960.

Rosenzweig, M.R., and Porter, L.W. (Eds.): *Annual Review of Psychology.* Palo Alto, Annual Reviews, 1980.

Rossi, R.J., and Gilmartin, K.J.: *The Handbook of Social Indicators: Sources, Characteristics, and Analysis.* New York, Garland STPM Press, 1980.

Rotter, G.S.: Clock-speed as in independent variable in psychological research. *J Gen Psychol, 81:*45-52, 1969.

Rotter, J.B.: Generalized expectancies for internal versus external control of reinforcement. *Psychological Monographs, 80:* 1-28 (whole No. 609), 1966.

Bibliography

Rubin, I.: *Sexual Life in the Later Years*. New York, Human Sciences Press, A Siecus Publication, 1970.

Sapora, A.V., and Mitchell, E.D.: *The Theory of Play and Recreation*, 3rd ed. New York, Ronald, 1961.

Scheingold, L.D., and Wagner, N.N.: *Sound Sex and the Aging Heart*. New York, Human Sciences Press, 1974.

Scheuch, Erwin K.: Die Verwendung von Zeit in West und Osteuropa. In Scheuch, Erwin K., and Meyersohn, Rolf (Eds.): *Soziologie der Freizeit*. Koeln, Kiepenheuer & Witsch, 1972(a).

Scheuch, Erwin K.: Die Problematik der Freizeit in der Massengesellschaft. In Scheuch, Erwin K., and Meyersohn, Rolf (Eds.): *Soziologie der Freizeit*. Koeln, Kiepenheuer, & Witsch, 1972(b).

Schiff, William, and Thayer, Stephen: Cognitive and affective factors in temporal experience: judgments of intrinsically and extrinsically motivated successful and unsuccessful performance. *Percept Mot Skills, 30:*895-902, 1970.

Schiller, Friedrich: *Essays, Aesthetic and Philosophical*. London, George Bell and Sons, 1875.

Schmitz-Scherzer, R., and Strödel, I.: Age-dependency of leisure-time activities. *Hum Dev, 14:*47-50, 1971.

Schnarch, David M.: The connotative definitions of leisure and work-related concepts, and their variations in various societal groups. Honors thesis, The City College of The City University of New York, Psychology Department, 1969.

Select Committee on Aging, U.S. House of Representatives.: *Mandatory Retirement: The Social and Human Cost of Enforced Idleness*. Washington, D.C., U.S. Government Printing Office, 1977.

Selye, Hans: *The Stress of Life*. New York, McGraw, 1956.

Sessoms, Douglas H.: and Oakley, Sidney R.: Recreation, leisure, and the alcoholic. *Journal of Leisure Research, 1:*21-31, 1969.

Sheldon, E.G., and Moore, W.E. (Eds.): *Indicators of Social Change*. New York, Russell Sage, 1968.

Simmons, J.L., and Winograd, B.: *It's Happening: A Portrait of the Youth Scene Today*. Santa Barbara, Marc-Laird Publications, 1966.

Singer, J.L.: *The Child's World of Make-Believe: Experimental Studies of Imaginative Play*. New York, Academica, 1973.

Skinner, B.F.: *Beyond Freedom and Dignity*. New York, Bantam Books, 1971.

Slavson, S.R.: *Recreation and the Total Personality*. New York, Ass Pr, 1948.

Sleet, David A.: An interdisciplinary research index on play. Ann Arbor, University Microfilms, Manuscript Abstracts Division, 1971.

Slivken, K.: Development of a leisure ethic scale. Master's thesis, University of Illinois, 1976.

Smigel, Erwin O. (Ed.): *Work and Leisure*. New Haven, Coll & U Pr, 1963.

285

Smith, Patricia C.: The curve of output as a criterion of boredom. *J Appl Psychol, 37:*69-74, 1953.

Smith, Patricia C.: The prediction of individual differences in susceptibility to industrial monotony. *J Appl Psychol, 39:* 322-329, 1955.

Smith, Stephen L.J.: Sex and surveys: bias in responses to participation questions. *Leisure Information Newsletter, 6,* 2:10-11, 1979.

Smith, Stephen L.J., and Haley, A.J. Ratio ex Machina: notes on leisure research. *Journal of Leisure Research, 11:*139-143, 1979.

Social Indicators, 1973. Washington, D.C., U.S. Office of Management and Budget, 1973.

Social Indicators, 1976. Washington, D.C., U.S. Department of Commerce, 1977.

Sorokin, P., and Berger, C.: *Time-Budgets of Human Behavior.* Cambridge, Harvard U Pr, 1939.

Spencer, H. (1862): *First Principles.* (Preface dated 1862.) New York, Appleton, 1895.

Spreitzer, E.A., and Snyder, E.E.: Work orientation, meaning of leisure and mental health. *Journal of Leisure Research, 6:*207-219, 1974.

Srole, L., Langner, T.S., Michael, S.T., Opler, M.K., and Rennie, T.A.: *Mental Health in the Metropolis: The Midtown Manhattan Study.* New York, McGraw-Hill, 1962.

Stefflre, B., and Matheny, K.B.: *The Function of Counseling Theory.* New York, Houghton Mifflin, 1968.

Stein, Morris I., and Neulinger, John: A typology of self-descriptions. In Katz, M.M., Cole, J.O., and Barton, W.E. (Eds.): *The Role and Methodology of Classification in Psychiatry and Psychopathology.* Washington, D.C., Government Printing Office, 1965, pp. 390-403.

Steiner, I.D.: Three kinds of reported choice. In Perlmutter, L.C., and Monty, R.A. (Eds.): *Choice and Perceived Control.* New York, Wiley, 1979.

Stinchcombe, A.L.: Environment the cumulation of events. In *Science, Heritability, and IQ.* Cambridge, MA, Harvard Educational Review, 1969, pp. 28-39.

Strumpel, B.: Economic life styles, values and subjective welfare. In Strumpel, B. (Ed.): *Economic Means for Human Needs, Social Indicators of Well-Being and Discontent.* Ann Arbor, Mich., Institute of Social Research, Survey Research Center, 1976(a).

Strumpel, B. (Ed.): *Economic Means for Human Needs, Social Indicators of Well-Being and Discontent.* Ann Arbor, Mich., Institute of Social Research, Survey Research Center, 1976(b).

Sutherland, Willard C.: A philosophy of leisure. *The Annals of the Am Acad Pol Soc Sci, 313:*1-3, 1957.

Sutton-Smith, B.: Children's play: some sources of play theorizing. *New Directions for Child Development, 9:*1-16, 1980.

Bibliography

Sutton-Smith, B., Roberts, J.M., and Kozelka, R.M.: Game involvement in adults. *J Soc Psychol, 60:*15-30, 1963.

Szalai, Alexander: Trends in comparative time budget research. *American Behavioral Scientist, 9:*3-8, 1966. Also December issue, Special Appendix.

Szalai, Alexander (Ed.): *The Use of Time.* The Hague, Mouton, 1972.

Takeo Doi: On the concept of *yutori.* Paper presented at the workshop on creative leisure for children and families, 1979 World Congress on Mental Health, World Federation for Mental Health, Salzburg, Austria, July, 1979.

Taylor, Graham C.: Work and leisure in the age of automation. *Humanitas, Journal of the Institute of Man, 3:*57-65, 1967.

Taylor, Lester D.: Combining the 1960-61 BLS survey of consumer expenditures and OBE time series data in projecting personal consumption expenditures. Unpublished manuscript, 1967.

Teaff, J.D., Ernst, N.W., and Ernst, M.: An elderly leisure attitude schedule. Paper presented at 28th Annual Meeting of the Gerontological Society, Louisville, October, 1975. See also *The Gerontologist, 15,* 5, Part II: 54,1975.

Thomas, W.I., and Znaniecki, F.: *The Polish Peasant in Europe and America.* Boston, Badger, 1918-1920, 5 Vols.

Thurstone, L.L., and Chave, E.J.: *The Measurement of Attitude.* Chicago, U of Chicago Pr, 1929.

Tinsley, D.J.: Book review of *Leisure Counseling: An Aspect of Leisure Education.* In *Journal of Leisure Research, 12:*93-95, 1980.

Tinsley, H.E.A., and Kass, R.A.: Leisure activities and need satisfaction: a replication and extension. *Journal of Leisure Research, 10:*191-202, 1978.

Toffler, A.: *Future Shock.* New York, Bantam, 1970.

Triandis, H.C.: *Attitude and Attitude Change.* New York, Wiley, 1971.

Turner, C.F., and Krauss, E.: Fallible indicators of the subjective state of the nation. *American Psychologist, 33:* 456-470, 1978.

Twardzik, L.F.: New goals, our future's key. *Parks & Recreation, 15,* 10: October, 1980, 56-58, 73.

Underwood, B.J.: *Psychological Research.* New York, Appleton, 1957.

U.S. Department of Health, Education, and Welfare: *Toward a Social Report.* Washington, D.C., U.S. Government Printing Office, 1969.

U.S. Department of Labor: *Dictionary of Occupational Titles.* Washington, D.C., U.S. Employment Service, 1949.

U.S. Senate: "S.843: Full opportunity and social accounting act." *Am Psychol, 22:*974-976, 1967.

U.S. Senate: "Full opportunity act," House of Representatives Bill No. 9483. 91st Congress, 1st Session, March, 1969.

Van Dusen, R.A. (Ed.): *Social Indicators, 1973: A Review Symposium.* New York, Social Science Research Council, 1974.

Veblen, Thorstein: *The Theory of the Leisure Class.* New York, The New American Library, 1953 (copyright 1899).

Walker, E.L.: Curiosity: tedium or titillation? Presented at the Eastern Psychological Association Convention, Atlantic City, April, 1959.

Walton, D.: Drug addiction and habit formation: an attempted integration. *Journal of Mental Science, 106:*1195-1229, 1960.

Ward, J.A., Co.: Mutual broadcasting, 1954 study. As described in de Grazia, Sebastian: *Of Time, Work, and Leisure.* New York, Twentieth Century Fund, 1962.

Warner, W.L., and Lunt, Paul S.: *The Social Life of a Modern Community.* New Haven, Yale U Pr, 1941 ("Yankee City Series," Vol.1).

Weber, M.: *The Protestant Ethic and the Spirit of Capitalism,* (Translated T. Parsons). New York, Scribners, 1952.

Weiss, Paul: A philosophical definition of leisure. In Charlesworth, James J. (Ed.): *Leisure in America: Blessing or Curse?* Philadelphia, Am Acad Pol Soc Sci, 1964.

Wessman, Alden E.: Personality and the subjective experience of time. *J Pers Assess, 37:*103-114, 1973.

White, R.C.: Social class differences in the uses of leisure. *Am J Sociol, 61:*145-150, 1955.

White, R.W.: Motivation reconsidered: the concept of competence. *Psychology Review, 66:*297-333, 1959.

Wilcox, L.D., Brooks, R.M., Beal, G.M., and Klonglan, G.E.: *Social Indicators and Societal Monitoring: An Annotated Bibliography.* San Francisco, Jossey-Bass, 1972.

Wilensky, Harold L.: Work, careers, and social integration. *International Social Science Journal, 12:*543-560, 1960.

Wilensky, Harold L.: The uneven distribution of leisure: the impact of economic growth on "free time." *Social Problems, 9:* No. 1, 1961. Also in Smigel, Erwin O. (Ed.): *Work and Leisure.* New Haven, Col & U Pr, 1963, pp. 107-145.

Wilson, James A., and Byham, William C. (Eds.): *The Four-Day Workweek: Fad or Future?* Proceedings of a conference conducted by the Graduate School of Business, University of Pittsburgh, 1973.

Winckler, Margit M.: The effects of fantasy on attitudes related to leisure and work. Unpublished honors thesis, The City College of the City University of New York, Psychology Department, 1972.

Witt, P.A.: Factor structure of leisure behavior for high school age youth in three communities. *Journal of Leisure Research, 3:*213-219, 1971.

Wolfbein, Seymour L.: The changing length of working life. In Larrabee, Eric, and Meyersohn, Rolf (Eds.): *Mass Leisure.* Glencoe, Free Pr, 1958.

Woody, Thomas: Leisure in the light of history. *The Annals of the Am Acad Pol Soc Sci, 313:*4-10, 1957.

Wylie, Ruth C.: *The Self Concept.* Lincoln, U of Nebr Pr, 1961.

Yarrow, L.J.: Maternal deprivation: toward an empirical and conceptual re-evaluation. *Psychol Bull, 58:*459-490, 1961.

Yarrow, L.J.: Separation from parents during early childhood. In Hoffman, M.L., and Hoffman, L.W. (Eds.): *Review of Child Development Research.* New York, Russell Sage, 1964, Vol. 1, pp. 89-137.

Yoesting, D.R., and Burdge, R.J.: Utility of a leisure orientation scale. *Iowa State Journal of Research, 50:*345-356, 1976.

Yoesting, D.R, and Burkhead, D.L.: Significance of childhood recreation experience on adult leisure behavior: an exploratory analysis. *Journal of Leisure Research, 5:*25-36, 1973.

Yoesting, D.R., and Christensen, J.E.: Reexamining the significance of childhood recreation patterns on adult leisure behavior. *Leisure Sciences, 1:*219-229, 1978.

Yuskaitis, J.: Leisure attitudes in relation to locus of control orientation under conditions of work and retirement. Unpublished M.A. thesis, The City College of New York, 1981.

Zarit, S. H.: Gerontology — Getting better all the time. In Zarit, S.H. (Ed.): *Readings in Aging and Death: Contemporary Perspectives.* New York, Harper and Row, 1977.

Zborowski, M., and Eyde, L.: Aging and social participation. *J Gerontol, 17:*424-430, 1962.

Zeisel, Joseph S.: The workweek in American industry 1850-1956. *Monthly Labor Review, 81:*23-29, 1958. Also described in Larrabee, Eric, and Meyersohn, Rolf (Eds.): *Mass Leisure.* Glencoe, Free Pr, 1958, pp. 145-153.

Zigler, E.: Research in personality structure in the retardate. In Ellis, N.R. (Eds.): *International Review of Research in Mental Retardation.* New York, Acad Pr, 1966, Vol. 1, pp. 77-108.

Zubek, J.P.: *Sensory Deprivation: Fifteen Years of Research.* New York, Appleton, 1969.

Zuckerman, M., and Cohen, N.: Sources of reports of visual and auditory sensations in perceptual isolation experiment. *Psychol Bull, 62:*1-20, 1964.

Zuzanek, J.: Social differences in leisure behavior: measurement and interpretation. *Leisure Sciences, 1:* 271-293, 1978.

AUTHOR INDEX

A

Aaronsen, B.S., 191
Abelson, R.P., 166
Ajzen, I., 69
Allport, G.W., 7, 155, 156
Alsikafe, M., 67, 125
Anderson, H.H., 10
Appley, M.H., 193
Aquinas, Saint Thomas, 2
Aristotle, 2, 179
Armstrong, J.S., 74
Arnold, N., 199
Aronson, E., 176
Ausubel, D.P., 100

B

Backman, S., 173, 180, 181
Baker, R., 242
Ballachey, E.L., 114, 156
Barnett, L.A., 10, 187
Barret, W., vi
Bartley, S.H., 193
Bauer, R.A., 147
Beaman, J., 57
Bennett, M.K., 146
Berelson, B., 81
Berg, C., 66, 136, 226
Berger, B.M., 113
Berger, C., 4, 40, 41, 44, 88, 219
Bergler, R., 118
Berkowitz, L., 174
Berlyne, D.E., 9, 10
Berman, J.J., 175
Bexton, W.H., 195
Biderman, A.D., 147
Bird, J.W., 135
Bird, L.P., 135
Bishop, D.W., 47, 57, 96, 122, 178, 179, 180
Bogardus, E.S., 6
Borow, H., 162, 163
Bradburn, N.M., 147
Braly, K.W., 127, 225

Brayley, L.S., 192
Brehm, J.W., 166
Breit, M., 61-67, 74, 101, 136, 166, 229
Brightbill, C.K., 5, 10, 109, 215
Brim, O.G., Jr., 119, 161
Bronfenbrenner, U., 169
Brown, P.D., 127, 227
Brown, P.J., 57
Brownwell, B., 10
Bryan, H., 67, 125
Buchholz, R.A., 67, 125
Bull, N.C., 113, 192
Bultena, G.L., 51
Burch, W.R., Jr., 12, 13, 113, 139
Burdge, R.J., 57, 67, 68, 96, 122, 123
Burkhead, D.L., 163
Burton, T.L., 57, 105, 178
Byham, W.C., 51

C

Cahoon, R.L., 191
Calabresi, R., 192
Calder, B.J., 187
Campbell, A., 109
Campbell, D.T., 68, 175
Cantril, H., 147
Caplovitz, D., 147
Carlsmith, J.M., 176
Cartwright, D., 177
Casler, L., 195
Caverly, M., 233, 240
Charlesworth, J.C., 215
Chave, E.J., 97
Cheek, N.H., Jr., 13, 139
Christensen, J.E., 163
Cicchetti, C.J., 93-95
Clarke, A.C., 93, 122
Clausen, J.A., 129
Clawson, M., 5
Coffman, T.L., 225
Cohen, J., 192
Cohen, N., 195
Collins, B.E., 166

291

293

SUBJECT INDEX